Advanced Italian

Edited by

Laura Riggio and Giuseppe Manca

LIVING LANGUAGE®

Content in this program has been modified and enhanced from Starting Out in Italian and Complete Course Italian: The Basics, both published in 2008.

Living Language and colophon are registered trademarks of Random House, Inc.

Published in the United States by Living Language, an imprint of Random House, Inc.

www.livinglanguage.com

Editor: Laura Riggio
Production Editor: Ciara Robinson
Production Manager: Tom Marshall
Interior Design: Sophie Chin
Illustrations: Sophie Chin

First Edition

Library of Congress Cataloging-in-Publication Data

Advanced Italian / edited by Laura Riggio and Giuseppe Manca.—1st ed.
p.   cm.
ISBN 978-0-307-97158-6
1. Italian language—Textbooks for foreign speakers—English.   2. Italian language—Grammar.
3. Italian language—Spoken Italian.   I. Riggio, Laura.   II. Manca, Giuseppe.
PC1129.E5A38 2011
458.2′421—dc23   2011021875

This book is available at special discounts for bulk purchases for sales promotions or premiums. Special editions, including personalized covers, excerpts of existing books, and corporate imprints, can be created in large quantities for special needs. For more information, write to Special Markets/ Premium Sales, 1745 Broadway, MD 3-1, New York, New York 10019 or e-mail specialmarkets@ randomhouse.com.

PRINTED IN THE UNITED STATES OF AMERICA

10 9 8 7 6 5 4 3 2 1

Acknowledgements

Thanks to the Living Language team: Amanda D'Acierno, Christopher Warnasch, Suzanne McQuade, Laura Riggio, Erin Quirk, Amanda Munoz, Fabrizio LaRocca, Siobhan O'Hare, Sophie Chin, Sue Daulton, Alison Skrabek, Carolyn Roth, Ciara Robinson, and Tom Marshall.

Course Outline

COURSE

OUTLINE

COURSE

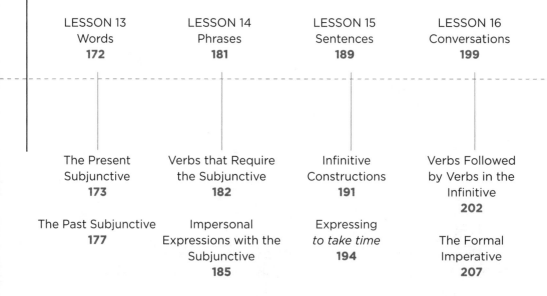

OUTLINE

How to Use This Course

Benvenuto! Welcome to *Living Language Advanced Italian*!

Before we begin, let's take a quick look at what you'll see in this course.

CONTENT

Advanced Italian is a continuation of *Intermediate Italian*. Now that you've mastered the basics with *Essential* and *Intermediate Italian,* you'll take your Italian even further with a comprehensive look at irregular verbs, advanced verb tenses, and complex sentences.

UNITS

There are four units in this course. Each unit has four lessons arranged in a "building block" structure: the first lesson will present essential *words*, the second will introduce longer *phrases*, the third will teach *sentences*, and the fourth will show how everything works together in everyday *conversations*.

At the beginning of each unit is an introduction highlighting what you'll learn in that unit. At the end of each unit you'll find the Unit Essentials, which reviews the key information from that unit, and a self-graded Unit Quiz, which tests what you've learned.

LESSONS

There are four lessons per unit for a total of 16 lessons in the course. Each lesson has the following components:

- **Introduction** outlining what you will cover in the lesson.

- **Word Builder 1** (first lesson of the unit) presenting key words and phrases.

- **Phrase Builder 1** (second lesson of the unit) introducing longer phrases and expressions.

- **Sentence Builder 1** (third lesson of the unit) teaching sentences.

- **Conversation 1** (fourth lesson of the unit) for a natural dialogue that brings together important vocabulary and grammar from the unit.

- **Take It Further** providing extra information about the new vocabulary you just saw, expanding on certain grammar points, or introducing additional words and phrases.

- **Word/Phrase/Sentence/Conversation Practice 1** practicing what you learned in Word Builder 1, Phrase Builder 1, Sentence Builder 1, or Conversation 1.

- **Grammar Builder 1** guiding you through important Italian grammar that you need to know.

- **Work Out 1** for a comprehensive practice of what you saw in Grammar Builder 1.

- **Word Builder 2/Phrase Builder 2/Sentence Builder 2/Conversation 2** for more key words, phrases, or sentences, or a second dialogue.

- **Take It Further** for expansion on what you've seen so far and additional vocabulary.

- **Word/Phrase/Sentence/Conversation Practice 2** practicing what you learned in Word Builder 2, Phrase Builder 2, Sentence Builder 2, or Conversation 2.

- **Grammar Builder 2** for more information on Italian grammar.

- **Work Out 2** for a comprehensive practice of what you saw in Grammar Builder 2.

- **Tip** or **Culture Note** for a helpful language tip or useful cultural information related to the lesson or unit.

- **Drive It Home** reviewing important grammar and vocabulary from the lesson.

- **How Did You Do?** outlining what you learned in the lesson.

UNIT ESSENTIALS

You will see **Unit Essentials** at the end of every unit. This section summarizes and reviews the key information from the unit, but with missing vocabulary information for you to fill in. In other words, each Unit Essentials works as both a study guide and a blank "cheat sheet." Once you complete it, you'll have your very own reference for the most essential vocabulary and grammar from the unit.

UNIT QUIZ

After each Unit Essentials, you'll see a **Unit Quiz.** The quizzes are self-graded so it's easy for you to test your progress and see if you should go back and review.

PROGRESS BAR

You will see a **Progress Bar** on each page that has course material. It indicates your current position within the unit and lets you know how much progress you're making. Each line in the bar represents a Grammar Builder section.

AUDIO

Look for the symbol ⊳ to help guide you through the audio as you're reading the book. It will tell you which track to listen to for each section that has audio. When you see the symbol, select the indicated track and start listening. If you don't see the symbol, then there isn't any audio for that section. You'll also see ⏸, which will tell you where that track ends.

You can listen to the audio on its own, when you're on the go, to brush up on your pronunciation or review what you've learned in the book.

PRONUNCIATION GUIDE, GRAMMAR SUMMARY, GLOSSARY

At the back of this book you will find a **Pronunciation Guide, Grammar Summary,** and **Glossary**. The Pronunciation Guide provides information on Italian pronunciation and the phonetics system used in this course. The Grammar Summary contains a brief overview of key Italian grammar from *Essential* and *Intermediate Italian*. The Glossary (Italian–English and English–Italian) includes all of the essential words from *Essential* and *Intermediate Italian,* as well as additional vocabulary.

FREE ONLINE TOOLS

Go to **www.livinglanguage.com/languagelab** to access your free online tools. The tools are organized around the units in this course, with audiovisual flashcards, and interactive games and quizzes. These tools will help you to review and practice the vocabulary and grammar that you've seen in the units, as well as provide some bonus words and phrases related to the unit's topic.

More on Using the Past
and Imperfect Tenses

The Pronoun **ci**

Modal verbs, **sapere**, and **conoscere**
in the past or imperfect

Double Object Pronouns

Unit 1:
Getting Around Italy

If you intend to travel in Italy, there are amazing choices: the seaside, the Alps, beautiful alpine lakes, little towns built on rocky hills, beautiful cities rich in art and history, and more. Are you ready to learn how to explain what you want to a travel agent? By the end of this unit, you'll know:

☐ vocabulary related to nature

☐ more on using past tenses

☐ vocabulary related to travel and tourism

☐ how to express *must*, *want*, *can*, and *know* in the past

☐ how to say *there* using the pronoun ci

☐ how to form sentences with both direct and indirect objects

☐ ways to compare things using *as*

☐ ways to compare things using *more than* and *less than*

☐ how to say *the most* and *the least*

☐ how to say *I had gone*

Lesson 1: Words

By the end of this lesson, you'll know:

- ☐ vocabulary related to nature

- ☐ more on using past tenses

- ☐ vocabulary related to travel and tourism

- ☐ how to express *must, want, can,* and *know* in the past

Word Builder 1

▶ 1A Word Builder 1 (CD 7, Track 1)

(il) mare	*sea, seaside*
(la) spiaggia	*beach*
(la) montagna	*mountains*
(la) campagna	*country, countryside*
(la) gita	*day trip/short trip*
(la) nuvola	*cloud*
(il) sole	*sun*
(la) pioggia	*rain*
(il) vento	*wind*
(il) tuono	*thunder*
(il) fulmine	*lightning*
(la) neve	*snow*

⏸

More on Using the Past
and Imperfect Tenses

The Pronoun **ci**

Modal verbs, **sapere**, and **conoscere**
in the past or imperfect

Double Object Pronouns

✎ Word Practice 1

A. Translate the following words into English.

1. (la) **nuvola** _____

2. (la) **neve** _____

3. (la) **gita** _____

4. (la) **spiaggia** _____

5. (il) **fulmine** _____

B. Translate the following words into Italian.

1. *mountains* _____

2. *rain* _____

3. *sea* _____

4. *sun* _____

5. *wind* _____

ANSWER KEY
A. 1. *cloud*; 2. *snow*; 3. *day trip*; 4. *beach*; 5. *lightning*
B. 1. (la) **montagna**; 2. (la) **pioggia**; 3. (il) **mare**; 4. (il) **sole**; 5. (il) **vento**

Grammar Builder 1

▶ 1B Grammar Builder 1 (CD 7, Track 2)

MORE ON USING THE PAST AND IMPERFECT TENSES

In Lessons 15 and 19 of *Intermediate Italian*, we studied the past tense and the imperfect, both used to speak of events that occurred in the past. However, while the past is a narrative tense, the imperfect is a descriptive tense. When we want to speak about a past action that occurred in a specific moment in time, no matter how long it lasted, we use the **passato**, while when we want to describe the circumstances associated with a past action, we use the **imperfetto**. In other words, the **imperfetto** expresses the physical or psychological circumstances surrounding the action, which is expressed by the **passato**.

As we saw in Lesson 19, the **imperfetto** is used to express a habitual action in the past, as well as a progressive action in the past.

Quando andavo in montagna facevo molte escursioni.
When I used to go to the mountains, I would hike a lot.

Mentre camminavo improvvisamente ha cominciato a piovere.
I was walking, when all of a sudden it started to rain.

In addition, the **imperfetto** is used to express age, time, weather, and a physical or emotional state in the past.

Quando avevo dieci anni andavo sempre al lago.
When I was ten, I would always go to the lake.

Erano le 11:30 quando finalmente siamo partiti.
It was 11:30 when we finally left.

Il sole splendeva e non c'era una nuvola in cielo.
The sun was shining and there wasn't a single cloud in the sky.

Ero molto felice.
I was very happy.

Ⅱ

Modal verbs, **sapere**, and **conoscere**
in the past or imperfect

Double Object Pronouns

✎ Work Out 1

Complete the following sentences using either the past or the imperfect of the
verbs in parentheses as appropriate.

1. _____ (Essere) l'una quando il treno finalmente _____

   (arrivare).

2. Voi non _____ (andare) al parco perché

   _____ (piovere) molto forte.

3. Loro _____ (mangiare) quando Enrico

   _____ (entrare) in casa.

4. Mentre lui _____ (dormire) Mariella _____

   (leggere) un libro.

5. Noi _____ (avere) dieci anni quando _____

   _____ (venire) a vivere in America.

ANSWER KEY

1. era, è arrivato; 2. siete andati/e, pioveva; 3. mangiavano, è entrato; 4. dormiva, leggeva;
5. avevamo, siamo venuti/e

Word Builder 2

▶ 1C Word Builder 2 (CD 7, Track 3)

(il) viaggio	trip
(l')isola	island
(la) Sardegna	Sardinia
(la) Sicilia	Sicily
(la) storia	story, history
(la) cultura	culture

(il) tempio	temple
greco	Greek
arabo	Arab
barocco	baroque
selvaggio	wild
entrambi/entrambe	both (of them)

Word Practice 2

Match the following expressions.

1. greco
2. (il) tempio
3. arabo
4. (la) cultura
5. (la) Sardegna
6. entrambi/entrambe
7. (l')isola
8. selvaggio

a. Sardinia
b. both (of them)
c. temple
d. island
e. wild
f. Greek
g. Arab
h. culture

ANSWER KEY
1. f; 2. c; 3. g; 4. h; 5. a; 6. b; 7. d; 8. e

More on Using the Past
and Imperfect Tenses

The Pronoun **ci**

Modal verbs, **sapere**, and **conoscere**
in the past or imperfect

Double Object Pronouns

Grammar Builder 2

▶ 1D Grammar Builder 2 (CD 7, Track 4)

MODAL VERBS, SAPERE, AND CONOSCERE IN THE PAST OR IMPERFECT

Modal verbs (dovere, volere, and potere) have slightly different meanings when used in the past or the imperfect. Generally, the past has a stronger meaning than the imperfect, as exemplified in the following sentences:

Dovevo andare a cena a casa di amici dei miei genitori.
I was supposed to go to dinner at my parents' friends' house. (I didn't necessarily go)

Sono dovuta andare a cena a casa di amici dei miei genitori.
I had to go to dinner at my parents' friends' house. (I did go)

Volevo fare un viaggio in Sicilia.
I wanted to take a trip to Sicily. (I didn't necessarily go)

Ho voluto fare un viaggio in Sicilia.
I wanted to take a trip to Sicily. (I did go)

Potevo andare in montagna.
I could have gone to the mountains. (I had the means and opportunity, but I didn't necessarily go)

Sono potuto andare in montagna.
I managed to go to the mountains.

Also, the verbs sapere and conoscere have a slightly different meaning when used in the past or the imperfect.

Advanced Italian

When used in the imperfect, **conoscere** means *to be familiar with*, while in the past it means *to meet (for the first time)*.

Non conoscevo Giuseppe Nannini, ma l'ho conosciuto ieri sera.
I didn't know Giuseppe Nannini, but I met him last night.

Used in the imperfect, **sapere** means *to be aware*, while in the past it means *to find out*.

Non sapevo che volevi andare in vacanza con Gigi.
I didn't know you wanted to go on vacation with Gigi.

Hanno saputo che lui è già partito.
They found out that he has already left.

Ⓘ

✎ Work Out 2

Complete the following sentences with either the past or the imperfect of the verbs in parentheses.

1. **Lui ha vinto un milione di euro alla lotteria e** _____

   (potere) permettersi di fare un viaggio di un anno intorno al mondo.

2. **Noi** _____ **(dovere) andare in Italia quest'estate, ma Mirko**

   si è ammalato e così non andremo.

3. **"Tu** _____ **(sapere) che Franco si è fidanzato?" Sì, l'** _____

   _____ **(sapere) la settimana scorsa.**

Modal verbs, **sapere**, and **conoscere**
in the past or imperfect

Double Object Pronouns

4. Quando ho visto quel vestito, l' _____ (volere) comprare

a tutti i costi!

5. Quando ha cominciato a piovere, loro _____

(dovere) interrompere la passeggiata.

ANSWER KEY
1. ha potuto; 2. dovevamo; 3. sapevi, ho saputo; 4. ho voluto; 5. hanno dovuto

✎ Drive It Home

Complete the following sentences using either the past or the imperfect of the
verbs in parentheses.

1. Quando Paolo (arrivare) _____ io (guardare)

_____ la televisione.

2. Quando lui (essere) _____ un bambino (avere) _____ molti

giocattoli.

3. Mentre lei (cucinare) _____ suo fratello (preparare)

_____ il caffè.

4. Quando noi (arrivare) _____ in campagna il

sole (splendere) _____.

5. Ieri alla festa di Laura io (essere) _____ molto annoiato, ma poi (conoscere)

_____ Franco e insieme (divertirsi) _____

_____ tanto.

6. Lei (volere) _____ venire al cinema con noi, invece (andare) _____

_____ al bar con Gino.

7. Loro non (sapere) _____ che oggi è il mio compleanno.

8. Quando Franco non (lavorare) _____, non (potere)

_____ noleggiare la macchina spesso.

9. Io (sapere) _____ finalmente dove Maria compra

quei dolci buonissimi.

10. (volere) _____ pagare il conto io, ma non (avere) _____

abbastanza soldi e così (dovere) _____ pagare Bruno.

ANSWER KEY

1. è arrivato, guardavo; 2. era, aveva; 3. cucinava, preparava; 4. siamo arrivati, splendeva; 5. ero, ho conosciuto, ci siamo divertiti; 6. voleva, è andata; 7. sapevano; 8. lavorava, poteva; 9. ho saputo; 10. Volevo, avevo, ha dovuto

How Did You Do?

Let's see how you did in this lesson. By now, you should know:

☐ vocabulary related to nature (Still unsure? Jump back to page 13.)

☐ more on using past tenses (Still unsure? Jump back to page 14.)

☐ vocabulary related to travel and tourism (Still unsure? Jump back to page 16.)

☐ how to express *must, want, can,* and *know* in the past
(Still unsure? Jump back to page 18.)

✎ Word Recall

A. Translate the following words into English.

1. (il) sole _____

2. (la) pioggia _____

3. (la) neve _____

More on Using the Past
and Imperfect Tenses

The Pronoun **ci**

Modal verbs, **sapere**, and **conoscere**
in the past or imperfect

Double Object Pronouns

4. (l')isola _____

5. barocco _____

B. Translate the following words into Italian.

1. *wild* _____

2. *trip* _____

3. *lightning* _____

4. *Greek* _____

5. *beach* _____

ANSWER KEY
A. 1. *sun*; 2. *rain*; 3. *snow*; 4. *island*; 5. *baroque*
B. 1. **selvaggio**; 2. **(il) viaggio**; 3. **(il) fulmine**; 4. **greco**; 5. **(la) spiaggia**

Lesson 2: Phrases

By the end of this lesson, you'll know:

☐ how to say *there* using the pronoun **ci**

☐ how to form sentences with both direct and indirect objects

Phrase Builder 1

▶ 2A Phrase Builder 1 (CD 7, Track 5)

Ci va.	*He/she goes there.*
Ne parla.	*He/she speaks about it.*
Beato te!	*Lucky you!*

Sto per ...	I'm about to ...
raccogliere funghi	to pick mushrooms
più adatto	more appropriate
del solito	than usual
mai più	never again
al mare	at the beach
al lago	at the lake
in montagna	to the mountains
in campagna	to the country

(II)

✎ Phrase Practice 1

Match the following expressions.

1. raccogliere funghi
2. mai più
3. Beato te!
4. più adatto
5. Ne parla.
6. Ci va.
7. al lago
8. al mare

a. *Lucky you!*
b. *He/she speaks about it.*
c. *never again*
d. *at the lake*
e. *at the beach*
f. *to pick mushrooms*
g. *He/she goes there.*
h. *more appropriate*

ANSWER KEY
1. f; 2. c; 3. a; 4. h; 5. b; 6. g; 7. d; 8. e

More on Using the Past
and Imperfect Tenses

The Pronoun **ci**

Modal verbs, **sapere**, and **conoscere**
in the past or imperfect

Double Object Pronouns

Grammar Builder 1

 2B Grammar Builder 1 (CD 7, Track 6)

THE PRONOUN CI

You have already encountered the pronoun ci in different functions: as a direct
object pronoun (*us*), as an indirect object pronoun (*to us*), and as a reflexive
pronoun (*ourselves*). You have also encountered it in the expression c'è and
ci sono where it expresses a location and has the meaning of *there*. With this
function it replaces the preposition a (or da, in, and su) + a place.

"Vai spesso in montagna?" "Sì, ci vado spesso."
"Do you often go to the mountains?" "Yes, I go there a lot/often."

"Vieni a casa mia stasera?" "Sì, ci vengo."
"Are you coming to my house tonight?" "Yes, I'm coming (there)."

Ci can also be used to replace a prepositional phrase introduced by a, su, or in,
even if it doesn't refer to location.

"Pensi di fare una vacanza in Europa?" "Oh, sì, ci penso spesso!"
"Do you think about taking a vacation to Europe?" "Oh, yes, I often think about it."

"Credi a quello che ci ha raccontato Mario?" "Non, non ci credo affatto."
"Do you believe what Mario told us?" "No, I don't believe it at all."

The pronoun ne means *of/about it* or *of/about them*. It is used to replace a
partitive *some* construction, including one introduced by a number, or expression
indicating quantity.

Non me ne hai mai parlato.
You never spoke to me about it.

"Puoi comprare delle riviste?" "Quante ne devo comprare?"
"Can you buy some magazines?" "How many (of them) shall I buy?"

"Quanti viaggi fai quest'anno?" "Ne faccio due."
"How many trips are you taking this year?" "I'm taking two (trips)."

Ne also replaces a noun or expression introduced by the preposition di.

"Hai bisogno di aiuto?" "No, non ne ho bisogno."
"Do you need help?" "No, I don't need any."

(II)

✎ Work Out 1

Complete the following sentences with either ci or ne.

1. Se vuoi andare in Sicilia _____ possiamo andare insieme.

2. Non preoccuparti, _____ penso io!

3. Mi hanno offerto dei soldi, ma io non _____ ho bisogno.

4. Sapevo che non c'erano più mele e così _____ ho comprato un chilo.

5. Stasera andiamo in discoteca, _____ vieni anche tu?

6. "Vuoi ancora un po' di vino?" "No grazie, non _____ voglio più."

ANSWER KEY
1. ci; 2. ci; 3. ne; 4. ne; 5. ci; 6. ne

More on Using the Past
and Imperfect Tenses

The Pronoun **ci**

Modal verbs, **sapere**, and **conoscere**
in the past or imperfect

Double Object Pronouns

Phrase Builder 2

▶ 2C Phrase Builder 2 (CD 7, Track 7)

fare un viaggio	to take a trip; to go on a trip
in macchina	by car
in treno	by train
in aereo	by plane
fare una foto	to take a picture
insieme a te	(together) with you
Te ne voglio parlare.	I want to talk with you about it. I want to discuss it with you.
Gliele do.	I give them to him/to her.
Posso mandargliele.	I can send them to him/to her.
in ogni caso	in any event
più culture	more/different cultures
più selvaggia	wilder
testa o croce	heads or tails

✎ Phrase Practice 2

A. Translate the following phrases into English.

1. fare una foto _____

2. Gliele do. _____

3. insieme a te _____

4. testa o croce _____

B. Translate the following phrases into Italian.

1. *by plane* _____

2. *I want to talk with you about it.* _____

3. *in any event* _____

4. *to take a trip; to go on a trip* _____

ANSWER KEY

A. 1. *to take a picture*; 2. *I give them to him/to her.* 3. *(together) with you*; 4. *heads or tails*
B. 1. **in aereo**; 2. **Te ne voglio parlare.** 3. **in ogni caso**; 4. **fare un viaggio**

Grammar Builder 2

⊳ 2D Grammar Builder 2 (CD 7, Track 8)

DOUBLE OBJECT PRONOUNS

So far you have learned to replace either a direct or an indirect object with a pronoun (see Lessons 16 and 17 of *Intermediate Italian*). However, sentences often contain both a direct and an indirect object as in **Mando una lettera a mio zio** (*I send a letter to my uncle*), where **una lettera** is the direct object and **a mio zio** is the indirect object. Both objects can be replaced by a pronoun, called a double object pronoun.

	+ LO	+ LA	+ LI	+ LE	+ NE*
mi	me lo	me la	me li	me le	me ne
ti	te lo	te la	te li	te le	te ne
ci	ce lo	ce la	ce li	ce le	ce ne
vi	ve lo	ve la	ve li	ve le	ve ne
gli	glielo	gliela	glieli	gliele	gliene
le/Le	glielo	gliela	glieli	gliele	gliene

* Ne is included in this chart, even though it's not a direct object pronoun, because it behaves the same as direct object pronouns.

More on Using the Past
and Imperfect Tenses

The Pronoun **ci**

Modal verbs, **sapere**, and **conoscere**
in the past or imperfect

Double Object Pronouns

As you can see from the chart, the indirect object pronoun always precedes the direct object pronoun. In addition, some spelling changes occur to the indirect object pronouns: when followed by a direct object pronoun, the indirect object pronoun ending -i changes to -e. Also, the indirect object pronouns gli, le, and Le change to glie, which is attached to the direct object's pronoun, forming a single word. Please note that in double object pronouns there is no difference between *to her* and *to him*. The position of double object pronouns is the same as for single object pronouns.

Faccio un viaggio e volevo parlartene.
I'm taking a trip and I wanted to talk to you about it/discuss it with you.

Ho sentito una barzelletta divertente e ve la voglio raccontare.
I want to tell you a funny joke I heard.

"Dove hai comprato questa borsa?" "Me l'ha regalata mia madre."
"Where did you buy this purse?" "My mother gave it to me as a present."

In compound tenses the past participle agrees in gender and number with the preceding direct object.

Giuseppe mi ha chiesto di fare delle foto e io gliele ho promesse.
Giuseppe asked me to take some pictures and I promised him I would.

(II)

✎ Work Out 2

Complete the following sentences using a double object pronoun.

1. Hai parlato a Vittorio del viaggio? No, non _____ ho parlato.

2. Ti fa dei regali il tuo ragazzo? Sì _____ fa molti.

3. Vi siete ricordati di comprare il pane? Sì, _____ siamo ricordati.

4. Hai dato la rivista a tuo padre? No, non _____ ho ancora data.

5. Mi mandi quella lettera per favore? Sì, _____ mando domani.

6. Più tardi ti racconto una fiaba. _____ puoi raccontare subito?

ANSWER KEY
1. gliene; 2. me ne; 3. ce ne; 4. gliel'; 5. te la; 6. Me la

✎ Drive It Home

Answer the following questions using the pronoun ci, ne, or the direct object pronouns as needed.

1. A che ora vai al cinema? _____ alle quattro.

2. Quanti amici hai invitato? _____ sette.

3. Vieni al museo con me domani? Sì, _____ volentieri.

4. Hai dato il giornale a Paolo? No, _____.

5. Ti ha scritto l'email tuo fratello? Sì, _____.

6. Insegni i pronomi agli studenti oggi? Sì, _____.

7. Mi prometti che penserai a ciò che ti ho detto? Sì, _____ prometto,

_____ penserò.

8. Quante volte siete andate al ristorante il mese scorso? _____

_____ sei volte.

9. Ci racconti il film che hai visto? Va bene, _____.

10. Quanti fiori hai comprato a Giulia? _____

due dozzine.

More on Using the Past
and Imperfect Tenses

The Pronoun **ci**

Modal verbs, **sapere**, and **conoscere**
in the past or imperfect

Double Object Pronouns

ANSWER KEY

1. Ci vado; 2. Ne ho invitati; 3. ci vengo; 4. non gliel'ho dato; 5. me l'ha scritta; 6. glieli insegno;
7. te lo, ci; 8. Ci siamo andate; 9. ve lo racconto; 10. Gliene ho comprate

How Did You Do?

Let's see how you did in this lesson. By now, you should know:

☐ how to say *there* using the pronoun **ci** (Still unsure? Jump back to page 24.)

☐ how to form sentences with both direct and indirect objects
   (Still unsure? Jump back to page 27.)

✎ Word Recall

A. Translate the following phrases into English.

1. **Gliele do.** _____

2. **in ogni caso** _____

3. **mai più** _____

4. **sto per ...** _____

5. **fare una foto** _____

B. Translate the following phrases into Italian.

1. *more appropriate* _____

2. *He/she speaks about it.* _____

3. *to the country* _____

4. *I can send them to him/to her.* _____

5. *to pick mushrooms* _____

ANSWER KEY
A. 1. *I give them to him/to her.* 2. *in any event*; 3. *never again*; 4. *I'm about to …* ; 5. *to take a picture*
B. 1. **più adatto**; 2. **Ne parla**. 3. **in campagna**; 4. **Posso mandargliele/li**. 5. **raccogliere funghi**

Lesson 3: Sentences

By the end of this lesson, you'll know:

☐ ways to compare things using *as*

☐ ways to compare things using *more than* and *less than*

Sentence Builder 1

▶ 3A Sentence Builder 1 (CD 7, Track 9)

Sto per andare in vacanza.	*I'm about to go on vacation.*
Non ci andrò mai più.	*I'll never go there again.*
Non ne hai mai parlato.	*You never talked about it.*
Quando andavo in montagna facevo escursioni.	*When I used to go to the mountains, I would hike.*
Sembrava la giornata migliore di tutte.	*It seemed like the ideal day.*
Mentre camminavo il cielo si è riempito di nuvole.	*While I was walking, the sky filled with clouds.*
Tuonava e un fulmine è caduto vicino a me.	*It was thundering, and lightning struck near me.*
Il mare non è così interessante come la montagna.	*The beach is not as interesting as the mountains.*

More on Using the Past
and Imperfect Tenses

The Pronoun **ci**

Modal verbs, **sapere**, and **conoscere**
in the past or imperfect

Double Object Pronouns

✎ Sentence Practice 1

A. Translate the following sentences into English.

1. **Quando andavo in montagna facevo escursioni.** _____

_____

2. **Non ci andrò mai più.** _____

_____

3. **Il mare non è così interessante come la montagna.** _____

_____

B. Translate the following sentences into Italian.

1. *It was thundering, and lightning struck near me.* _____

_____

2. *You never talked about it.* _____

_____

3. *I'm about to go on vacation.* _____

_____

ANSWER KEY

A. 1. *When I used to go to the mountains, I would hike.* 2. *I'll never go there again.* 3. *The beach is not as interesting as the mountains.*

B. 1. Tuonava e un fulmine è caduto vicino a me. 2. Non ne hai mai parlato. 3. Sto per andare in vacanza.

Grammar Builder 1

▶ 3B Grammar Builder 1 (CD 7, Track 10)

COMPARATIVES OF EQUALITY

To express a comparative of equality (*as/so ... as; as much/as many ... as*) Italian uses either **così ... come, tanto ... quanto**, or **sia ... che**. The first part of the comparison (**così** or **tanto**) is often omitted.

Il mare non è (così) interessante come la montagna.
The beach is not as interesting as the mountains.

La Sicilia è (tanto) bella quanto ricca di storia.
Sicily is as beautiful as it is rich in history.

When two nouns are compared, **tanto ... quanto** must be used, and they must agree in gender and number with the nouns they modify.

Lui sembra avere tanti giorni di lavoro quante vacanze.
He seems to have as many working days as vacation days.

⏸

✎ Work Out 1

Form complete sentences with the given expressions, using a comparative of equality. Don't forget to conjugate the verb.

1. **Mario/avere/libri/CD/.** _____

_____

More on Using the Past
and Imperfect Tenses

The Pronoun **ci**

Modal verbs, **sapere**, and **conoscere**
in the past or imperfect

Double Object Pronouns

2. Noi/essere/stanchi/felici/. _____

_____

3. Loro/mangiare/pasta/carne/. _____

_____

4. Voi/viaggiare/in Europa/in Asia/. _____

_____

5. La campagna/non essere/divertente/mare/. _____

_____

ANSWER KEY

1. Mario ha tanti libri quanti CD. 2. Noi siamo tanto stanchi quanto felici. 3. Loro mangiano tanta pasta quanta carne. 4. Voi viaggiate (così) in Europa come in Asia. 5. La campagna non è così divertente come il mare.

Sentence Builder 2

▶ 3C Sentence Builder 2 (CD 7, Track 11)

Quando hai chiamato ero già uscita.	*When you called I had already gone out/left.*
Sono dovuta andare a cena a casa di amici dei miei genitori.	*I had to go to dinner at my parents' friends' house.*
Sia in Sicilia che in Sardegna ci sono spiagge bellissime.	*There are beautiful beaches in both Sicily and Sardinia.*
La Sicilia ha una storia più ricca della Sardegna.	*Sicily has a richer history than Sardinia.*
In Sicilia si sono alternate più culture che in Sardegna.	*In Sicily there have been more cultures than in Sardinia.*
La natura è più selvaggia in Sardegna che in Sicilia.	*Nature is wilder in Sardinia than in Sicily.*

| I nuraghi sono forse più antichi di qualsiasi monumento in Sicilia. | *Nuraghi are perhaps more ancient than any monument in Sicily.* |
| Giuseppe mi ha chiesto di fare delle foto e io gliele ho promesse. | *Giuseppe asked me to take some pictures and I promised him that I would.* |

Ⓘ

✎ Sentence Practice 2

Match the following expressions.

1. La natura è più selvaggia in Sardegna che in Sicilia.
2. I nuraghi sono forse più antichi di qualsiasi monumento in Sicilia.
3. La Sicilia ha una storia più ricca della Sardegna.
4. Giuseppe mi ha chiesto di fare delle foto e io gliele ho promesse.
5. Sia in Sicilia che in Sardegna ci sono spiagge bellissime.
6. Quando hai chiamato ero già uscita.

a. *Sicily has a richer history than Sardinia.*
b. *There are beautiful beaches in both Sicily and Sardinia.*
c. *When you called I had already gone out/left.*
d. *Nuraghi are perhaps more ancient than any monument in Sicily.*
e. *Nature is wilder in Sardinia than in Sicily.*
f. *Giuseppe asked me to take some pictures and I promised him that I would.*

ANSWER KEY
1. e; 2. d; 3. a; 4. f; 5. b; 6. c

More on Using the Past
and Imperfect Tenses

The Pronoun **ci**

Modal verbs, **sapere**, and **conoscere**
in the past or imperfect

Double Object Pronouns

Grammar Builder 2

▶ 3D Grammar Builder 2 (CD 7, Track 12)

COMPARATIVES OF INEQUALITY

The comparison of inequality can be either of superiority (*more, -er … than*) or
of inferiority (*less … than*). They are expressed in Italian by più … and by meno
… respectively. *Than* can either be translated as di or che. Di is used in front of
numbers, or when two entities are compared in terms of the same quality or action.

La Sicilia ha una storia più ricca della Sardegna.
Sicily has a richer history than Sardinia.

I treni sono meno cari degli aerei.
Trains are less expensive than planes.

Che is used when comparing two entities of the same quality (expressed by
nouns, adjectives, verbs, or adverbs).

La natura è più selvaggia in Sardegna che in Sicilia.
Nature is wilder in Sardinia than in Sicily.

È più comodo viaggiare in macchina che in treno.
It's more comfortable to travel by car than by train.

⏸

✎ Work Out 2

Complete the following sentences with either di or che. Don't forget to combine di with the article when necessary.

1. La campagna è più noiosa _____ il mare.

2. In Italia è più costoso viaggiare in macchina _____ in treno.

3. Noi viaggiamo meno _____ voi.

4. Il biglietto aereo costa più _____ 1.500 dollari.

5. Tu viaggi più in Europa _____ in Asia.

6. La Toscana ha più opere d'arte _____ le altre regioni in Italia.

ANSWER KEY
1. La campagna è più noiosa del mare. 2. In Italia è più costoso viaggiare in macchina che in treno. 3. Noi viaggiamo meno di voi. 4. Il biglietto aereo costa più di 1.500 dollari. 5. Tu viaggi più in Europa che in Asia. 6. La Toscana ha più opere d'arte delle altre regioni in Italia.

✎ Drive It Home

Complete the following sentences with the appropriate form of di, che, or quanto.

1. A Venezia d'estate ci sono più turisti _____ veneziani.

2. L'italiano è più difficile _____ lo spagnolo.

3. Tu leggi più libri_____ giornali.

4. Il mio amico Luigi è tanto simpatico _____ generoso.

5. La macchina di Giulio è più veloce _____ la tua.

6. Roma è tanto bella _____ Parigi.

7. I film di Fellini sono più interessanti _____ quelli di Rossellini.

More on Using the Past
and Imperfect Tenses

The Pronoun **ci**

Modal verbs, **sapere**, and **conoscere**
in the past or imperfect

Double Object Pronouns

8. La torta che fa mia madre è decisamente _____ buona _____ la mia.

9. Luigi è _____ alto quanto grasso.

10. A casa ho tanti CD _____ libri.

ANSWER KEY
1. che; 2. dello; 3. che; 4. quanto; 5. della; 6. quanto; 7. di; 8. più, della; 9. tanto; 10. quanti

Culture Note

Not too many people outside of Italy travel to Sardinia, perhaps because it is isolated and inconvenient to reach. Sardinia, however, offers some of the cleanest and most beautiful beaches in Europe, and it's certainly worth the trip!

How Did You Do?

Let's see how you did in this lesson. By now, you should know:

☐ ways to compare things using *as* (Still unsure? Jump back to page 33.)

☐ ways to compare things using *more than* and *less than*
(Still unsure? Jump back to page 36.)

Word Recall

A. Translate the following sentences into English.

1. Il mare non è così interessante come la montagna. _____

   _____

2. La natura è più selvaggia in Sardegna che in Sicilia. _____

   _____

3. Sia in Sicilia che in Sardegna ci sono spiagge bellissime. _____

   _____

4. Sto per andare in vacanza. _____

_____

5. Non ne hai mai parlato. _____

_____

B. Translate the following sentences into Italian.

1. *Sicily has a richer history than Sardinia.* _____

_____

2. *When you called I had already gone out/left.* _____

_____

3. *I had to go to dinner to my parents' friends' house.* _____

_____

4. *I'll never go there again.* _____

_____

5. *While I was walking, the sky filled with clouds.* _____

_____

ANSWER KEY

A. 1. *The beach is not as interesting as the mountains. 2. Nature is wilder in Sardinia than in Sicily. 3. There are beautiful beaches in both Sicily and Sardinia. 4. I'm about to go on vacation. 5. You never talked about it.*
B. 1. **La Sicilia ha una storia più ricca della Sardegna.** 2. **Quando hai chiamato ero già uscita.**
3. **Sono dovuta andare a cena a casa di amici dei miei genitori.** 4. **Non ci andrò mai più.** 5. **Mentre camminavo il cielo si è riempito di nuvole.**

More on Using the Past
and Imperfect Tenses

The Pronoun **ci**

Modal verbs, **sapere**, and **conoscere**
in the past or imperfect

Double Object Pronouns

Lesson 4: Conversations

By the end of this lesson, you'll know:

☐ how to say *the most* and *the least*

☐ how to say *I had gone*

ⒶⒶ Conversation 1

▶ 4A Conversation 1 (CD 7, Track 13 - Italian; Track 14 - Italian and English)

Gabriele:	Ciao Paolo, come va?
Paolo:	Molto bene, sto per andare finalmente in vacanza.
Gabriele:	Beato te, vai di nuovo in montagna?
Paolo:	No, non ci andrò mai più! Non sai cosa mi è successo l'anno scorso?
Gabriele:	No, non me ne hai mai parlato.
Paolo:	Allora, sai che mi piace molto camminare e quando andavo in montagna ogni giorno facevo delle escursioni (sulle montagne) o passeggiavo nei boschi per raccogliere funghi. Un giorno l'anno scorso mi sono svegliato ed era una giornata bellissima, splendeva il sole e non c'era una nuvola in cielo. Ero molto felice perché volevo fare un'escursione più lunga del solito e questa sembrava la giornata ideale. Dopo circa tre ore, mentre camminavo, improvvisamente il cielo si è riempito di nuvole e ha cominciato a piovere. Tuonava e lampeggiava e un fulmine è caduto a due metri da me e ha distrutto un albero! In quel momento ho deciso di non andare mai più in montagna!
Gabriele:	E allora dove vai in vacanza?
Paolo:	Vado al mare! Non è così interessante come la montagna, ma non è nemmeno così pericoloso.

Gabriele:	Hello Paolo, how's it going?
Paolo:	Very well, I'm finally about to go on vacation.
Gabriele:	Lucky you; are you going to the mountains again?
Paolo:	No, I'll never go there again! Don't you know what happened to me last year?
Gabriele:	No, you never told me about it.
Paolo:	Well, you know I like to walk a lot, and when I used to go to the mountains every day, I would hike (on mountains) or walk in the woods to pick up mushrooms. One day last year, I woke up and it was a gorgeous day: the sun was shining and there wasn't a cloud in the sky. I was very happy because I wanted to take a longer hike than usual, and that seemed like the perfect day. After about three hours, while I was walking, all of a sudden the sky filled with clouds and it began to rain. It was thundering and lightning, and lightning struck and destroyed a tree two meters away from me. At that precise moment, I decided never to go to the mountains again!
Gabriele:	So, where are you going on vacation?
Paolo:	I'm going to the seaside/beach! It's not as interesting as the mountains, but it's not as dangerous either.

Notes:

Stare per + infinitive translates to the idiomatic expression *to be about to*: l'aereo sta per decollare (*the plane is about to take off*).

The verb fare is used idiomatically to express weather conditions: fa caldo/ freddo (*it is hot/cold*), fa bello/brutto (*it's good/bad [weather]*).

More on Using the Past
and Imperfect Tenses

The Pronoun **ci**

Modal verbs, **sapere**, and **conoscere**
in the past or imperfect

Double Object Pronouns

✎ Conversation Practice 1

Fill in the blanks in the following sentences with the missing words in the word bank.
If you're unsure of the answer, listen to the conversation on your audio one more time.

c'era, camminavo, così interessante come, ci andrò, sai, mai più, sono svegliato,
più lunga del solito, facevo, si è riempito, sto per

1. Molto bene, _____ andare finalmente in vacanza.

2. No, non _____ mai più!

3. _____ che mi piace molto camminare.

4. Quando andavo in montagna ogni giorno _____ delle escursioni.

5. Un giorno l'anno scorso mi _____ ed era

   una giornata bellissima.

6. Ero molto felice perché volevo fare un'escursione _____

   _____ .

7. Mentre _____ , improvvisamente il cielo _____

   _____ di nuvole e ha cominciato a piovere.

8. In quel momento ho deciso di non andare _____ in montagna!

9. Non _____ una nuvola in cielo.

10. Il mare non è _____ la

    montagna.

ANSWER KEY
1. sto per; 2. ci andrò; 3. Sai; 4. facevo; 5. sono svegliato; 6. più lunga del solito; 7. camminavo, si è
riempito; 8. mai più; 9. c'era; 10. così interessante come

Grammar Builder 1

⊳ 4B Grammar Builder 1 (CD 7, Track 15)

SUPERLATIVES

There are two superlatives in Italian: the relative superlative (*more/less beautiful than*), and the absolute superlative (*the most/least beautiful*).

The relative superlative is formed by placing the appropriate definite article in front of the comparatives **più** or **meno**, or by using a noun + **più** or **meno**. Italian uses **di** or **fra/tra** to express the English *in* or *of* in superlative constructions.

Sembrava la giornata più adatta di tutte.
It seemed like the ideal day.

Cortina è la cittadina più famosa delle Dolomiti.
Cortina is the best known town in the Dolomites.

L'aereo è il mezzo di trasporto più veloce (di tutti).
Airplanes are the fastest means of transportation (of all).

The absolute superlative is formed by adding the appropriate form of the suffix -ssimo (-ssima, -ssimi, -ssime) to the masculine plural form of the adjective: **bello → belli → bellissimo/a/i/e**; **felice → felici → felicissimo/a/i/e**.

Era una giornata bellissima.
It was a very beautiful/gorgeous day.

Ho fatto un viaggio interessantissimo.
I went on a very interesting trip.

More on Using the Past
and Imperfect Tenses

The Pronoun **ci**

Modal verbs, **sapere**, and **conoscere**
in the past or imperfect

Double Object Pronouns

The absolute superlative can also be expressed by preceding an adjective with the adverb molto.

Ero molto felice.
I was very happy.

Abbiamo visto monumenti molto antichi.
We saw very ancient monuments.

(II)

✎ Work Out 1

Rewrite the following sentences following the example:

**Marco è un ragazzo gentile. → Marco è il ragazzo più gentile del mondo. →
Marco è un ragazzo gentilissimo.**

1. Loro sono ragazzi simpatici. _____

   _____

2. Questo è un viaggio lungo. _____

   _____

3. L'Eurostar è un treno veloce. _____

   _____

4. Questo è un libro noioso. _____

   _____

5. Questa è una modella bella. _____

   _____

ANSWER KEY

1. (Loro) sono i ragazzi più simpatici del mondo. (Loro) sono ragazzi simpaticissimi. 2. Questo è il viaggio più lungo del mondo. Questo è un viaggio lunghissimo. 3. L'Eurostar è il treno più veloce del mondo. L'Eurostar è un treno velocissimo. 4. Questo è il libro più noioso del mondo. Questo è un libro noiosissimo. 5. Questa è la modella più bella del mondo. Questa è una modella bellissima.

Conversation 2

▶ 4C Conversation 2 (CD 7, Track 16 - Italian; Track 17 - Italian and English)

Mario:	Ciao Giulietta, ti ho chiamata ieri sera, ma non c'eri.
Giulietta:	Sì, ho ricevuto il tuo messaggio; quando hai chiamato ero già uscita. Sono dovuta andare a cena a casa di amici dei miei genitori. Lì ho conosciuto Giuseppe Nannini, lo conosci?
Mario:	No. Scusa se cambio discorso, ma volevo chiederti se vuoi fare un viaggio con me quest'estate.
Giulietta:	Dove hai in progetto di andare?
Mario:	Non lo so, pensavo di andare in Sicilia o in Sardegna, ma volevo parlartene e decidere insieme a te.
Giulietta:	Sono due isole molto belle, simili e diverse allo stesso tempo, sarà una decisione difficile. Vuoi andare in treno o in aereo?
Mario:	Come vuoi, non importa, ma prima dobbiamo decidere che cosa vogliamo fare, sia in Sicilia che in Sardegna ci sono spiagge bellissime, ma la Sicilia ha una storia più ricca della Sardegna. In Sicilia si sono alternate più culture che in Sardegna. Ci sono molti templi e teatri greci da visitare, molti edifici con influenze arabe e molte chiese barocche. La natura è più selvaggia in Sardegna che in Sicilia e in Sardegna ci sono i famosi nuraghi, i monumenti archeologici forse più antichi di qualsiasi monumento in Sicilia. In ogni caso, in Sicilia o in Sardegna dovrò fare molte foto: Giuseppe mi ha chiesto se posso mandargliene perché vuole usarle nella sua agenzia di viaggi ed io gliele ho promesse.
Giulietta:	Mi sembrano entrambi due posti meravigliosi, e non so proprio quale scegliere. Perché non facciamo testa o croce?

More on Using the Past
and Imperfect Tenses

The Pronoun **ci**

Modal verbs, **sapere**, and **conoscere**
in the past or imperfect

Double Object Pronouns

Mario:	Hi, Giulietta, I called you last night, but you were not there.
Giulietta:	Yes, I got your message; when you called I had already left. I had to go to my parents' friends' house for dinner. There I met Giuseppe Nannini; do you know him?
Mario:	No. Excuse me if I change the subject, but I wanted to ask you if you would like to take a trip with me this summer.
Giulietta:	Where were you thinking of going?
Mario:	I don't know. I was thinking of going to Sicily, or Sardinia, but I wanted to talk to you about it, and decide with you.
Giulietta:	They are two very beautiful islands, similar and different at the same time; it is going to be a difficult decision. Do you want to go by train or by plane?
Mario:	I'll leave that up to you, it doesn't matter to me; but first we must decide what we want to do. There are beautiful beaches in both Sicily and Sardinia. Sicily has a richer history than Sardinia. In Sicily there have been more cultures than in Sardinia. There are many Greek temples and theaters to visit, many buildings with Arab influences, and many Baroque churches. Nature is wilder in Sardinia than in Sicily, and in Sardinia there are the famous nuraghi, archeological monuments perhaps more ancient than any monument in Sicily. In any event, either in Sicily or in Sardinia I will have to take many pictures because Giuseppe asked me if I can send him some as he wants to use them for his travel agency and I promised him that I will.
Giulietta:	They both seem like wonderful places, I wouldn't know which one to choose. Why don't we flip a coin?

Notes:

Tempio (*temple*) has an irregular plural: templi.

Sia … che expresses the English *both … and.*

✎ Conversation Practice 2

Translate the expressions written in parentheses in the following sentences.

1. Ciao Giulietta, *(I called you last night)* _____

   _____, ma *(you were not there)* _____.

2. Vuoi andare *(by train or by plane)* _____?

3. Prima *(we must)* _____ decidere che cosa *(we want)*

   _____ fare.

4. *(both)* _____ in Sicilia *(and)* _____ in Sardegna *(there are)*

   _____ spiagge bellissime.

5. La Sicilia *(has a richer history than)* _____

   _____ Sardegna.

6. In Sicilia si sono alternate *(more cultures than)* _____

   _____ in Sardegna.

7. La natura è *(wilder)* _____ in Sardegna che in Sicilia.

8. In ogni caso, in Sicilia o in Sardegna *(I will have to take)* _____

   _____ molte foto.

9. Giuseppe mi ha chiesto se posso *(send him some)* _____

   perché vuole *(to use them)* _____ nella sua agenzia di viaggi.

10. Perché non *(we flip a coin)* _____

    _____?

More on Using the Past
and Imperfect Tenses

The Pronoun **ci**

Modal verbs, **sapere**, and **conoscere**
in the past or imperfect

Double Object Pronouns

ANSWER KEY

1. ti ho chiamata ieri sera, non c'eri; 2. in treno o in aereo; 3. dobbiamo, vogliamo; 4. Sia, che, ci sono; 5. ha una storia più ricca della; 6. più culture che; 7. più selvaggia; 8. dovrò fare; 9. mandargliene, usarle; 10. facciamo testa o croce

Grammar Builder 2

▶ 4D Grammar Builder 2 (CD 7, Track 18)

THE PAST PERFECT

The trapassato prossimo, or past perfect (*had* + past participle) is used to express an action that happened before another action in the past. It is formed with the imperfect of the auxiliary verb essere or avere followed by the past participle of the main verb. The same agreement rules of the passato prossimo apply to the trapassato prossimo.

io avevo viaggiato	*I had traveled*	io ero andato/a	*I had gone*
tu avevi viaggiato	*you had traveled*	tu eri andato/a	*you had gone*
lui aveva viaggiato	*he had traveled*	lui era andato	*he had gone*
lei aveva viaggiato	*she had traveled*	lei era andata	*she had gone*
Lei aveva viaggiato	*you (fml.) had traveled*	Lei era andato/a	*you (fml.) had gone*
noi avevamo viaggiato	*we had traveled*	noi eravamo andati/e	*we had gone*
voi avevate viaggiato	*you had traveled*	voi eravate andati/e	*you had gone*
loro/Loro avevano viaggiato	*they had traveled; you (fml.pl.) had traveled*	loro/Loro erano andati/e	*they had gone; you (fml. pl.) had gone*

Quando hai chiamato ero già uscita.
When you called, I had already left.

Non siamo andati a Assisi perché loro l'avevano già visitata.
We didn't go to Assisi because they had already been there.

Ⓘ

✎ Work Out 2

Translate the following sentences.

1. *When we arrived at the station the train had already left.* _____

   _____

2. *I didn't eat because I had already eaten.* _____

   _____

3. *When we called they had already left (the house).* _____

   _____

4. *He didn't go to Venice because he had already been there.* _____

   _____

5. *She didn't come to the theater with us because she had already seen that comedy.*

   _____

ANSWER KEY
1. Quando siamo arrivati alla stazione il treno era già partito. 2. Non ho mangiato perché avevo già
mangiato. 3. Quando abbiamo chiamato (loro) erano già usciti. 4. Non è andato a Venezia perché
c'era già stato. 5. Non è venuta a teatro con noi perché aveva già visto quella commedia.

Modal verbs, **sapere**, and **conoscere**
in the past or imperfect

Double Object Pronouns

✎ Drive It Home

Translate the following sentences using the superlatives appropriately.

1. *This is the most interesting book I have ever read.* _____

    _____

2. *This is the most beautiful car in the show.* _____

    _____

3. *The nuraghi are the most ancient monuments I know.* _____

    _____

4. *Sicily is the biggest island in the Mediterranean.* _____

    _____

5. *This pasta is really very good.* _____

    _____

6. *When I started eating he had not arrived yet.* _____

    _____

7. *We saw a movie that he had already seen.* _____

    _____

8. *On Monday they bought what they hadn't bought yet the day before.* _____

    _____

9. *When you received my postcard I had already returned.* _____

    _____

10. *I just told you what had happened last week.* _____

ANSWER KEY

1. Questo è il libro più interessante che ho mai letto. 2. Questa è la macchina più bella della mostra. 3. I nuraghi sono i monumenti più antichi che conosco. 4. La Sicilia è l'isola più grande del Mediterraneo. 5. Questa pasta è davvero buonissima. 6. Quando ho cominciato a mangiare lui non era ancora arrivato. 7. Abbiamo visto un film che lui aveva già visto. 8. Lunedì hanno comprato quello che non avevano ancora comprato il giorno prima. 9. Quando hai ricevuto la mia cartolina io ero già ritornato. 10. Ti ho appena raccontato quello che era successo la settimana scorsa.

How Did You Do?

Let's see how you did in this lesson. By now, you should know:

☐ how to say *the most* and *the least* (Still unsure? Jump back to page 43.)

☐ how to say *I had gone* (Still unsure? Jump back to page 48.)

✎ Word Recall

A. Translate the following sentences into English.

1. **Ti ho chiamata ieri sera.** _____

_____

2. **Dove hai in progetto di andare?** _____

_____

3. **Scusa se cambio discorso.** _____

_____

4. **Sto per andare finalmente in vacanza.** _____

_____

5. Non me ne hai mai parlato. _____

_____

B. Translate the following sentences into Italian.

1. *I got your message.* _____

_____

2. *I was thinking of going to Sicily or Sardinia.* _____

_____

3. *I wanted to talk to you about it.* _____

_____

4. *The sun was shining and there wasn't a cloud in the sky.* _____

_____

5. *I decided never to go to the mountains again!* _____

_____

ANSWER KEY
A. 1. *I called you last night.* 2. *Where were you thinking of going?* 3. *Excuse me if I change the subject.*
4. *I'm finally about to go on vacation.* 5. *You never told me about it.*
B. 1. **Ho ricevuto il tuo messaggio.** 2. **Pensavo di andare in Sicilia o in Sardegna.** 3. **Volevo
parlartene.** 4. **Splendeva il sole e non c'era una nuvola in cielo.** 5. **Ho deciso di non andare mai più
in montagna!**

Don't forget to practice and reinforce what you've
learned by visiting **www.livinglanguage.com/
languagelab** for flashcards, games, and quizzes!

Unit 1 Essentials

Vocabulary Essentials

Test your knowledge of the key material in this unit by filling in the blanks in the following charts. Once you've completed these pages, you'll have tested your retention, and you'll have your own reference for the most essential vocabulary.

NATURE

	sea, seaside
	beach
	mountains
	country, countryside

[pg. 13]

WORDS RELATED TO WEATHER

	cloud
	sun
	rain
	wind
	thunder
	lightning
	snow

[pg. 13]

TRAVEL AND TOURISM

	trip
	island
	Sardinia
	Sicily
	story, history
	culture
	temple
	Greek
	Arab
	baroque

[pg. 16–17]

DESTINATIONS

	at the beach
	at the lake
	to the mountains
	to the country

[pg. 23]

TRAVEL PHRASES

	to take a trip; to go on a trip
	by car
	by train
	by plane
	to take a picture

[pg. 26]

Advanced Italian

If you're having a hard time remembering this vocabulary, don't forget to check out the supplemental flashcards for this unit online. Go to **www.livinglanguage. com/languagelab** for a great way to help you practice vocabulary.

Grammar Essentials

Here is a reference of the key grammar that was covered in Unit 1. Make sure you understand the summary and can use all of the grammar in it.

PAST AND IMPERFECT TENSES

• The passato expresses completed actions that took place once or a specific number of times in the past.

• When describing the circumstances associated with a past action use the imperfetto.

• Modal verbs (dovere, volere, and potere) have slightly different meanings when used in the past or the imperfect. The past states an action that actually took place, while the imperfect expresses an intention that was not pursued.

• conoscere means *to be familiar with* in the imperfect and *to meet (for the first time)* in the past.

• sapere means *to be aware* in the imperfect and *to find out* in the past.

THE PRONOUNS CI AND NE

ci

• Replaces the preposition a (or da, in, and su) + a place.

• Can replace a prepositional phrase introduced by a, su, or in, even if it doesn't refer to location.

ne

• Means *of/about it* or *of/about them*. Used to replace the partitive *some* construction, including one introduced by a number, or expression indicating quantity.

• Replaces a noun or expression introduced by the preposition di.

DOUBLE OBJECT PRONOUNS

	+ LO	+ LA	+ LI	+ LE	+ NE*
mi	me lo	me la	me li	me le	me ne
ti	te lo	te la	te li	te le	te ne
ci	ce lo	ce la	ce li	ce le	ce ne
vi	ve lo	ve la	ve li	ve le	ve ne
gli	glielo	gliela	glieli	gliele	gliene
le/Le	glielo	gliela	glieli	gliele	gliene

COMPARATIVES OF EQUALITY

• To express a comparative of equality (*as/so … as; as much/as many … as*) use either **così … come**, **tanto … quanto**, or **sia … che**.

• Note that the first part of the comparison (**così** or **tanto**) is often omitted.

• When two nouns are compared, **tanto … quanto** must be used, and must agree in gender and number with the nouns they modify.

COMPARATIVES OF INEQUALITY

• Can be either of superiority (*more, -er … than*) or of inferiority (*less … than*) and are expressed by **più …** and by **meno …**. *Than* can either be translated as **di** or **che**.

• **di** is used in front of numbers, or when two entities are compared in terms of the same quality or action.

• **che** is used when comparing two entities of the same quality (expressed by nouns, adjectives, verbs, or adverbs).

SUPERLATIVES

- The relative superlative is formed by placing the appropriate definite article in front of the comparatives più or meno, or by using noun + più or meno. Italian uses di or fra/tra to express the English *in* or *of* in superlative constructions.

- The absolute superlative is formed by adding the appropriate form of the suffix -ssimo (-ssima, -ssimi, -ssime) to the masculine plural form of the adjective: bello→belli→bellissimo/a/i/e; felice→felici→felicissimo/a/i/e.

- The absolute superlative can also be expressed by preceding an adjective with the adverb molto.

THE PAST PERFECT

The trapassato prossimo, or past perfect (*had* + past participle) is used to express an action that happened before another action in the past. It is formed with the imperfect of the auxiliary verb essere or avere followed by the past participle of the main verb. The same agreement rules as in the passato prossimo apply to the trapassato prossimo.

io avevo viaggiato	*I had traveled*	io ero andato/a	*I had gone*
tu avevi viaggiato	*you had traveled*	tu eri andato/a	*you had gone*
lui aveva viaggiato	*he had traveled*	lui era andato	*he had gone*
lei aveva viaggiato	*she had traveled*	lei era andata	*she had gone*
Lei aveva viaggiato	*you (fml.) had traveled*	Lei era andato/a	*you (fml.) had gone*
noi avevamo viaggiato	*we had traveled*	noi eravamo andati/e	*we had gone*
voi avevate viaggiato	*you had traveled*	voi eravate andati/e	*you had gone*
loro/Loro avevano viaggiato	*they had traveled; you (fml. pl.) had traveled*	loro/Loro erano andati/e	*they had gone; you (fml. pl.) had gone*

Unit 1 Quiz

Let's put the most essential Italian words and grammar points you've learned so far to practice in a few exercises. It's important to be sure that you've mastered this material before you move on. Score yourself at the end of the review and see if you need to go back for more practice, or if you're ready to move on to Unit 2.

A. Complete the following sentences using either the past or the imperfect of the verbs in parentheses as appropriate.

1. _____ (Essere) le tre quando l'aereo finalmente _____

   _____ (partire).

2. Loro non _____ (andare) al mare perché _____

   (fare) molto freddo.

3. Mentre lui _____ (cucinare) Mariella _____

   (guardare) la televisione.

B. Complete the following sentences with either the past or the imperfect of the verbs in parentheses.

1. Lei _____ (dovere) andare alla biblioteca ieri sera, ma si

   è ammalata e così non _____ (andare).

2. "Tu _____ (sapere) che Franco è ritornato dall'Italia?"

   "Sì, l' _____ (sapere) la settimana scorsa."

3. Quando ho saputo del concerto, _____ (volere) comprare i biglietti a tutti i costi!

C. Complete the following sentences with either **ci** or **ne**.

1. Se vai al supermercato più tardi _____ vengo anch'io.

2. "Vuoi dello zucchero nel caffè?" "Sì, grazie. _____ prendo due cucchiaini."

D. Complete the following sentences using a double object pronoun.

1. "Hai comprato il libro a tuo padre?" "Sì, _____ ho già comprato."

2. "Dai, dimmi come si chiama la tua ragazza." "No, non _____ dico!"

3. "Più tardi ti do il regalo." "Perché non _____ dai adesso?"

E. Form complete sentences with the given expressions, using a comparative of equality.

1. Loro bevono/il vino bianco/il vino rosso/. _____

   _____

2. Gli piace/la campagna/la montagna/. _____

   _____

F. Complete the following sentences with either **di** or **che**, combining **di** with the article when necessary.

1. La lezione di filosofia è più interessante _____ la lezione di storia.

2. In Italia è più pericoloso viaggiare in macchina _____ in treno.

G. Rewrite the following sentences following the example.

> Marco è un ragazzo gentile.→Marco è il ragazzo più gentile del mondo.→Marco è gentilissimo.

1. Loro sono studenti bravi. _____

   _____

2. Questa è una esperienza avventurosa. _____

   _____

H. Translate the following sentences.

1. *When they arrived at the appointment their friends had already left.* _____

   _____

2. *She didn't drink any wine because she had already drank two beers.* _____

   _____

3. *Before eating we waited for the guests who hadn't arrived yet.* _____

   _____

ANSWER KEY
A. 1. Erano, è partito; 2. sono andati/e, faceva; 3. cucinava, guardava
B. 1. doveva, è andata; 2. sapevi, ho saputo; 3. ho voluto
C. 1. ci; 2. Ne
D. 1. gliel'; 2. te lo; 3. me lo
E. 1. tanto il vino bianco quanto il vino rosso; 2. tanto la campagna quanto la montagna
F. 1. della; 2. che
G. 2. Loro sono gli studenti più bravi del mondo. Loro sono bravissimi. 3. Questa è l'esperienza più avventurosa del mondo. Questa esperienza è avventurosissima.
H. 1. Quando sono arrivati all'appuntamento i loro amici erano già andati via. 2. Lei non ha bevuto del vino perché aveva già bevuto due birre. 3. Prima di mangiare abbiamo aspettato gli ospiti che non erano ancora arrivati.

How Did You Do?

Give yourself a point for every correct answer, then use the following key to tell whether you're ready to move on:

0-7 points: It's probably a good idea to go back through the lesson again. You may be moving too quickly, or there may be too much "down time" between your contact with Italian. Remember that it's better to spend 30 minutes with Italian three or four times a week than it is to spend two or three hours just once a week. Find a pace that's comfortable for you, and spread your contact hours out as much as you can.

8-12 points: You would benefit from a review before moving on. Go back and spend a little more time on the specific points that gave you trouble. Re-read the Grammar Builder sections that were difficult, and do the work out one more time. Don't forget about the online supplemental practice material, either. Go to **www.livinglanguage.com/languagelab** for games and quizzes that will reinforce the material from this unit.

13-17 points: Good job! There are just a few points that you could consider reviewing before moving on. If you haven't worked with the games and quizzes on **www.livinglanguage.com/languagelab**, please give them a try.

18-20 points: Great! You're ready to move on to the next unit.

points

Unit 2:
Getting Around Town

Now that you're finally in Italy, you might want to reserve a room in a hotel, and start walking around all those beautiful cities. Here you are going to learn how to talk to a hotel receptionist, and also how to ask for directions so that you won't get lost. Don't forget to bring your maps! By the end of this unit, you'll know:

☐ useful words related to directions

☐ how to express something that happened in the past and is still going on

☐ key vocabulary for checking into a hotel

☐ ways to emphasize exclamations

☐ how to give directions

☐ how to say *let's go there*

☐ how to say *I would*

☐ how to say *I would have*

☐ how to change the meaning of a word by adding a suffix

☐ how to say *first, second,* and *third*

Lesson 5: Words

By the end of this lesson, you'll know:

☐ useful words related to directions

☐ how to express something that happened in the past and is still going on

☐ key vocabulary for checking into a hotel

☐ ways to emphasize exclamations

Word Builder 1

▶ 5A Word Builder 1 (CD 7, Track 19)

(il) colloquio	interview
trasferirsi	to move, to transfer
esperto	expert
(il/la) finalista	finalist (male or female)
metro	meter
centimetro	centimeter
chilometro	kilometer
voltare	to turn
girare	to turn
destra	right
sinistra	left
lungo	along
avanti	ahead

⏸

✎ Word Practice 1

A. Translate the following words into English.

1. **(il) colloquio** _____

2. **chilometro** _____

3. **destra** _____

4. **avanti** _____

B. Translate the following words into Italian.

1. *left* _____

2. *to turn* _____

3. *to move* _____

4. *along* _____

ANSWER KEY
A. 1. *interview*; 2. *kilometer*; 3. *right*; 4. *ahead*
B. 1. **sinistra**; 2. **girare**; 3. **trasferirsi**; 4. **lungo**

Grammar Builder 1
▶ 5B Grammar Builder 1 (CD 7, Track 20)

EXPRESSING DURATION OF AN ACTION

To express the duration of an action that began in the past and is still going on in the present, Italian uses the present tense + **da** + time expression.

Non ti vedo da molto tempo.
I haven't seen you in a long time.

Studiamo italiano da due mesi.
We have been studying Italian for two months.

Non vanno al cinema da Natale.
They haven't gone to the movies since Christmas.

To ask for how long an action has been going on, Italian uses da quanto tempo + present.

Da quanto tempo non vedi Maria?
How long has it been since you've seen Maria?

⏸

✎ Work Out 1

Translate the following sentences into Italian.

1. *I haven't seen him for a long time.* _____

   _____

2. *We have been traveling for two months.* _____

   _____

3. *He hasn't eaten since last night.* _____

   _____

4. *You haven't come to my house since December.* _____

   _____

5. *For how long have you been working in this store?* _____

   _____

ANSWER KEY

1. Non lo vedo da molto tempo. 2. Viaggiamo da due mesi. 3. Non mangia da ieri sera. 4. Non vieni a casa mia da dicembre. 5. Da quanto tempo lavori in questo negozio?

Word Builder 2

5C Word Builder 2 (CD 7, Track 21)

controllare	to check
prenotare	to reserve
(la) fiera	trade fair
affollato	crowded
disponibile	available
(la) camera matrimoniale	double room (one queen-size bed)
(la) camera doppia	double room (two twin-size beds)
(la) camera singola	single room (one twin bed)
(il) piano	floor (of a building)
(l')asciugamano	towel
(la) saponetta	soap (bar)
(la) carta igienica	toilet paper
(l')aria condizionata	air conditioning
(la) valigia	suitcase

✎ Word Practice 2

Match the following expressions:

1. **prenotare**	a. *trade fair*
2. **(la) saponetta**	b. *double room (one queen-size bed)*
3. **(la) fiera**	c. *toilet paper*
4. **(l')aria condizionata**	d. *available*
5. **(la) camera matrimoniale**	e. *to reserve*
6. **(la) carta igienica**	f. *floor (of a building)*
7. **disponibile**	g. *air conditioning*
8. **(il) piano**	h. *soap (bar)*
9. **(la) valigia**	i. *towel*
10. **(l')asciugamano**	l. *suitcase*

ANSWER KEY
1. e; 2. h; 3. a; 4. g; 5. b; 6. c; 7. d; 8. f; 9. l; 10. i

Grammar Builder 2

▶ 5D Grammar Builder 2 (CD 7, Track 22)

DISJUNCTIVE PRONOUNS

Direct and indirect object pronouns also have emphatic forms, known as disjunctive pronouns.

me	*me*	a me	*to me*
te	*you*	a te	*to you*
lui	*him*	a lui	*to him*
lei	*her*	a lei	*to her*
Lei	*you (fml.)*	a Lei	*to you (fml.)*
noi	*us*	a noi	*to us*
voi	*you*	a voi	*to you (pl.)*

loro	them	a loro	to them
Loro	you (fml. pl.)	a Loro	to you (fml. pl.)

They are used for emphasis immediately after a verb or in exclamations.

Hanno chiamato te, ma non hanno chiamato me!
They called you, but they didn't call me!

Non lo do a te, lo do a lui.
I'm not giving it to you, I'm giving it to him.

They are always used after the prepositions **per**, **con**, and **tra/fra**.

Perché non vieni con me a Napoli?
Why don't you come to Naples with me?

Il dottor Benaglia mi ha detto che lavori per lui.
Dr. Benaglia told me you work for him.

Ⅱ

✎ Work Out 2

Replace the underlined expression with a disjunctive pronoun.

1. **Esci con** *Mariella* **stasera?** _____

_____

2. **Noi lavoriamo per** *il direttore dell'albergo.* _____

_____

3. **Quando hanno chiamato hanno chiesto di parlare con** *Franco e Mariella*. _____

_____

4. **Vieni con** *me e Giorgio* **al mare?** _____

_____

5. **Posso venire a cena da** *te e Francesca*? _____

_____

ANSWER KEY
1. Esci con lei stasera? 2. Noi lavoriamo per lui. 3. Quando hanno chiamato hanno chiesto di
parlare con loro. 4. Vieni con noi al mare? 5. Posso venire a cena da voi?

✎ Drive It Home
Translate the following sentences from English into Italian.

1. *I have been studying for two hours.* _____

_____

2. *I haven't seen Giorgio since last Sunday.* _____

_____

3. *How long have you being learning Italian?* _____

_____

4. *How long have you being waiting?* _____

_____

5. *We have being working here for a very long time.* _____

_____

6. *I only told you, not her!* _____

   _____

7. *I ordered this pizza for all of us.* _____

   _____

8. *Why do you have to give it to him, don't you want to give it to me?* _____

   _____

9. *Between you and me maybe we know barely ten words of Spanish.* _____

   _____

10. *All right, I'll come to the movies with you tonight.* _____

    _____

ANSWER KEY

1. **Studio da due ore.** 2. **Non vedo Giorgio da domenica scorsa.** 3. **Da quanto tempo impari l'italiano?** 4. **Da quanto tempo aspetti?** 5. **Lavoriamo qui da moltissimo tempo.** 6. **L'ho detto solo a te, non a lei!** 7. **Ho ordinato questa pizza per tutti noi.** 8. **Perché lo devi dare a lui, non vuoi darlo a me?** 9. **Tra me e te forse conosciamo appena dieci parole di spagnolo.** 10. **Va bene, vengo al cinema con te stasera.**

🔅 Tip!

Bologna is one of the best-kept secrets in Italy. Everybody traveling from northern to southern Italy goes through Bologna, but very few people stop there. Those who do, however, always think of Bologna as one of their favorite places in Italy. Bologna is known as **la grassa** (*the fat one*) for its renowned food, **la rossa** (*the red one*) for the color of its buildings and roofs, or, alternately, for its leftist political leanings, **la dotta** (*the learned one*) for its famous university, and **la turrita** (*the towered one*) for the more than 100 towers that used to be in this city. Only a few of these towers are still standing, the most famous ones are the **Torre degli Asinelli** and the **Torre della Garisenda** which stand right next to each other in the center of the city.

How Did You Do?

Let's see how you did in this lesson. By now, you should know:

☐ useful words related to directions (Still unsure? Jump back to page 64.)

☐ how to express something that happened in the past and is still going on (Still unsure? Jump back to page 65.)

☐ key vocabulary for checking into a hotel (Still unsure? Jump back to page 67.)

☐ ways to emphasize exclamations (Still unsure? Jump back to page 68.)

✎ Word Recall

A. Translate the following words into English.

1. **voltare** _____

2. **(la) fiera** _____

3. **(la) saponetta** _____

4. **destra** _____

5. **(la) camera singola** _____

B. Translate the following words into Italian.

1. *interview* _____

2. *crowded* _____

3. *available* _____

4. *air conditioning* _____

5. *to check* _____

ANSWER KEY

A. 1. *to turn*; 2. *trade fair*; 3. *soap bar*; 4. *right*; 5. *single room*
B. 1. **(il) colloquio**; 2. **affollato**; 3. **disponibile**; 4. **(l')aria condizionata**; 5. **controllare**

Lesson 6: Phrases

By the end of this lesson, you'll know:

☐ how to give directions

☐ how to say *Let's go there.*

Phrase Builder 1

▷ 6A Phrase Builder 1 (CD 7, Track 23)

da una vita	*for a very long time; since always; since forever*
riuscire a	*to manage to; to be able to*
Fammi vedere.	*Let me see.*
Va' avanti.	*Go ahead.*
a destra	*to/on the right*
a sinistra	*to/on the left*
Sono in ritardo.	*I'm late.*
È tardi.	*It's late.*
Sono in anticipo.	*I'm early.*
È presto.	*It's early.*
fra tre quarti d'ora	*in forty-five minutes*

⏸

✎ Phrase Practice 1

Match the following expressions.

1. Va' avanti.	a. *for a very long time*
2. fra tre quarti d'ora	b. *Go ahead.*
3. Sono in anticipo.	c. *Let me see.*
4. È presto.	d. *to be able to*
5. Fammi vedere.	e. *I'm late.*
6. da una vita	f. *in forty-five minutes*
7. riuscire a	g. *I'm early.*
8. Sono in ritardo.	h. *It's early.*

ANSWER KEY

1. b; 2. f; 3. g; 4. h; 5. c; 6. a; 7. d; 8. e

Grammar Builder 1

▶ 6B Grammar Builder 1 (CD 7, Track 24)

THE INFORMAL IMPERATIVE

The imperative is used to give a command or to make a suggestion. The forms
of the informal imperative in Italian are the same as those of the present tense,
with the exception of the **tu** form of first conjugation verbs (**-are**), which ends
in **-a** rather than **-i**. Thus verbs that are irregular in the present tense are also
irregular in the imperative. Notice that an exclamation point normally follows an
imperative in Italian.

	CANTARE (TO SING)	PRENDERE (TO TAKE)	DORMIRE (TO SLEEP)	PULIRE (TO CLEAN)
(tu)	canta	prendi	dormi	pulisci
(noi)	cantiamo	prendiamo	dormiamo	puliamo
(voi)	cantate	prendete	dormite	pulite

Gira a sinistra!
Turn left!

Cammina lungo via Zamboni!
Walk along Zamboni Street!

Prendiamo l'autobus!
Let's take the bus!

Andare, **dare**, **fare**, **stare**, and **dire** have also an irregular **tu** imperative form which is very often used instead of the regular one: **va'**, **da'**, **fa'**, **sta'**, and **di'**. But their other imperative forms are regular: **andiamo, andate**; **diamo, date**; **facciamo, fate**; **stiamo, state**; **diciamo, dite**.

Va' avanti cento metri!
Go ahead for one hundred meters.

Sta' attento!
Pay attention!; Be careful!; Watch it!; Watch out!

Essere and **avere** have an irregular imperative form: **essere: sii, siamo, siate**; **avere: abbi, abbiamo, abbiate**.

Sii gentile!
Be kind!

Abbiate pazienza!
Be patient!

The negative imperative is formed by placing **non** in front of the imperative. However, the **tu** negative imperative is formed by **non** + infinitive.

Non fate rumore!
Don't make any noise!

Non usciamo stasera!
Let's not go out tonight!

Non mangiare troppi dolci!
Don't eat too many sweets!

The infinitive is often used when giving directions to the general public in signs, public notices, recipes, etc.

Mescolare bene tutti gli ingredienti.
Mix all ingredients thoroughly.

Non calpestare l'erba.
Do not step on the grass.

⏸

✎ Work Out 1

In your opinion, these people must, or mustn't do certain things. Tell them to do, or not do these things, following the example: **I ragazzi devono studiare→Studiate!**

1. **Mario deve imparare l'italiano.** _____

_____

2. **Mirella non deve mangiare troppi dolci.** _____

_____

3. **Noi dobbiamo andare al museo.** _____

_____

4. **I ragazzi devono prenotare l'albergo.** _____

_____

5. **Giorgio deve fare le valige.** _____

_____

6. **Le signore non devono spendere troppi soldi.** _____

_____

7. **Franco non deve accettare quel lavoro.** _____

_____

8. **Noi dobbiamo fare più sport.** _____

_____

ANSWER KEY
1. **Impara l'italiano!** 2. **Non mangiare troppi dolci!** 3. **Andiamo al museo!** 4. **Prenotate l'albergo!**
5. **Fa' le valige!** 6. **Non spendete troppi soldi!** 7. **Non accettare quel lavoro!** 8. **Facciamo più sport!**

Phrase Builder 2

▶ 6C Phrase Builder 2 (CD 7, Track 25)

Siamo pieni.	*We're full.*
avere bisogno di	*to need*
a partire da	*starting from*
per quale data?	*for which date/day?*
Va meglio.	*It's better.*
lo stesso	*the same*
al secondo piano	*on/to the second floor*

in fretta	in a hurry, quickly
all'ultimo minuto	at the last minute
Andiamoci.	Let's go there.

Phrase Practice 2

A. Translate the following phrases into English.

1. **lo stesso** _____

2. **a partire da** _____

3. **in fretta** _____

4. **al secondo piano** _____

B. Translate the following phrases into Italian.

1. *at the last minute* _____

2. *We're full.* _____

3. *It's better.* _____

4. *For which date?* _____

ANSWER KEY

A. 1. *the same*; 2. *starting from*; 3. *quickly*; 4. *on the second floor*

B. 1. **all'ultimo minuto**; 2. **Siamo pieni.** 3. **Va meglio.** 4. **Per quale data?**

Grammar Builder 2

 6D Grammar Builder 2 (CD 8, Track1)

THE INFORMAL IMPERATIVE AND PRONOUNS

Direct and indirect object pronouns, reflexive pronouns, and **ci** when used as an adverb meaning *there*, are all attached to the end of the informal imperative. With the negative imperative, the pronouns can either precede the imperative, or be attached to it.

Andiamoci!
Let's go there!

Parlagliene!
Speak with/to him about it!

Non mandarle questa lettera! (Non le mandare questa lettera!)
Don't send this letter to her!

Before attaching a pronoun to **va'**, **da'**, **fa'**, **sta'**, and **di'**, remember to drop the apostrophe and to double the first consonant of the pronoun, with the exception of **gli**, which does not double the consonant.

Fammi vedere che ore sono!
Let me see what time it is!

Digli la verità!
Tell him the truth!

Vacci!
Go there!

(II)

✎ Work Out 2

Replace the underlined object(s) with a pronoun or a double pronoun.

1. **Da'** *il libro a tuo cugino*! _____

2. **Parlate** *a vostra madre*! _____

3. **Non mangiate** *tutta la pasta*! _____

4. **Dite** *la verità a noi*! _____

5. **Ordiniamo** *un caffè*! _____

6. **Va'** *in via Zamboni*! _____

7. **Mandiamo** *una lettera al nostro amico*! _____

8. **Non leggere** *quel giornale*! _____

   ANSWER KEY
   1. Daglielo! 2. Parlatele! 3. Non mangiatela! (Non la mangiate!) 4. Ditecela! 5. Ordiniamolo! 6. Vacci!
   7. Mandiamogliela! 8. Non leggerlo! (Non lo leggere!)

✎ Drive It Home

Turn the following sentences from positive into negative and viceversa,
substituting the nouns with the appropriate pronouns and double pronouns.

1. **Finisci le verdure!** _____

   _____

2. **Date il regalo a vostro fratello!** _____

   _____

3. **Non andate al cinema stasera!** _____

_____

4. **Non diamo il regalo a Franco!** _____

_____

5. **Non spedire la lettera ai tuoi genitori!** _____

_____

6. **Per favore mandate i fiori al vostro amico!** _____

_____

7. **Mangia la minestra!** _____

_____

8. **Non mandare un'email a Luigi, telefonagli!** _____

_____

9. **Ricordiamo a Giulio l'ora dell'appuntamento!** _____

_____

10. **Porta fuori il cane ora!** _____

_____

ANSWER KEY
1. **Non finirle!** 2. **Non dateglielo!** 3. **Andateci stasera!** 4. **Diamoglielo!** 5. **Spediscigliela!** 6. **Non mandateglieli!** 7. **Non mangiarla!** 8. **Mandagliela, non telefonargli!** 9. **Non ricordiamoglielo!** 10. **Non portarlo fuori ora!**

⊕ Culture Note

The University of Bologna was founded in 1088 and is the most ancient university in the Western world. It was famous for its instruction in law and medicine, and is still one of the most prestigious public universities in Italy.

How Did You Do?

Let's see how you did in this lesson. By now, you should know:

☐ how to give directions (Still unsure? Jump back to page 74.)

☐ how to say *Let's go there.*(Still unsure? Jump back to page 79.)

✎ Word Recall

Translate the following expressions into Italian.

1. *Let me see.* _____

2. *on the right* _____

3. *at the last minute* _____

4. *the same* _____

5. *I'm late.* _____

6. *to need* _____

7. *starting from* _____

8. *in forty-five minutes* _____

9. *It's better.* _____

10. *I'm early.* _____

ANSWER KEY

1. Fammi vedere. 2. a destra; 3. all'ultimo minuto; 4. lo stesso; 5. Sono in ritardo. 6. avere bisogno di;
7. a partire da; 8. fra tre quarti d'ora; 9. Va meglio. 10. Sono in anticipo.

Lesson 7: Sentences

By the end of this lesson, you'll know:

☐ how to say *I would*

☐ how to say *I would have*

Sentence Builder 1

▶ 7A Sentence Builder 1 (CD 8, Track 2)

Abito qui da un anno.	*I have been living here for a year.*
Ho saputo che ti eri trasferito.	*I found out that you had moved.*
Avresti tempo di prendere un caffè?	*Would you have time for a coffee?*
Non vorrei arrivare in ritardo.	*I wouldn't want to arrive late.*
Mi faresti un favore?	*Would you do me a favor?*
Va' avanti cento metri.	*Go ahead for one hundred meters.*
Gira a sinistra e cammina lungo via Zamboni.	*Turn left and walk along Zamboni Street.*
Fammi vedere che ore sono.	*Let me see what time it is.*
Andiamoci!	*Let's go there!*

⏸

✎ Sentence Practice 1

A. Translate the following sentences into English.

1. **Non vorrei arrivare in ritardo.** _____

2. **Mi faresti un favore?** _____

3. **Andiamoci!** _____

B. Translate the following sentences into Italian.

1. *Go ahead for one hundred meters.* _____

2. *Would you have time for a coffee?* _____

3. *I have been living here for a year.* _____

ANSWER KEY

A. 1. *I wouldn't want to arrive late.* 2. *Would you do me a favor?* 3. *Let's go there!*
B. 1. **Va' avanti cento metri.** 2. **Avresti tempo di prendere un caffè?** 3. **Abito qui da un anno.**

Grammar Builder 1

▶ 7B Grammar Builder 1 (CD 8, Track 3)

THE PRESENT CONDITIONAL

The conditional mood expresses possible or hypothetical actions or states and translates into English as *would* + verb. Just like in English, there are two conditional tenses: present conditional and past conditional.

The present conditional is formed, just like the future tense, by dropping the final -e from the infinitive. Then the conditional endings -ei, -esti, -ebbe, -emmo, -este, -ebbero are added. As in the future, in verbs of the first conjugation, the -a of the infinitive ending changes to -e:

parlare *(to speak)*	prendere *(to take)*	dormire *(to sleep)*	pulire *(to clean)*
io parlerei	io prenderei	io dormirei	io pulirei
tu parleresti	tu prenderesti	tu dormiresti	tu puliresti
lui parlerebbe	lui prenderebbe	lui dormirebbe	lui pulirebbe
lei/Lei parlerebbe	lei/Lei prenderebbe	lei/Lei dormirebbe	lei/Lei pulirebbe

noi parleremmo	noi prenderemmo	noi dormiremmo	noi puliremmo
voi parlereste	voi prendereste	voi dormireste	voi pulireste
loro/Loro parlerebbero	loro/Loro prenderebbero	loro/Loro dormirebbero	loro/Loro pulirebbero

The present conditional is used to express actions that would occur in the present or in the future, if not for conditions or uncertainties that prevent them from occurring.

Prenderei un caffè, ma non ho tempo.
I would have a coffee, but I don't have time.

Usciremmo con voi, ma abbiamo già un altro impegno.
We would go out with you, but we already have a previous engagement.

Verbs with irregularities in the future (Lesson 19 of *Intermediate Italian*) maintain the same irregularities in the conditional.

Andrei in vacanza, ma non ho abbastanza soldi.
I would go on vacation, but I don't have enough money.

Vorrei dormire, ma non ho tempo.
I would like to sleep, but I don't have time.

The present conditional can also be used to express polite requests and wishes. This is particularly true when using the conditional of **dovere**, **potere**, and **volere**.

Vorrei sapere se avete una camera disponibile.
I would like to know if you have a room available.

Potrei prenotare una stanza?
Could I reserve a room?

Ⓘ

✎ Work Out 1

Fill in the blanks with the present conditional of the verbs in parentheses.

1. Io _____ (uscire) volentieri con te, ma ho troppo lavoro.

2. Loro _____ (venire) a cena da noi, ma domani hanno

   già un impegno.

3. Noi _____ (comprare) quella macchina, ma non

   abbiamo abbastanza soldi.

4. Lui _____ (dovere) studiare, ma non ne ha voglia.

5. Voi lo _____ (invitare), ma lui non viene mai.

6. Tu mi _____ (potere) chiamare un po' più spesso!

ANSWER KEY

1. uscirei; 2. verrebbero; 3. compreremmo; 4. dovrebbe; 5. invitereste; 6. potresti

Sentence Builder 2

▶ 7C Sentence Builder 2 (CD 8, Track 4)

Ho appena saputo che ho bisogno di venire a Bologna.	I've just found out (that) I need to come to Bologna.
Vorrei sapere se avete una camera disponibile.	I would like to know if you have a room available.
Avrebbe dovuto chiamare prima.	You should have called sooner.
Ho una camera doppia, Le andrebbe bene?	I have a double room, would that be good for you?
La camera è al secondo piano.	The room is on the third floor.

Non avrei mai pensato di trovare una camera.	I would have never thought I would find a room.
A che ora pensa di arrivare?	At what time do you expect to arrive/ get here?
Sarebbe un problema se arriviamo domani mattina?	Would it be a problem if we arrive tomorrow morning?

Ⓜ

✎ Sentence Practice 2

Fill the blanks translating into Italian the parts indicated in parentheses.

1. Ho appena saputo che *(I need to come to Bologna)* _____

   _____.

2. La camera è *(on the third floor)* _____.

3. Ho una camera doppia, *(would that be good for you)* _____

   _____?

4. *(Would it be a problem)* _____ se

   arriviamo domani mattina?

5. *(At what time)* _____ pensa di arrivare?

6. *(I would like to know)* _____ se avete una camera

   disponibile.

ANSWER KEY
1. ho bisogno di venire a Bologna. 2. al secondo piano; 3. Le andrebbe bene; 4. Sarebbe un
problema; 5. A che ora; 6. Vorrei sapere

Grammar Builder 2

 7D Grammar Builder 2 (CD 8, Track 5)

THE PAST CONDITIONAL

The past conditional is formed with the conditional of **essere** or **avere**, followed by the past participle. Just as is the case with the present perfect, past participles of **essere** verbs must agree with the subject.

io avrei parlato	io sarei arrivato/a
tu avresti parlato	ti saresti arrivato/a
lui avrebbe parlato	lui sarebbe arrivato
lei avrebbe parlato	lei sarebbe arrivata
Lei avrebbe parlato	Lei sarebbe arrivato/a
noi avremmo parlato	noi saremmo arrivati/e
voi avreste parlato	voi sareste arrivati/e
loro/Loro avrebbero parlato	loro/Loro sarebbero arrivati/e

The past conditional in Italian is the same as the phrase *would have ...* in English.

Ti avrei telefonato, ma non ho avuto tempo.
I would have called you, but I didn't have time.

In English, when expressing a future action from the point of view of the past, we use the present conditional; Italian uses the past conditional.

Ha detto che sarebbe arrivato presto.
He said he would arrive early.

Ha deciso che avrebbero mangiato fuori.
He decided they would eat out.

When using **dovere**, **potere**, and **volere** in the past conditional, they mean *should have, could have,* and *would have liked* respectively. They are all followed by the main verb in the infinitive form, and the main verb determines which auxiliary to use.

Avrebbe dovuto chiamare prima.
You should have called sooner.

Saremmo dovuti restare di più.
We should have stayed longer.

✎ Work Out 2

Fill in the blank with the present or past conditional of the verb in parentheses as appropriate.

1. Io _____ (prendere) un aperitivo con te, ma ho fretta.

2. Noi _____ (venire) a casa tua, ma siamo tornati tardi.

3. Loro vi _____ (invitare), ma non vi

   hanno trovato.

4. Lui ti _____ (scrivere), ma non ha il tuo indirizzo.

5. Voi gli _____ (offrire) il lavoro, ma lui non è molto

   interessato.

6. Tu _____ (partire) con noi, ma dovevi

   finire quel lavoro.

ANSWER KEY
1. prenderei; 2. saremmo venuti; 3. avrebbero invitato; 4. scriverebbe; 5. offrireste; 6. saresti partito/a

✎ Drive It Home

A. Translate the following sentences into English.

1. **L'estate prossima vorrei andare al mare.** _____

   _____

2. **Sarebbero venuti anche loro, ma erano occupati.** _____

   _____

3. **Avrei dovuto prenotare una stanza, ma ci ho pensato troppo tardi.** _____

   _____

4. **Ieri vi ho detto chiaramente che sarei arrivato stamattina alle dieci.** _____

   _____

5. **Avrei mangiato la torta ma ero davvero pieno.** _____

   _____

B. Translate the following sentences into Italian.

1. _You should have eaten the dessert, it was delicious._ _____

   _____

2. _He should have seen the movie after having read the book._ _____

   _____

3. _Would it be possible to put one more bed in the room?_ _____

   _____

4. _He told me he would buy the smaller apartment._ _____

   _____

5. *Could you tell Gianni to come early?* _____

_____

ANSWER KEY

A. 1. *Next summer I would like to go to the beach.* 2. *They would have also come but they were busy.* 3. *I should have reserved a room but I thought about it too late.* 4. *Yesterday I clearly told you that I would come this morning at ten o'clock.* 5. *I would have eaten the cake but I was really full.*

B. 1. Avresti dovuto mangiare il dolce, era delizioso. 2. Avrebbe dovuto vedere il film dopo aver letto il libro. 3. Sarebbe possibile mettere un altro letto nella camera? 4. Mi ha detto che avrebbe comprato l'appartamento più piccolo. 5. Potresti dire a Gianni di venire presto?

Culture Note

Bologna gave birth to many famous artists, most notably Guido Reni, the brothers Annibale and Agostino Carracci, Lodovico Carracci, Giovanni Barbieri, known as il Guercino, and Giorgio Morandi.

How Did You Do?

Let's see how you did in this lesson. By now, you should know:

☐ how to say *I would* (Still unsure? Jump back to page 84.)

☐ how to say *I would have* (Still unsure? Jump back to page 88.)

Word Recall

A. Translate the following sentences into English.

1. Vorrei sapere se avete una camera disponibile. _____

_____

2. Abito qui da un anno. _____

_____

3. **Mi faresti un favore?** _____

_____

4. **Sarebbe un problema se arriviamo domani mattina?** _____

_____

5. **Avrebbe dovuto chiamare prima.** _____

_____

B. Translate the following sentences into Italian.

1. *Go ahead for one hundred meters.* _____

_____

2. *I need to come to Bologna.* _____

_____

3. *Let's go there!* _____

_____

4. *Would you have time for a coffee?* _____

_____

5. *At what time do you expect to arrive/get here?* _____

_____

ANSWER KEY

A. 1. *I would like to know if you have a room available.* 2. *I have been living here for a year.* 3. *Would you do me a favor?* 4. *Would it be a problem if we arrive tomorrow morning?* 5. *You should have called sooner.*
B. 1. **Va' avanti cento metri.** 2. **Ho bisogno di venire a Bologna.** 3. **Andiamoci!** 4. **Avresti tempo di prendere un caffè?** 5. **A che ora pensa di arrivare?**

Lesson 8: Conversations

By the end of this lesson, you'll know:

☐ how to change the meaning of a word by adding a suffix

☐ how to say *first, second,* and *third*

Conversation 1

▶ 8A Conversation 1 (CD 8, Track 6 - Italian; Track 7 - Italian and English)

Giorgio:	Paola! Sei tu? Non posso crederci! Non ti vedo da una vita! Che cosa fai qui a Bologna?
Paola:	Sono qui per un colloquio di lavoro! E tu?
Giorgio:	Io abito qui da un anno. Non lo sapevi?
Paola:	No, ho saputo che ti eri trasferito, ma non sapevo che abitavi a Bologna.
Giorgio:	Dove vai per il colloquio?
Paola:	Alla Pinacoteca. Cercano un esperto d'arte medievale e sono una delle finaliste.
Giorgio:	Avresti tempo di prendere un caffè con me? C'è un ottimo bar qui vicino.
Paola:	Fammi vedere che ore sono, non vorrei arrivare in ritardo … no, mi dispiace, non ho tempo, il colloquio è fra tre quarti d'ora. Anzi, mi faresti un favore?
Giorgio:	Certamente, se posso.
Paola:	Sapresti dirmi come arrivare alla Pinacoteca da qui? È in via Belle Arti.

Giorgio: È molto facile: va' avanti cento metri fino a via Rizzoli. Volta a destra e davanti a te vedrai le due Torri. Quando arrivi sotto le due Torri, gira a sinistra e cammina lungo via Zamboni quasi fino in fondo, sulla sinistra troverai via Belle Arti. Da qui sono solo circa dieci minuti a piedi.

Paola: Beh, allora ho anche il tempo di bere un caffè in quel famoso bar. Andiamo!

Giorgio: Paola! Is that you? I can't believe it! I haven't seen you in ages! What are you doing here in Bologna?

Paola: I'm here for a job interview, and you?

Giorgio: I've lived here for a year. You didn't know?

Paola: No, I heard that you had moved, but I didn't know you lived in Bologna.

Giorgio: Where do you have your interview?

Paola: At the Pinacoteca. They're looking for an expert in medieval art, and I'm one of the finalists.

Giorgio: Would you have time to have coffee with me? There is a very good café nearby.

Paola: Let me see what time it is, I wouldn't want to be late … no, I'm sorry, I don't have time, the interview is in forty-five minutes. Would you do me a favor, though?

Giorgio: Certainly, if I can.

Paola: Could you tell me how to get to the Pinacoteca from here? It's on via Belle Arti.

Giorgio: It's very easy: go ahead for one hundred meters up to via Rizzoli. Turn right, and you'll see the two towers in front of you. When you get under the two towers, turn left and walk along via Zamboni almost until the end, and on your left you'll find via Belle Arti. It's about a ten-minute walk from here.

Paola: Well, then I should have time for a coffee in that café. Let's go there.

Notes:

Riuscire a + infinitive is often used in Italian instead of potere to indicate *to be able to* or *to succeed in doing something.*

Da una vita idiomatically indicates *for a very long time (in ages).*

Different from other means of transportation that use the preposition in, piedi is used with the preposition a, a piedi, to indicate *on foot (walking).*

✎ Conversation Practice 1

Translate the expressions written in parentheses in the following sentences.

1. Non posso crederci! *(I haven't seen you in ages)* _____

   _____!

2. Sono qui per *(a job interview)* _____.

3. *(I've lived)* _____ qui da un anno.

4. Ho saputo che *(you had moved)* _____.

5. *(I didn't know)* _____ che abitavi a Bologna.

6. *(Let me see)* _____ che ore sono.

7. *(I wouldn't want to)* _____ arrivare in ritardo.

8. *(Would you do me)* _____ un favore?

9. *(Go ahead for one hundred meters)* _____

   _____ fino a via Rizzoli.

10. *(Turn left)* _____ e cammina lungo via Zamboni.

ANSWER KEY

1. Non ti vedo da una vita; 2. un colloquio di lavoro; 3. Io abito; 4. ti eri trasferito; 5. Non sapevo;
6. Fammi vedere; 7. Non vorrei; 8. Mi faresti; 9. Va' avanti cento metri; 10. Gira a sinistra

Grammar Builder 1

▶ 8B Grammar Builder 1 (CD 8, Track 8)

SUFFIXES

In Italian it is possible to slightly change the meaning of a word by adding a suffix to that word. These suffixes give emphasis to the size or quality of that word, or express the speaker's feeling concerning a person or object. Since there are no specific rules governing these suffixes, it is better to learn to recognize the suffixes before using them. Please note that when adding a suffix most nouns maintain their gender, and that the final vowel is dropped before adding a suffix.

Three main categories of suffixes exist:

- **-ino**, **-etto**, and **-ello** are called diminutives, indicating smallness or cuteness, or used to express the speaker's affection.

  Tuo figlio è proprio carino!
  Your son is really cute!

- **-one**, **-ona**, **-oni**, and **-one** *(f. pl.)* express largeness.

  Suo marito è un omone.
  Her husband is a big man.

- **-accio**, **-astro**, and **-ucolo** express ugliness, roughness, or other negative qualities.

  Non dire quelle parolacce!
  Don't say those/such bad words.

⏸

✎ Work Out 1

Change the underlined words into a word with a suffix.

1. Marco è un *ragazzo piccolo*. _____

   _____

2. Mirko è un *ragazzo cattivo*. _____

   _____

3. Loro hanno una bella *casa piccola*. _____

   _____

4. I bambini giocano con le *macchine piccole*. _____

   _____

5. Tu stai leggendo un *libro molto grosso*. _____

   _____

ANSWER KEY
1. Marco è un ragazzino. 2. Mirko è un ragazzaccio. 3. Loro hanno una bella casetta. 4. I bambini giocano con le macchinine. 5. Tu stai leggendo un librone.

◖ Conversation 2

▶ 8C Conversation 2 (CD 8, Track 9 - Italian; Track 10 - Italian and English)

Receptionist:	Buon giorno, Hotel International, desidera?
Signora Bianchini:	Buon giorno, vorrei sapere se avete una camera disponibile per me e mio marito.
Receptionist:	Per quando?
Signora Bianchini:	Per due notti a partire da domani sera.
Receptionist:	Signora, controllo, ma siamo molto pieni. Avrebbe dovuto chiamare prima perché questa settimana c'è la fiera del mobile e Bologna è affollatissima.

Signora Bianchini:	Sì, lo so, ma purtroppo ho appena appreso di dover venire a Bologna.
Receptionist:	Signora, è la Sua giornata fortunata. Non ho una camera matrimoniale, ma ho una camera doppia, Le andrebbe bene lo stesso?
Signora Bianchini:	Certamente, anzi, per noi va meglio.
Receptionist:	Signora, la camera è al secondo piano ed è un po' rumorosa, ma è spaziosa e ha l'aria condizionata.
Signora Bianchini:	Per me non è un problema. Abitiamo al terzo piano e anche il nostro appartamento è rumoroso. Non avrei mai pensato di trovare una stanza così in fretta all'ultimo minuto!
Receptionist:	Signora, lei è molto accomodante. A che ora pensa di arrivare?
Signora Bianchini:	Per Lei sarebbe un problema se arriviamo domani mattina?
Receptionist:	No signora, se la camera non è pronta può lasciare le valigie alla reception.
Signora Bianchini:	Grazie allora, a domani.

Receptionist:	*Good morning, Hotel International, how can I help you?*
Signora Bianchini:	*Good morning, I'd like to know if you have a room available for my husband and I.*
Receptionist:	*For which date?*
Signora Bianchini:	*For two nights, starting tomorrow night.*
Receptionist:	*Madam, I will check, but we're very full. You should have called earlier because this is furniture-fair week, and Bologna is very crowded.*
Signora Bianchini:	*Yes, I know, but unfortunately I've just found out that I need to come to Bologna.*
Receptionist:	*Madam, you're lucky. I don't have a room with a queen-size bed, but I have one with two single beds; would that be okay by you?*
Signora Bianchini:	*Certainly, actually we'd prefer it.*

Receptionist:	Madam, the room is on the third floor, and it's a bit noisy, but it's spacious and it has air conditioning.
Signora Bianchini:	It's fine by me. We live on the fourth floor and our apartment is also noisy. I would have never thought I would be able to find a room so quickly at last minute notice!
Receptionist:	Madam, you're very accommodating. At what time do you think you'll be checking in?
Signora Bianchini:	Would it be a problem if we check in tomorrow morning?
Receptionist:	No Madam, if the room is not ready, you can leave your luggage with reception.
Signora Bianchini:	Thank you, until tomorrow then.

Ⅱ

Notes:

Two different words translate the English word *floor* in Italian: piano is the floor of a building with different floors, while pavimento is the floor inside a house or apartment, the surface on which we walk.

✎ Conversation Practice 2

Fill in the blanks in the following sentences with the missing words in the word bank. If you're unsure of the answer, listen to the conversation on your audio one more time.

Desidera, vorrei sapere, avrebbe dovuto, una camera doppia, secondo piano, problema, avrei mai pensato, pensa

1. Buongiorno, Hotel International, _____?

2. Buon giorno, _____ se avete una camera disponibile.

3. _____ chiamare prima perché questa settimana c'è la fiera del mobile.

4. Ho _____, Le andrebbe bene lo stesso?

5. La camera è al _____ ed è un po' rumorosa.

6. Per me non è un _____.

7. Non _____ di trovare una stanza così in fretta all'ultimo minuto!

8. A che ora _____ di arrivare?

ANSWER KEY

1. desidera; 2. vorrei sapere; 3. Avrebbe dovuto; 4. una camera doppia; 5. secondo piano;
6. problema; 7. avrei mai pensato; 8. pensa

Grammar Builder 2

▶ 8D Grammar Builder 2 (CD 8, Track 11)

ORDINAL NUMBERS

The ordinal numbers from first to tenth are as follows:

primo	*first*
secondo	*second*
terzo	*third*
quarto	*fourth*
quinto	*fifth*
sesto	*sixth*
settimo	*seventh*
ottavo	*eighth*
nono	*ninth*
decimo	*tenth*

Beginning with **undicesimo** (*eleventh*), ordinal numbers are formed by dropping the last vowel of the cardinal number, and by adding **-esimo**. If the cardinal number ends in **-tre**, then the final **-e** of the cardinal number is retained, as in **ventitreesimo**.

Remember that ordinal numbers are adjectives, and they must agree in gender and number with the noun they modify. Where English uses a superscript *-st, -nd, -rd*, or *-th* for ordinal numbers, Italian uses a degree symbol: **1°, 2°**, etc.

✎ Work Out 2

Spell out the number given in parentheses.

1. **Giulio è il suo (3°) figlio.** _____

2. **Loro festeggiano il loro (43°) anniversario di matrimonio.** _____

3. **Ieri sera abbiamo ascoltato la (9°) sinfonia di Beethoven.** _____

4. **Questo è il (18°) anno che lavoro in quest'ufficio.** _____

5. **Mia figlia fa la (5°) elementare.** _____

ANSWER KEY
1. **terzo**; 2. **quarantatreesimo**; 3. **nona**; 4. **diciottesimo**; 5. **quinta**

✎ Drive It Home

A. Modify the following nouns with a suffix instead of an adjective.

1. **Una macchina grande.** _____

2. **Un tavolo piccolo.** _____

3. **Una brutta giornata.** _____

4. **Un gatto carino.** _____

5. **Una canzone brutta.** _____

B. Translate the following sentences spelling out the ordinal numbers.

1. *This is the 3rd time I'm calling you.* _____

_____

2. *I live on the 14th floor.* _____

_____

3. *In Italy Sunday is considered the 7th day of the week.* _____

_____

4. *Today is my 33rd birthday.* _____

_____

5. *When I was in 5th grade I was very shy.* _____

_____

ANSWER KEY
A. 1. una macchinona; 2. un tavolino; 3. una giornataccia; 4. un gattino/gattuccio; 5. una canzonaccia
B. 1. Questa è la terza volta che ti chiamo. 2. Abito al tredicesimo piano. 3. In Italia, la domenica è
considerata il settimo giorno della settimana. 4. Oggi è il mio trentatreesimo compleanno.
5. Quando ero in quinta elementare ero molto timido/a.

How Did You Do?

Let's see how you did in this lesson. By now, you should know:

☐ how to change the meaning of a word by adding a suffix
   (Still unsure? Jump back to page 96.)

☐ how to say *first, second,* and *third* (Still unsure? Jump back to page 100.)

✎ Word Recall

A. Translate the following sentences into English.

1. **Avete una camera disponibile?** _____

   _____

2. **Per quando?** _____

   _____

3. **Avrebbe dovuto chiamare prima.** _____

   _____

4. **Siamo molto pieni.** _____

   _____

5. **Dove vai per il colloquio?** _____

   _____

B. Translate the following sentences into Italian.

1. *Would that be okay by you?* _____

   _____

2. *It has air conditioning.* _____

   _____

3. *I can't believe it!* _____

   _____

4. *Would you have time to have coffee with me?* _____

   _____

5. *On your left you'll find via Belle Arti.* _____

Don't forget to practice and reinforce what you've learned by visiting **www.livinglanguage.com/languagelab** for flashcards, games, and quizzes!

Unit 2 Essentials

Vocabulary Essentials

Test your knowledge of the key material in this unit by filling in the blanks in the following charts. Once you've completed these pages, you'll have tested your retention, and you'll have your own reference for the most essential vocabulary.

WORDS RELATED TO A JOB INTERVIEW

	interview
	to move, to transfer
	expert
	finalist (male or female)

[pg. 64]

MEASUREMENT

	meter
	centimeter
	kilometer

[pg. 64]

LOCATION

	to turn
	right
	left

[pg. 64]

	along
	ahead

[pg. 64]

BOOKING A HOTEL ROOM

	to check
	to reserve
	crowded
	available
	double room (one queen-size bed)
	double room (two twin-size beds)
	single room (one twin bed)
	floor (of a building)
	towel
	soap (bar)
	toilet paper
	air conditioning
	suitcase

[pg. 67]

EXPRESSIONS OF DURATION AND TIME

	for a very long time; since always; since forever
	I'm late.
	It's late.
	I'm early.

[pg. 73]

	It's early.
	in forty-five minutes

[pg. 73]

Don't forget: if you're having a hard time remembering this vocabulary, check out the supplemental flashcards for this unit online, at **www.livinglanguage. com/languagelab**.

Grammar Essentials

Here is a reference of the key grammar that was covered in Unit 2. Make sure you understand the summary and can use all of the grammar in it.

EXPRESSING DURATION OF AN ACTION

- To express duration use the present tense + da + time expression.

- To ask for how long an action has been going on, use da quanto tempo + present.

DISJUNCTIVE PRONOUNS

- Always used after the prepositions per, con, and tra/fra.

me	me	a me	to me
te	you	a te	to you
lui	him	a lui	to him
lei	her	a lei	to her
Lei	you (fml.)	a Lei	to you (fml.)
noi	us	a noi	to us
voi	you	a voi	to you (pl.)
loro	them	a loro	to them
Loro	you (fml. pl.)	a Loro	to you (fml. pl.)

THE INFORMAL IMPERATIVE

- Used to give a command or make a suggestion.

- Formed the same way as the present tense, with the exception of the **tu** form of first conjugation verbs (**-are**), which ends in **-a** rather than **-i**.

Note:
1. **Andare**, **dare**, **fare**, **stare**, and **dire** have an irregular **tu** imperative form: **va'**, **da'**, **fa'**, **sta'**, and **di'**. But their other imperative forms are regular.

2. **Essere** and **avere** have an irregular imperative form:
   essere: **sii**, **siamo**, **siate**
   avere: **abbi**, **abbiamo**, **abbiate**

3. The negative imperative is formed by placing **non** in front of the imperative. However, the **tu** negative imperative is formed by **non** + infinitive.

4. The infinitive is often used when giving directions to the general public in signs, public notices, recipes, etc.

THE INFORMAL IMPERATIVE AND PRONOUNS

- Direct and indirect object pronouns, reflexive pronouns, and **ci** when used as an adverb meaning there are all attached to the end of the informal imperative.

- With the negative imperative, the pronouns can either precede the imperative, or be attached to it.

- Before attaching a pronoun to **va'**, **da'**, **fa'**, **sta'**, and **di'**, remember to drop the apostrophe and to double the first consonant of the pronoun, with the exception of **gli**, which does not double the consonant.

SUFFIXES

- **-ino**, **-etto**, and **-ello** are called diminutives, indicating smallness or cuteness, or used to express the speaker's affection.

- **-one**, **-ona**, **-oni**, and **-one** (*f. pl.*) express largeness.

- **-accio**, **-astro**, and **-ucolo** express ugliness, roughness, or other negative qualities.

ORDINAL NUMBERS

primo	*first*	sesto	*sixth*
secondo	*second*	settimo	*seventh*
terzo	*third*	ottavo	*eighth*
quarto	*fourth*	nono	*ninth*
quinto	*fifth*	decimo	*tenth*

- Beginning with **undicesimo** (eleventh) ordinal numbers are formed by dropping the last vowel of the cardinal number, and by adding **-esimo**. If the cardinal number ends in **-tre**, then the final **-e** of the cardinal number is retained, as in **ventitreesimo**.

- Ordinal numbers are adjectives, and must agree in gender and number with the noun they modify. Italian also uses a degree symbol: 1°, 2°, etc.

THE PRESENT CONDITIONAL

- Expresses possible or hypothetical actions or states and translated into English as *would* + verb.

- Formed like the future tense, by dropping the final **-e** from the infinitive.

- In verbs of the first conjugation, the **-a** of the infinitive ending changes to **-e**.

- Verbs with irregularities in the future maintain the same irregularities in the conditional.

Conditional Endings

io -ei	noi -emmo
tu -esti	voi -este
lui/lei/Lei -ebbe	loro/Loro -ebbero

THE PAST CONDITIONAL

- The past conditional is formed with the conditional of essere or avere, followed by the past participle. Remember that past participles of essere verbs must agree with the subject.

- When using dovere, potere, and volere in the past conditional, they are all followed by the main verb in the infinitive form, and the main verb determines which auxiliary to use.

VERBS IN THE INFORMAL IMPERATIVE

CANTARE *(TO SING)*	
(tu) canta	*(you) sing*
(noi) cantiamo	*let's sing*
(voi) cantate	*(you pl.) sing*

PRENDERE *(TO TAKE)*	
prendi	*(you) take*
prendiamo	*let's take*
prendete	*(you pl.) take*

DORMIRE *(TO SLEEP)*	
dormi	*(you) sleep*
dormiamo	*let's sleep*
dormite	*(you pl.) sleep*

PULIRE *(TO CLEAN)*	
pulisci	*(you) clean*
puliamo	*let's clean*
pulite	*(you pl.) clean*

VERBS IN THE PRESENT CONDITIONAL

PARLARE *(TO SPEAK)*			
io parlerei	*I would speak*	noi parleremmo	*we would speak*
tu parleresti	*you would speak*	voi parlereste	*you would speak*
lui/lei/Lei parlerebbe	*he/she would speak, you (fml.) would speak*	loro/Loro parlerebbero	*they would speak, you (fml. pl.) would speak*

PRENDERE *(TO TAKE)*			
io prenderei	*I would take*	noi prenderemmo	*we would take*
tu prenderesti	*you would take*	voi prendereste	*you would take*
lui/lei/Lei prenderebbe	*he/she would take, you (fml.) would take*	loro/Loro prenderebbero	*they would take, you (fml. pl.) would take*

DORMIRE *(TO SLEEP)*			
io dormirei	*I would sleep*	noi dormiremmo	*we would sleep*
tu dormiresti	*you would sleep*	voi dormireste	*you would sleep*
lui/lei/Lei dormirebbe	*he/she would sleep, you (fml.) would sleep*	loro/Loro dormirebbero	*they would sleep, you (fml. pl.) would sleep*

PULIRE *(TO CLEAN)*			
io pulirei	*I would clean*	noi puliremmo	*we would clean*
tu puliresti	*you would clean*	voi pulireste	*you would clean*
lui/lei/Lei pulirebbe	*he/she would clean, you (fml.) would clean*	loro/Loro pulirebbero	*they would clean, you (fml. pl.) would clean*

VERBS IN THE PAST CONDITIONAL

PARLARE *(TO SPEAK)*			
io avrei parlato	*I would have spoken*	noi avremmo parlato	*we would have spoken*
tu avresti parlato	*you would have spoken*	voi avreste parlato	*you would have spoken*
lui/lei/Lei avrebbe parlato	*he/she would have spoken, you (fml.) would have spoken*	loro/Loro avrebbero parlato	*they would have spoken, you (fml. pl.) would have spoken*

ARRIVARE *(TO ARRIVE)*			
io sarei arrivato/a	*I would have arrived*	noi saremmo arrivati/e	*we would have arrived*
tu saresti arrivato/a	*you would have arrived*	voi sareste arrivati/e	*you would have arrived*
lui/lei/ Lei sarebbe arrivato/a	*he/she would have arrived, you (fml.) would have arrived*	loro/Loro sarebbero arrivati/e	*they would have arrived, you (fml. pl.) would have arrived*

Unit 2 Quiz

Let's put the most essential Italian words and grammar points you've learned so far to practice in a few exercises. It's important to be sure that you've mastered this material before you move on. Score yourself at the end of the review and see if you need to go back for more practice, or if you're ready to move on to Unit 3.

A. Translate the following sentences into Italian.

1. *They haven't talked to her for a long time.* _____

_____

2. *For how long have you been reading this book?* _____

_____

B. Replace the underlined expression with a disjunctive pronoun.

1. Mangi *con Giovanni* stasera? _____

_____

2. Ora non posso telefonare *a Luisa*? _____

_____

C. In your opinion, these people must, or mustn't do certain things. Tell them to do, or not do these things, following the example: **I ragazzi devono studiare → studiate!**

1. Voi dovete studiare di più! _____

   _____

2. Giorgio non deve mangiare tutto il cioccolato. _____

   _____

3. Noi dobbiamo bere solo acqua a cena. _____

   _____

D. Replace the underlined object(s) with a pronoun or a double pronoun.

1. Non bevete tutto *il vino*! _____

   _____

2. Di' *la verità a me*! _____

   _____

3. Perché non mandate mai *le cartoline a noi* quando siete in vacanza? _____

   _____

4. Diamo *il regalo a Laura* stasera! _____

   _____

E. Fill in the blanks with the present conditional of the verbs in parentheses.

1. Io _____ (andare) al mare con voi, ma devo lavorare.

2. Noi _____ (ritornare) a casa più tardi, ma nostra

   mamma (preoccuparsi) _____.

3. Lui _____ (volere) andare in vacanza in montagna, ma sua moglie non sa sciare.

F. Fill in the blank with the present or past conditional of the verb in parentheses as appropriate.

1. Io _____ (comprare) la televisione più grande, ma era troppo cara.

2. Loro _____ (rimanere) alla festa , ma hanno dovuto prendere il treno delle dieci.

3. Lui ti _____ (chiamare), ma ha lasciato il telefonino a casa.

G. Change the underlined words into a word with a suffix.

1. Quando ero piccolo giocavo con i piccoli *treni*. _____

2. Ieri faceva *brutto tempo*, fortunatamente avevamo un *ombrello grandissimo*. ___

_____

H. Spell out the ordinal numbers given in parentheses in English.

1. Nella gara di corsa Franco è arrivato (*1st*), Giorgio (*3rd*), Lina (*8th*), Luisa (*12th*) e Francesco, poverino, (*32nd*). _____

_____

How Did You Do?

Give yourself a point for every correct answer, then use the following key to tell whether you're ready to move on:

0-7 points: It's probably a good idea to go back through the lesson again. You may be moving too quickly, or there may be too much "down time" between your contact with Italian. Remember that it's better to spend 30 minutes with Italian three or four times a week than it is to spend two or three hours just once a week. Find a pace that's comfortable for you, and spread your contact hours out as much as you can.

8-12 points: You would benefit from a review before moving on. Go back and spend a little more time on the specific points that gave you trouble. Re-read the Grammar Builder sections that were difficult, and do the work out one more time. Don't forget about the online supplemental practice material, either. Go to **www.livinglanguage.com/languagelab** for games and quizzes that will reinforce the material from this unit.

13-17 points: Good job! There are just a few points that you could consider reviewing before moving on. If you haven't worked with the games and quizzes on **www.livinglanguage.com/languagelab**, please give them a try.

18-20 points: Great! You're ready to move on to the next unit.

 **points**

ANSWER KEY
A. 1. **Loro non le parlano da molto tempo**; 2. **Da quanto tempo leggi questo libro?**
B. 1. **Mangi con lui stasera?** 2. **Ora non posso telefonarle?**
C. 1. **Studiate di più!** 2. **Giorgio, non mangiare tutto il cioccolato!** 3. **Beviamo solo acqua a cena!**
D. 1. **Non bevetelo tutto!** 2. **Dimmela!** 3. **Perché non ce le mandate mai quando siete in vacanza?**
4. **Diamoglielo stasera!**
E. 1. **andrei**; 2. **ritorneremmo, si preoccuperebbe**; 3. **vorrebbe**
F. 1. **avrei comprato**; 2. **sarebbero rimasti**; 3. **avrebbe chiamato**
G. 1. **trenini**; 2. **un tempaccio, ombrellone**
H. 1. **primo, terzo, ottava, dodicesima, trentaduesimo**

Unit 3:
Talking About Health

God forbid you might get sick while traveling in Italy! However, just in case you need to, we want to make sure you are going to be able to communicate with **un medico** (*a doctor*). By the end of this unit, you'll be able to:

☐ name the different parts of the body

☐ form plurals of words like *eyelash* and *knee*

☐ talk about your health

☐ form plurals of words like *climate* and *planet*

☐ describe your symptoms

☐ use words like *who, whom,* and *whose*

☐ say words like *slowly* and *rarely*

☐ express *one another* and *each other*

☐ use the words *some* and *any*

☐ use words like *many* and *none*

Lesson 9: Words

By the end of this lesson, you'll be able to:

☐ name the different parts of the body

☐ form plurals of words like *eyelash* and *knee*

☐ talk about your health

☐ form plurals of words like *climate* and *planet*

Word Builder 1

▶ 9A Word Builder 1 (CD 8, Track 12)

(l')ospedale	*hospital*
(il) pronto soccorso	*emergency room*
(la) testa	*head*
(il) collo	*neck*
(l')occhio	*eye*
(il) naso	*nose*
(la) bocca	*mouth*
(la) schiena	*back*
(lo) stomaco	*stomach*
(la) pancia	*belly*
(l')intestino	*intestine*
(la) gamba	*leg*
(il) piede	*foot*
(l')infarto	*heart attack*

Ⅱ

✎ Word Practice 1

A. Translate the following words into English.

1. (la) testa _____

2. (la) bocca _____

3. (la) pancia _____

4. (il) piede _____

5. (l')ospedale _____

6. (l')infarto _____

B. Translate the following words into Italian.

1. *stomach* _____

2. *leg* _____

3. *emergency room* _____

4. *neck* _____

5. *back* _____

6. *eye* _____

ANSWER KEY
A. 1. *head*; 2. *mouth*; 3. *belly*; 4. *foot*; 5. *hospital*; 6. *heart attack*
B. 1. (lo) stomaco; 2. (la) gamba; 3. (il) pronto soccorso; 4. (il) collo; 5. (la) schiena; 6. (l')occhio

Grammar Builder 1

▶ 9B Grammar Builder 1 (CD 8, Track 13)

IRREGULAR PLURALS OF NOUNS

In Lesson 1 of *Intermediate Italian*, you learned how to form the plural of nouns. There are, however, some nouns that have irregular plurals.

a. Nouns that end with an accent, such as **città**, **università**, **caffè**, etc., do not change in the plural: **una città → due città**.

b. Foreign words, which usually end in a consonant, such as **sport**, **film**, **weekend**, etc., do not change in the plural: **un film → due film**. Although the word **zoo** ends with a vowel, it's a foreign word, and its plural is **zoo**.

c. Words that are abbreviated, such as **cinematografo → cinema**; **fotografia → foto**; **motocicletta → moto**; **bicicletta → bici**, etc. do not change in the plural. Also, pay attention to the gender of these nouns, which is the gender of the original word: **il cinema → i cinema**.

d. A few words, particularly words indicating parts of the body, are masculine in the singular, but have an irregular feminine plural ending in **-a**:

il ciglio	**le ciglia**	*eyelash*
il sopracciglio	**le sopracciglia**	*eyebrow*
il braccio	**le braccia**	*arm*
il ginocchio	**le ginocchia/i ginocchi**	*knee*
il dito	**le dita**	*finger*
l'osso	**le ossa**	*bone*
l'uovo	**le uova**	*egg*

Reflexive Verbs of
Reciprocity

Indefinites Used as Either
Adjectives or Pronouns

il lenzuolo	le lenzuola	*bed sheets, bed linens*

L'orecchio (*ear*) has both a feminine and a masculine plural, respectively ending in -e/-i: **le orecchie/gli orecchi**. **La mano** (*hand*) is feminine but with an irregular ending in -o. The plural is also feminine, ending in -i: **la mano → le mani**.

(II)

✎ Work Out 1

Provide the singular article for the following nouns, and then change both article and noun to the plural.

1. braccio _____

2. foto _____

3. città _____

4. sport _____

5. zoo _____

6. mano _____

7. orecchio _____

8. lenzuolo _____

ANSWER KEY
1. il braccio, le braccia; 2. la foto, le foto; 3. la città, le città; 4. lo sport, gli sport; 5. lo zoo, gli zoo; 6. la mano, le mani; 7. l'orecchio, gli orecchi/le orecchie; 8. il lenzuolo, le lenzuola

Word Builder 2

9C Word Builder 2 (CD 8, Track 14)

(la) salute	*health*
(la) febbre	*fever*
(la) temperatura	*temperature*
(la) pressione	*pressure*
(il) sangue	*blood*
(il) cuore	*heart*
(il) polmone	*lung*
(il) fegato	*liver*
(il) rene	*kidney*
respirare	*to breathe*
(la) forma	*shape*
(l')elettrocardiogramma	*electrocardiogram*
mancino	*left-handed*
(l')atleta	*athlete*
sorprendere	*to surprise*

Word Practice 2

Match the following expressions.

1. (la) pressione — a. *fever*
2. respirare — b. *athlete*
3. (la) febbre — c. *to surprise*
4. (il) cuore — d. *liver*
5. mancino — e. *to breathe*

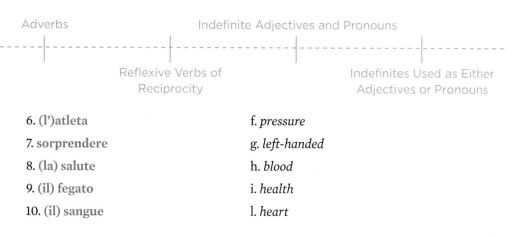
6. (l')atleta   f. *pressure*

7. sorprendere   g. *left-handed*

8. (la) salute   h. *blood*

9. (il) fegato   i. *health*

10. (il) sangue   l. *heart*

ANSWER KEY
1. f; 2. e; 3. a; 4. l; 5. g; 6. b; 7. c; 8. i; 9. d; 10. h

Grammar Builder 2

▷ 9D Grammar Builder 2 (CD 8, Track 15)

IRREGULAR SINGULAR NOUNS WITH REGULAR PLURAL FORMS

In Italian there are nouns with an irregular singular form, but a regular plural form:

A few masculine nouns, usually derived from Greek, have an irregular singular ending in -a. Many of these nouns are cognates. The plural form ends regularly in -i, just like the plural of all those nouns ending in -amma, such as **programma** (*program*), **telegramma** (*telegram*), **elettrocardiogramma** (*electrocardiogram*). Here are other common irregular nouns:

dramma	*drama*
aroma	*aroma*
diploma	*diploma*
panorama	*panorama*
poema	*poem*
problema	*problem*
clima	*climate*
pianeta	*planet*
sistema	*system*

Other irregular nouns include those nouns ending in -ista and -iatra (which usually indicate professions), and a few others such as collega (*colleague*) and astronauta (*astronaut*) that can be either masculine or feminine. The plural, however, ends regularly in -i in the masculine form, and in -e in the feminine form. Here are a few common nouns: atleta (*athlete*), giornalista (*journalist*), pianista (*pianist*), regista (*movie director*), turista (*tourist*), pediatra (*pediatrician*), psichiatra (*psychiatrist*).

✎ Work Out 2

Change the following sentences from the plural to the singular. Change everything possible.

1. I registi famosi hanno partecipato al Festival di Venezia. _____

2. Ci sono molti turisti a Roma. _____

3. Loro hanno molti problemi. _____

4. I programmi televisivi sono noiosi. _____

5. Sono due poemi epici famosi. _____

6. I giornalisti hanno scritto due articoli interessanti. _____

ANSWER KEY

1. Il regista famoso ha partecipato al Festival di Venezia. 2. C'è un turista a Roma. 3. Lui ha un problema. 4. Il programma televisivo è noioso. 5. È un poema epico famoso. 6. Il giornalista ha scritto un articolo interessante.

✎ Drive It Home

Change the following nouns into their plural form. Don't forget the appropriate article!

1. la foto _____

2. la città _____

3. il lenzuolo _____

4. il caffè _____

5. l'uovo _____

6. il problema _____

7. il sistema _____

8. il pianista _____

9. la pianista _____

10. il programma _____

ANSWER KEY

1. le foto; 2. le città; 3. le lenzuola; 4. i caffè; 5. le uova; 6. i problemi; 7. i sistemi; 8. i pianisti; 9. le pianiste; 10. i programmi

🌐 Culture Note

Although named by Americans, the "Mediterranean diet" has been a staple in many southern European countries, such as Italy, Spain, and Greece. In the past 50 years or so, however, due to the increased wealth of the country, Italy's diet has become less healthy, and as a consequence there has been an increase in obesity and other diet-related diseases. There has been an effort, both in Italy and the United States, to go back to a healthier way of eating.

How Did You Do?

Let's see how you did in this lesson. By now, you should be able to:

☐ name the different parts of the body (Still unsure? Jump back to page 118.)

☐ form plurals of words like *eyelash* and *knee* (Still unsure? Jump back to page 120.)

☐ talk about your health (Still unsure? Jump back to page 122.)

☐ form plurals of words like *climate* and *planet* (Still unsure? Jump back to page 123.)

✎ Word Recall

A. Translate the following words into English.

1. (l')elettrocardiogramma _____

2. (il) fegato _____

3. (il) pronto soccorso _____

4. respirare _____

5. (lo) stomaco _____

6. (il) rene _____

B. Translate the following words into Italian.

1. *heart* _____

2. *shape* _____

3. *temperature* _____

4. *health* _____

5. *intestine* _____

6. *mouth* _____

ANSWER KEY

A. 1. *electrocardiogram*; 2. *liver*; 3. *emergency room*; 4. *to breathe*; 5. *stomach*; 6. *kidney*
B. 1. **(il) cuore**; 2. **(la) forma**; 3. **(la) temperatura**; 4. **(la) salute**; 5. **(l') intestino**; 6. **(la) bocca**

Lesson 10: Phrases

By the end of this lesson, you'll be able to:

☐ describe your symptoms

☐ use words like *who*, *whom*, and *whose*

Phrase Builder 1

▷ 10A Phrase Builder 1 (CD 8, Track 16)

Sto bene.	I am well.
Mi sento bene.	I feel well.
Fa male.	It hurts.
ho un dolore a	I have a pain in; my … hurts
ho male a	I have a pain in; my … hurts
perdere tempo	to waste time
si telefona	one calls
si deve	one must
ogni volta	every time
nessuna idea	no idea

| tanto vale | (one) might as well |
| Sono preoccupato. | I'm worried. |

✎ Phrase Practice 1

A. Translate the following phrases into English.

1. nessuna idea _____

2. perdere tempo _____

3. fa male _____

4. tanto vale _____

B. Translate the following phrases into Italian.

1. *I am well.* _____

2. *one must* _____

3. *every time* _____

4. *I'm worried.* _____

ANSWER KEY
A. 1. *no idea*; 2. *to waste time*; 3. *it hurts*; 4. *(one) might as well*
B. 1. **Sto bene.** 2. **si deve**; 3. **ogni volta**; 4. **Sono preoccupato.**

Grammar Builder 1

▷ 10B Grammar Builder 1 (CD 8, Track 17)

THE IMPERSONAL CONSTRUCTION

The impersonal construction (the equivalent to the English *one, they,* or *people* + verb) is formed in Italian with the impersonal pronoun **si** followed by the verb in the third person singular.

Quando si telefona a un medico si deve aspettare molto.
When one calls a doctor one has to wait a long time.

Si legge che un dolore al braccio sinistro può essere un sintomo d'infarto.
One reads that a pain in the left arm can be a symptom of a heart attack.

If a plural noun follows the verb, then the verb is in the third person plural form.

In ospedale si mangia cibo molto leggero.
In the hospital one eats very light food.

In ospedale si curano molte malattie.
Hospitals (they) treat many diseases.

In compound tenses, the auxiliary in an impersonal construction is always **essere**, both with verbs that normally take **essere** as well as those that take **avere**.

Ieri si è mangiato molto.
Yesterday, people ate a lot.

Al Festival di Cannes si sono visti molti film interessanti.
People saw many interesting movies at the Cannes Festival.

(II)

✎ Work Out 1

Change the following sentences to the impersonal construction, following the example:

La gente mangia molta frutta in Italia → Si mangia molta frutta in Italia.

1. **A Bologna la gente mangia tagliatelle e lasagne.** _____

   _____

2. **La gente aspetta molto tempo dal dottore.** _____

   _____

3. **La gente deve fare molto sport.** _____

   _____

4. **La gente spende molti soldi in vacanza.** _____

   _____

5. **La gente deve usare meno la macchina.** _____

   _____

6. **Secondo le statistiche la gente ha letto molti libri l'anno scorso.** _____

   _____

7. **In Grecia di solito la gente va al mare d'estate.** _____

   _____

ANSWER KEY

1. A Bologna si mangiano tagliatelle e lasagne. 2. Si aspetta molto tempo dal dottore. 3. Si deve fare molto sport. 4. Si spendono molti soldi in vacanza. 5. Si deve usare meno la macchina. 6. Secondo le statistiche si sono letti molti libri l'anno scorso. 7. In Grecia di solito si va al mare d'estate.

Phrase Builder 2

▷ 10C Phrase Builder 2 (CD 8, Track 18)

Ho esagerato.	*I overreacted.*
si legge che …	*one reads that …*
avere la febbre	*to have a fever*
misurare la pressione	*to check blood pressure*
Faccio sport.	*I practice sports.*
in ottima forma	*in great shape*
chi fa sport …	*those who practice sports …*
con cui …	*with whom …*
è dovuto a …	*it's due to …*
visto che	*given that; since*

Ⅱ

✎ Phrase Practice 2

Match the following expressions:

1. si legge che …   a. *with whom …*

2. misurare la pressione   b. *given that*

3. visto che   c. *it's due to …*

4. Faccio sport.   d. *in great shape*

5. è dovuto a …   e. *to check blood pressure*

6. Ho esagerato.   f. *one reads that …*

7. con cui …   g. *I overreacted.*

8. in ottima forma   h. *I practice sports.*

ANSWER KEY
1. f; 2. e; 3. b; 4. h; 5. c; 6. g; 7. a; 8. d

Grammar Builder 2

▶ 10D Grammar Builder 2 (CD 8, Track 19)

RELATIVE PRONOUNS

A relative pronoun (*who, whom, whose, which, that*) connects a noun or a pronoun to a dependent clause. While in English the relative pronoun is often omitted, in Italian it must always be expressed.

I medici che lavorano al pronto soccorso sono molto gentili.
Doctors who work at the emergency room are very kind.

In the sentence above, **che** connects the noun **i medici** to the sentence **lavorano al pronto soccorso**. The relative pronouns are **che** (*that, which, who, whom*); **cui** (*which, whom*); and **chi** (*he/she who, the one who, whoever*).

che (*that, which, who, whom*) is invariable and is never used after a preposition.

Il medico che vedo normalmente è in vacanza.
The doctor (whom) I normally see is on vacation.

Gli esami che ha(i) fatto sono tutti normali.
The results of the tests you took are all normal./Your test results are all normal.

Cui (*which, whom*) is also invariable, and is always used after a preposition. **Cui** is also used in the expressions **la ragione/il motivo per cui** (*the reason why*), and **il modo in cui** (*the way in which*).

Sono uscito a cena con gli stessi amici con cui ho giocato a tennis.
I went out to dinner with my friends from the tennis game.

Mi piace il modo in cui quell'infermiera tratta i pazienti.
I like the way in which that nurse treats (her) patients.

chi (*he/she who, the one who, whoever*) is invariable, is only used for people, and always takes a verb in the singular. **Chi** is often found in proverbs and popular sayings.

Chi fa sport alla Sua/tua età raramente ha un infarto.
People who play sports at your age rarely have heart attacks.

Chi rompe, paga.
You break it, you buy it. (lit., The one who breaks, pays.)

(II)

✎ Work Out 2

Complete the following sentences with the appropriate relative pronoun.

1. **Mi fa male il braccio _____ mi sono rotto l'anno scorso.**

2. **Il medico di _____ mi parli sempre non accetta nuovi pazienti.**

3. **_____ non ingrassa ha meno problemi di salute.**

4. **Ho telefonato al medico _____ ha lo studio vicino a casa tua.**

5. **Quel signore _____ abbiamo incontrato ieri è un infermiere.**

6. **Non capisco il motivo per _____ devo aspettare così a lungo.**

7. **Chi è quella signora con _____ parlavi?**

ANSWER KEY
1. che; 2. cui; 3. Chi; 4. che; 5. che; 6. cui; 7. cui

✎ Drive It Home

A. Change the following sentences to the impersonal construction.

1. Quando uno sta male uno va dal dottore. _____

_____

2. Dicono che dimagrire fa bene alla salute. _____

_____

3. Quando uno compie gli anni è bene festeggiare. _____

_____

4. Di questi tempi la gente vede troppi film violenti. _____

_____

5. Per Natale in Italia la gente compra tanti regali. _____

_____

B. Complete the following sentences with the appropriate relative pronoun.

1. I libri _____ ho letto erano noiosi.

2. Lui è l'amico di _____ ti ho parlato.

3. _____ risponde a tutte le domande vince un premio.

4. Il cappotto _____ ho comprato ieri è molto caldo.

5. Questo è il motivo per _____ sono andato via presto.

ANSWER KEY
A. 1. Quando si sta male si va dal dottore. 2. Si dice che dimagrire fa bene alla salute. 3. Quando si compiono gli anni è bene festeggiare. 4. Di questi tempi si vedono troppi film violenti. 5. Per Natale si comprano tanti regali.
B. 1. che; 2. cui; 3. Chi; 4. che; 5. cui

⊕ Culture Note

In search of a healthy lifestyle, Italians have embraced **i prodotti d'erboristeria** (*herbal products*). There are numerous stores in Italy where you can buy not only vitamins and supplements, but also dried herbs that can be mixed according to individual needs.

How Did You Do?

Let's see how you did in this lesson. By now, you should be able to:

☐ describe your symptoms (Still unsure? Jump back to page 127.)

☐ use words like *who*, *whom*, and *whose* (Still unsure? Jump back to page 132.)

✎ Word Recall

A. Translate the following phrases into English.

1. **Sto bene.** _____

2. **Fa male.** _____

3. **Ho esagerato.** _____

4. **Sono preoccupato.** _____

5. **avere la febbre** _____

B. Translate the following phrases into Italian.

1. *to waste time* _____

2. *one must* _____

3. *every time* _____

4. *no idea* _____

5. *in great shape* _____

ANSWER KEY
A. 1. *I am well.* 2. *It hurts.* 3. *I overreacted.* 4. *I'm worried.* 5. *to have a fever*
B. 1. **perdere tempo**; 2. **si deve**; 3. **ogni volta**; 4. **nessuna idea**; 5. **in ottima forma**

Lesson 11: Sentences

By the end of this lesson, you'll be able to:

☐ say words like *slowly* and *rarely*

☐ express *one another* and *each other*

Sentence Builder 1

▶ 11A Sentence Builder 1 (CD 8, Track 20)

Ho un problema.	*I have a problem.*
Non mi sento bene.	*I don't feel good.*
Che cosa ti fa male?	*What hurts? Tell me about your ailment.*
Muoviti lentamente!	*Move slowly!*
Il medico che vedo normalmente è in vacanza.	*The doctor I normally see is on vacation.*
Ogni volta che si telefona si deve aspettare.	*Every time one calls, one has to wait.*
Tanto vale andare all'ospedale.	*One might as well go to the hospital.*
Ho male al braccio sinistro.	*My left arm hurts.*
Non ne ho (nessuna) idea.	*I have no idea (about it).*

⏸

Reflexive Verbs of
Reciprocity

Indefinites Used as Either
Adjectives or Pronouns

✎ Sentence Practice 1

Translate the following sentences into Italian.

1. *What hurts?* _____

   _____

2. *I have no idea.* _____

   _____

3. *I have a problem.* _____

   _____

4. *The doctor I normally see is on vacation.* _____

   _____

5. *One might as well go to the hospital.* _____

   _____

6. *Move slowly!* _____

   _____

7. *I don't feel good.* _____

   _____

8. *Every time one calls, one has to wait.* _____

   _____

ANSWER KEY

1. **Che cosa ti fa male?** 2. **Non ne ho nessuna idea.** 3. **Ho un problema.** 4. **Il medico che vedo normalmente è in vacanza.** 5. **Tanto vale andare all'ospedale.** 6. **Muoviti lentamente!** 7. **Non mi sento bene.** 8. **Ogni volta che si telefona si deve aspettare.**

Grammar Builder 1

⊳ 11B Grammar Builder 1 (CD 8, Track 21)

ADVERBS

Adverbs modify verbs, adjectives, and other adverbs, and are invariable. Some common adverbs are **bene** (*well*), **male** (*badly*), **molto** (*very*), **poco** (*little*), **presto** (*early*), **tardi** (*late*), **spesso** (*often*), **insieme** (*together*), **così** (*so*), and **volentieri** (*gladly*).

Many adverbs are formed by adding the suffix **-mente** to the feminine singular form of an adjective.
lento → lenta → lentamente
veloce → veloce → velocemente

Muoviti lentamente!
Move slowly!

Chi fa sport raramente ha un infarto.
People who practice sports rarely have heart attacks.

If the adjective ends in **-le** or **-re**, the final **-e** is dropped before **-mente** is added.

normale → normalmente
regolare → regolarmente

Il medico che vedo normalmente è in vacanza.
My regular physician is on vacation.

Faccio sport regolarmente.
I exercise regularly.

Some adjectives, such as **chiaro** (*clear, clearly*), **giusto** (*right*), **forte** (*loud, loudly*), **piano** (*slow/soft; slowly/softly*), **svelto** (*fast*), **vicino** (*nearby*), and **lontano** (*far*) can also be used as adverbs.

Lui abita molto lontano.
He lives very far away.

Non camminare così svelto.
Don't walk so fast.

Adverbs usually follow the verb. In compound tenses, however, **ancora** (*still, yet*), **già** (*already*), **mai** (*never*), **sempre** (*always*), **più** (*any more*), and **spesso** (*often*) are usually placed between the auxiliary and the past participle.

Ci siamo già conosciuti?
Have we already met?

Non sono mai stato in un ospedale.
I have never been in a hospital.

(II)

✎ Work Out 1

Translate the following sentences.

1. *She speaks very softly.* _____

_____

2. *I play tennis regularly.* _____

_____

3. *We run really fast.* _____

_____

4. *They haven't seen that movie yet.* _____

_____

5. *You play piano very well.* _____

_____

ANSWER KEY

1. **Lei parla molto piano.** 2. **Gioco a tennis regolarmente.** 3. **Corriamo molto forte (velocemente).**
4. **Non hanno ancora visto quel film.** 5. **Suoni il pianoforte molto bene.**

Sentence Builder 2

11C Sentence Builder 2 (CD 8, Track 22)

Ci siamo già conosciuti?	*Have we already met (each other)?*
Mi fa male il braccio sinistro.	*My left arm hurts.*
Vediamo se ha(i) la febbre.	*Let's see if you have a fever.*
Le misuro la pressione.	*I'll check your blood pressure.*
Controlliamo il cuore e i polmoni.	*Let's listen to your heart and lungs.*
Lei mi sembra in ottima forma.	*You appear to be in great shape.*
Chi fa sport raramente ha un infarto.	*People who practice sports rarely have heart attacks.*
Sono uscito con gli amici con cui ho giocato.	*I went out with my friends from the game.*
Il mal di testa è probabilmente dovuto alla cena abbondante.	*Your headache is probably due to the large dinner (you had).*

Reflexive Verbs of
Reciprocity

Indefinites Used as Either
Adjectives or Pronouns

✎ Sentence Practice 2

A. Translate the following sentences into English.

1. **Mi fa male il braccio sinistro.** _____

_____

2. **Chi fa sport raramente ha un infarto.** _____

_____

3. **Vediamo se hai la febbre.** _____

_____

4. **Sono uscito con gli amici con cui ho giocato.** _____

_____

B. Translate the following sentences into Italian.

1. *Your headache is probably due to the large dinner.* _____

_____

2. *You appear to be in great shape.* _____

_____

3. *Have we already met?* _____

_____

4. *Let's listen to your heart and lungs.* _____

_____

ANSWER KEY

A. 1. *My left arm hurts.* 2. *People who practice sports rarely have heart attacks.* 3. *Let's see if you have a fever.* 4. *I went out with my friends from the game.*

B. 1. Il mal di testa è probabilmente dovuto alla cena abbondante. 2. Lei mi sembra in ottima forma. 3. Ci siamo già conosciuti? 4. Controlliamo il cuore e i polmoni.

Grammar Builder 2

▷ 11D Grammar Builder 2 (CD 8, Track 23)

REFLEXIVE VERBS OF RECIPROCITY

You learned about reflexive verbs in Lesson 18 of *Intermediate Italian.* The reflexive structure is used idiomatically also to express reciprocity (*one another, each other*). In these cases the subject can only be plural. As with reflexive verbs, compound tenses are formed with **essere.** Some common verbs that express reciprocity are: **abbracciarsi** (*to hug*), **aiutarsi** (*to help each other*), **baciarsi** (*to kiss*), **conoscersi** (*to know each other*), **incontrarsi** (*to meet each other*), **salutarsi** (*to greet each other*), **telefonarsi** (*to call each other*), **vedersi** (*to see each other*).

Ci siamo già conosciuti?
Have we already met (each other)?

Loro si vedono oggi.
They see each other; they meet today.

ⓘ

✎ Work Out 2
Change the following sentences into the past tense.

1. **Ci vediamo spesso.** _____

_____

2. **Non si baciano ancora.** _____

_____

3. **Vi telefonate tutti i giorni.** _____

_____

4. **Non si salutano mai.** _____

_____

5. **Ci incontriamo regolarmente.** _____

_____

6. **Vi aiutate sempre.** _____

_____

ANSWER KEY
1. Ci siamo visti/e spesso. 2. Non si sono ancora baciati. 3. Vi siete telefonati/e tutti i giorni. 4. Non si sono mai salutati/e. 5. Ci siamo incontrati/e regolarmente. 6. Vi siete sempre aiutati/e.

✎ Drive It Home

Translate the following sentences into Italian.

1. _He walks very slowly._ _____

_____

2. _Let's go walking, it is not too far._ _____

_____

3. _He plays the piano very loudly._ _____

_____

4. _Do you often go to the movies?_ _____

_____

5. *The teacher speaks very clearly.* _____

_____

6. *We saw each other three times last week.* _____

_____

7. *They kissed in front of everybody.* _____

_____

8. *Agreed! Let's shake hands.* _____

_____

9. *After many years they still keep in touch.* _____

_____

10. *They got married last year.* _____

_____

ANSWER KEY

1. **Lui cammina molto lentamente.** 2. **Andiamo a piedi, non è troppo lontano.** 3. **Lui suona il piano molto forte.** 4. **Andate spesso al cinema?** 5. **Il professore parla molto chiaramente.** 6. **Ci siamo visti tre volte la settimana scorsa.** 7. **Si sono baciati di fronte a tutti.** 8. **D'accordo! Diamoci la mano.** 9. **Dopo tanti anni loro si tengono ancora in contatto.** 10. **Si sono sposati l'anno scorso.**

⊕ Culture Note

Italians have embraced **la medicina omeopatica** (*homeopathic medicine*). There are schools in Italy where medical doctors, pharmacists, or veterinarians can specialize in homeopathic medicine, and many people seek homeopathic treatment for their ailments. If you search **omeopatia** you will get a sense of how popular this therapeutic method is in Italy.

How Did You Do?

Let's see how you did in this lesson. By now, you should be able to:

☐ say words like *slowly* and *rarely* (Still unsure? Jump back to page 138.)

☐ express *one another* and *each other* (Still unsure? Jump back to page 142.)

✎ Word Recall

A. Translate the following sentences into English.

1. **Chi fa sport raramente ha un infarto.** _____

_____

2. **Non mi sento bene.** _____

_____

3. **Il mal di testa è probabilmente dovuto alla cena abbondante.** _____

_____

4. **Il medico che vedo normalmente è in vacanza.** _____

_____

5. **Ho male al braccio sinistro.** _____

_____

B. Translate the following sentences into Italian.

1. *Move slowly!* _____

_____

2. *One might as well go to the hospital.* _____

_____

3. *I have a problem.* _____

_____

4. *Have we already met?* _____

_____

5. *I'll check your blood pressure.* _____

_____

ANSWER KEY

A. 1. *People who practice sports rarely have heart attacks.* 2. *I don't feel good.* 3. *Your headache is probably due to the large dinner.* 4. *The doctor I normally see is on vacation.* 5. *My left arm hurts.*

B. 1. **Muoviti lentamente!** 2. **Tanto vale andare all'ospedale.** 3. **Ho un problema.** 4. **Ci siamo già conosciuti?** 5. **Le misuro la pressione.**

Lesson 12: Conversations

By the end of this lesson, you'll be able to:

☐ use the words *some* and *any*

☐ use words like *many* and *none*

ⓐ Conversation 1

▶ 12A Conversation 1 (CD 8, Track 24 - Italian; Track 25 - Italian and English)

Signor Pollini:	Luisa, ho un problema: non mi sento affatto bene; c'è qualcosa che non va e ho bisogno di vedere un medico.
Signora Pollini:	Cosa è successo, tu stai sempre bene, non hai mai niente. Che cosa ti senti? Che cosa ti fa male? Non ti agitare! Muoviti lentamente!
Signor Pollini:	Ho mal di testa, mal di stomaco e ho anche un dolore in fondo alla schiena. Da chi posso andare?

Signora Pollini: Non lo so, il medico che vedo normalmente è in vacanza e non conosco il suo sostituto, ma possiamo telefonargli.

Signor Pollini: No, non voglio perdere tempo. Ogni volta che si telefona a un medico si deve aspettare un sacco di tempo. E poi visto che non lo conosco di persona, tanto vale andare all'ospedale.

Signora Pollini: Ma stai davvero così male?

Signor Pollini: Sì, ma soprattutto sono preoccupato. Ti devo confessare che mi fa anche male il braccio sinistro … magari sto avendo un infarto!

Signora Pollini: Sergio, hai trentasette anni! Sei un atleta, come puoi pensare a un infarto!

Signor Pollini: Se non è un infarto, allora che cos'è?

Signora Pollini: Non ne ho nessuna idea. Ma se ti tranquillizza, ti accompagno al pronto soccorso.

Signor Pollini: Luisa, I have a problem: I don't feel well at all; something is not right and I need to see a doctor.

Signora Pollinu: What happened, you always feel well. There's never anything wrong with you. What do you feel? What hurts? Don't get nervous. Move slowly.

Signor Pollini: I have a headache, I have a stomachache, and I have a pain in my lower back. Who can I see?

Signora Pollini: I don't know; the doctor whom I normally see is on vacation, and I don't know his substitute, but we can call him.

Signor Pollini: No, I don't want to waste time. Every time one calls a doctor, one has to wait for a long time. Then, since I don't know him personally, I might as well go to the hospital.

Signora Pollini: Are you really that sick?

Signor Pollini: Yes, but above all I'm worried. I must confess that my left arm hurts as well … perhaps I'm having a heart attack!

Signora Pollini: Sergio, you're thirty-seven! You're an athlete, how can you think you're having a heart attack!

| Signor Pollini: | If it's not a heart attack, then what is it? |
| Signora Pollini: | I have no idea, but if it gives you peace of mind, I'll take you to the emergency room. |

Notes:

Both **fare male** and **avere male a/di** express that something hurts. **Fare male** works exactly like the verb **piacere: gli fa male lo stomaco**; but **ha male allo stomaco**. Note that Italian does not use the possessive adjective with parts of the body, but simply a definite article.

Fondo means bottom, and **in fondo a** is used to express at the bottom/end of something, such as **in fondo alla strada** (*at the end of the street*), **in fondo alla schiena** (*in the lower back*), **in fondo al bicchiere** (*at the bottom of the glass*), etc.

Tanto vale is an impersonal expression that can be translated into English as "subject + *might as well*." **Tanto vale andare in ospedale** (*one might as well go to the hospital*).

✎ Conversation Practice 1

Fill in the blanks in the following sentences with the missing words in the word bank. If you're unsure of the answer, listen to the conversation on your audio one more time.

ti fa, tanto vale, davvero, lentamente, normalmente, non mi sento, mal di stomaco, tempo, in fondo alla, non hai mai niente

1. Luisa, ho un problema: _____ affatto bene.

2. Cosa è successo, tu stai sempre bene, _____

   _____.

3. Che cosa _____ male?

4. Muoviti _____!

5. Ho mal di testa e _____.

6. Il medico che vedo _____ è in vacanza.

7. No, non voglio perdere _____.

8. Ho anche un dolore _____ schiena.

9. _____ andare all'ospedale.

10. Ma stai _____ così male?

ANSWER KEY
1. non mi sento; 2. non hai mai niente; 3. ti fa; 4. lentamente; 5. mal di stomaco; 6. normalmente;
7. tempo; 8. in fondo alla; 9. Tanto vale; 10. davvero

Grammar Builder 1

▶ 12B Grammar Builder 1 (CD 8, Track 26)

INDEFINITE ADJECTIVES AND PRONOUNS

Indefinite adjectives and pronouns indicate an indeterminate quality or quantity,
such as the English examples *some* or *any*. In Italian, some indefinites are used
strictly as adjectives, some are used strictly as pronouns, and others can be used
either as adjectives or pronouns.

The following indefinites can only be used as adjectives. They are invariable, and
they can only modify singular nouns, although they can also express plural meaning.

ogni (*each, every*)
qualche (*some*)
qualsiasi/qualunque (*any, any kind of*)

Ogni volta che si telefona a un medico si deve aspettare.
Every time one calls a doctor one has to wait.

Ho invitato qualche amico a cena. Mi hanno detto che mangiano di tutto.
I invited some friends for dinner. They told me they eat anything.

The following indefinites can only be used as pronouns, and they are singular.

chiunque (*anyone*)
niente/nulla (*nothing*)
ognuno/ognuna (*everyone*)
qualcosa (*something, anything*)
qualcuno (*someone, anyone*)
uno/una (*one*)

Non hai mai niente.
You have never had any health problems/suffered from any ailment.

C'è qualcosa che non va.
Something is not right.

Hai visto qualcuno che conosci a teatro ieri sera?
Did you see anyone you know at the theater, last night?

When an adjective follows **qualcosa** or **niente**, it is introduced by the preposition
di. When a verb follows **qualcosa** or **niente** it is introduced by the preposition **da**.

C'è qualcosa di bello da fare questo weekend?
Is there anything interesting/cool to do this weekend?

Alla festa non c'era niente di buono da mangiare.
There was nothing good to eat at the party.

Adverbs	Indefinite Adjectives and Pronouns
Reflexive Verbs of Reciprocity	Indefinites Used as Either Adjectives or Pronouns

✎ Work Out 1

Complete with either an indefinite adjective or pronoun.

1. In quel negozio non ho visto _____ che mi piaceva.

2. C'è _____ che parla inglese in quest'ospedale?

3. Gioco a tennis quasi _____ giorno.

4. _____ volta mangio dolci, ma di solito mangio frutta.

5. C'è _____ di interessante da fare stasera?

6. _____ sa cucinare in casa di Vittoria.

ANSWER KEY
1. niente/nulla; 2. qualcuno; 3. ogni; 4. Qualche; 5. qualcosa; 6. Chiunque

ᕮ Conversation 2

▶ 12C Conversation 2 (CD 9, Track 1 - Italian; Track 2 - Italian and English)

Medico:	Buongiorno, ci siamo già conosciuti?
Signor Pollini:	No, è la prima volta che vengo al pronto soccorso e forse non ce ne sarà bisogno, ma sono molto preoccupato … vede, mi fa male il braccio sinistro e si legge sempre che …
Medico:	Prima di tutto vediamo se ha la febbre … no, ha 36,7, la temperatura è normale. Adesso Le misuro la pressione … 120 su 70, è perfetta … Ascoltiamo il cuore e i polmoni. … Respiri profondamente … tutto sembra normale. … Guardi, Lei mi sembra in ottima forma, gli esami sono normali e mi sembra un tipo atletico. …
Signor Pollini:	Sì, faccio molto sport e gioco a tennis almeno due volte alla settimana.

Medico: Guardi, di solito chi fa sport alla sua età e non è in sovrappeso raramente ha un infarto, comunque Le faccio un elettrocardiogramma, così siamo sicuri. ... Anche l'elettrocardiogramma è normale. Mi dica, che cosa ha fatto ieri?

Signor Pollini: Vediamo, ho lavorato, poi ho giocato per due ore a tennis e poi sono uscito a cena con gli stessi amici con cui ho giocato ... beh, ora che ci penso celebravamo il compleanno di un amico e forse ho bevuto un po' troppo.

Medico: E forse ha anche giocato a tennis un po' troppo entusiasticamente! Ho notato che Lei è mancino e dopo due ore di tennis non mi sorprende che abbia male al braccio e alla schiena. Il mal di stomaco e il mal di testa sono probabilmente dovuti alla cena abbondante. Visto che non Le ho trovato nessun problema grave, Le consiglio di andare a casa e di farsi una bella dormita!

Doctor: Good morning, have we met before?

Signor Pollini: No, it's my first time at the emergency room, and perhaps I overreacted when I decided to come, but I'm very nervous ... you see, my left arm hurts and one always reads that ...

Doctor: First of all, let's see if you've a fever ... no, it's 36.7; your temperature is normal. Now I'm going to measure your blood pressure ... 120 over 70; it's perfect ... let's listen to your heart and lungs ... take a deep breath ... everything seems normal. ... Look, it seems to me that you are in excellent shape: all tests are normal, and you look athletic ...

Signor Pollini: Yes, I play a lot of sports and I play tennis at least twice a week.

Doctor: Look, usually people of your age who exercise a lot and who are not overweight rarely have heart attacks; in any case we'll do an electrocardiogram, just to make sure. ... Even the electrocardiogram is normal. Tell me, what did you do yesterday?

Adverbs

Indefinite Adjectives and Pronouns

Reflexive Verbs of
Reciprocity

Indefinites Used as Either
Adjectives or Pronouns

Signor Pollini:	Let's see; I worked, then I played tennis for two hours, and then I went out to dinner with my friends from the tennis game … well, now that I think about it we were celebrating a friend's birthday and perhaps I drank a bit too much.
Doctor:	And perhaps you also played tennis a bit too enthusiastically. I noticed that you're left handed, and after two hours of tennis I'm not surprised that your left arm and your back hurt. Your stomachache and headache are probably due to the big dinner. Since I haven't found any serious problem, I'll advise you to go home and take a nice long nap!

Notes:

Please note that respiri, guardi, mi dica are formal imperatives that will be explained in the next unit.

È dovuto/a; sono dovuti/e a translates to English as *it's/they are due to*. Il suo mal di testa è dovuto alla cena abbondante. *Your headache is due to the large dinner.*

Farsi una bella dormita (*to take a nice long nap*) and farsi una bella mangiata (*to have a nice big meal*) are idiomatic expressions using the past participle, mangiato, dormito, as feminine nouns.

Conversation Practice 2
Unscramble the following sentences.

1. **Buongiorno,/ci/già/conosciuti/siamo/?** _____

_____

2. Mi/fa/sinistro/il/braccio/male/. _____

_____

3. Prima/se/la/vediamo/di/tutto/ha/febbre/. _____

_____

4. Le/pressione/misuro/la/adesso/. _____

_____

5. Guardi,/in/Lei/mi/forma/ottima/sembra/. _____

_____

6. Gioco/a/settimana/almeno/due/tennis/alla/volte/. _____

_____

7. Mi/fatto,/che/cosa/ha/dica/ieri/? _____

_____

8. Anche/normale/l'/è/elettrocardiogramma/. _____

_____

9. Forse po'/ho/un/troppo/bevuto/. _____

_____

10. Le/di/consiglio/casa/a/andare/. _____

_____

ANSWER KEY

1. Buongiorno, ci siamo già conosciuti? 2. Mi fa male il braccio sinistro. 3. Prima di tutto vediamo
se ha la febbre. 4. Adesso Le misuro la pressione. 5. Guardi, Lei mi sembra in ottima forma.
6. Gioco a tennis almeno due volte alla settimana. 7. Mi dica, che cosa ha fatto ieri? 8. Anche
l'elettrocardiogramma è normale. 9. Forse ho bevuto un po' troppo. 10. Le consiglio di andare a casa.

Grammar Builder 2

▶ 12D Grammar Builder 2 (CD 9, Track 3)

INDEFINITES USED AS EITHER ADJECTIVES OR PRONOUNS

The following indefinites, some of which you have already encountered, may be
used as either adjectives or pronouns.

alcuni/alcune (*some, a few*)
certo/-a/-i/-e (*certain, certain ones*)
ciascuno/a (*each, each one*)
molto/-a/-i/-e (*much, many, a lot*)
nessuno/nessuna (*no, none, no one*)
parecchio/-a/-i/-e (*a lot, several*)
poco/-a/-chi/-che (*little, few*)
quanto/-a/-i/-e (*how much, how many*)
tanto/-a/-i/-e (*so much, so many*)
troppo/-a/-i/-e (*too much, too many*)

Non ho visto nessuno.
I didn't see anybody.

Non ho visto nessuna amica.
I didn't see any (of my) friends.

Lui lavora tanto.
He works a lot.

Lui ha tanti libri.
He has many books.

✎ Work Out 2

Replace the underlined expression with an indefinite pronoun.

1. *Alcune persone* **vanno sempre al pronto soccorso.** _____

2. **In quell'ospedale** *tutti gli infermieri* **sono gentili.** _____

3. *Molte persone* **leggono poco.** _____

4. **Hanno mangiato** *troppe cose* **in quel ristorante.** _____

5. *Molte persone evitano* **quel parco perché è pericoloso.** _____

ANSWER KEY
1. **Alcuni**; 2. **tutti**; 3. **Molti**; 4. **troppo**; 5. **Parecchi**

✎ Drive It Home

A. Translate the following sentences into English using the appropriate indefinite adjectives and pronouns.

1. **Sono andato al supermercato e non ho comprato nulla.** _____

   _____

2. **Avete visto qualcosa d'interessante?** _____

   _____

3. **Chiunque parla troppo è noioso.** _____

   _____

4. **Qualche volta ritorno a casa molto presto.** _____

   _____

5. **Non gli piace mai nulla!** _____

   _____

B. Translate the following sentences into Italian using the appropriate indefinite adjectives and pronouns.

1. *Is anybody there?* _____

_____

2. *Every time I drink too much I don't feel well.* _____

_____

3. *Nobody knows how old I am.* _____

_____

4. *Only some people were really happy to see you.* _____

_____

5. *Next year I'll give two presents to each one of you.* _____

_____

ANSWER KEY
A. 1. *I went to the supermarket and I didn't buy anything.* 2. *Did you see anything interesting?* 3. *Whoever speaks too much is boring.* 4. *Sometimes I go back home very early.* 5. *He never likes anything.*
B. 1. **C'è qualcuno lì?** 2. **Ogni volta che bevo troppo non sto bene.** 3. **Nessuno sa quanti anni ho.**
4. **Solo qualcuno era veramente contento di vederti.** 5. **L'anno prossimo vi do due regali ciascuno.**

✎ Culture Note

Before herbs and homeopathic medicine became popular, Italians have always believed in the healing power of water. Most Italians go to the terme (*spas*) every year to treat specific ailments, or simply to relax and detoxify. There are many terme in Italy.

How Did You Do?

Let's see how you did in this lesson. By now, you should be able to:

☐ use the words *some* and *any* (Still unsure? Jump back to page 149.)

☐ use words like *many* and *none* (Still unsure? Jump back to page 155.)

✎ Word Recall

Complete the following sentences translating the words and expressions suggested in parentheses.

1. Luisa, (*I have a problem*) _____: non mi

    sento affatto bene.

2. (*What happened*) _____, tu stai sempre bene.

3. Che cosa (*hurts*) _____?

4. (*I don't know*) _____ il suo sostituto, ma

    possiamo (*call him*) _____.

5. (*Every time*) _____ che si telefona a un medico

    (*one has to wait*) _____ un sacco di tempo.

6. (*It's the first time*) _____ che vengo al

    pronto soccorso.

7. (*It seems to me that you*) _____ in ottima forma.

8. Faccio molto sport e gioco a tennis (*at least twice a week*) _____

    _____.

9. *(Now that I think about it)* _____ **forse ho**

   bevuto un po' troppo.

10. **Forse ha anche giocato a tennis** *(a bit too enthusiastically)* _____

   _____.

ANSWER KEY

1. ho un problema; 2. Cosa è successo; 3. ti fa male 4. Non conosco, telefonargli; 5. Ogni volta, si deve aspettare; 6. È la prima volta; 7. Lei mi sembra; 8. almeno due volte alla settimana; 9. Ora che ci penso; 10. un po' troppo entusiasticamente

Don't forget to practice and reinforce what you've learned by visiting **www.livinglanguage.com/languagelab** for flashcards, games, and quizzes!

Unit 3 Essentials

Vocabulary Essentials

Test your knowledge of the key material in this unit by filling in the blanks in the following charts. Once you've completed these pages, you'll have tested your retention, and you'll have your own reference for the most essential vocabulary.

PARTS OF THE BODY

	head
	neck
	eye
	nose
	mouth
	back
	stomach
	belly
	intestine
	leg
	foot

[pg. 118]

HEALTH

	heart attack
	hospital
	emergency room

[pg. 118]

	health
	fever
	temperature
	pressure
	blood
	heart
	lung
	liver
	kidney
	to breathe
	shape
	electrocardiogram
	left-handed

[pg. 122]

SYMPTOMS

	I feel well.
	I am well.
	it hurts
	I have a pain in; my … hurts
	I have a pain in; my … hurts
	I'm worried.

[pg. 127–128]

AT THE DOCTOR'S

	I overreacted
	one reads that …
	to have a fever
	to check blood pressure
	I practice sports
	in great shape
	those who practice sports …
	with whom …
	it's due to …
	given that; since

[pg. 131]

Don't forget: if you're having a hard time remembering this vocabulary, check out the supplemental flashcards for this unit online, at **www.livinglanguage. com/languagelab**.

Grammar Essentials

Here is a reference of the key grammar that was covered in Unit 3. Make sure you understand the summary and can use all of the grammar in it.

IRREGULAR PLURALS OF NOUNS

- Nouns that end with an accent, such as città, università, caffè, etc. do not change in the plural.

- Foreign words, which usually end in a consonant, such as sport, film, week-end, etc., do not change in the plural. Although the word zoo ends with a vowel, it is a foreign word, and its plural is zoo.

- Words that are abbreviated, such as cinematografo → cinema; fotografia → foto; motocicletta → moto; bicicletta → bici, etc. do not change in the plural. Also, pay attention to the gender of these nouns, which is the gender of the original word: il cinema → i cinema.

- A few words, particularly words indicating parts of the body, are masculine in the singular, but have an irregular feminine plural ending in -a.

IRREGULAR SINGULAR NOUNS WITH REGULAR PLURAL FORMS

- A few masculine nouns, usually derived from Greek, have an irregular singular ending in -a. The plural form ends regularly in -i.

- Nouns ending in -ista and -iatra (which usually indicate professions), and a few others such as collega (*colleague*) and astronauta (*astronaut*) can be either masculine or feminine. The plural, however, ends regularly in -i in the masculine form, and in -e in the feminine form.

THE IMPERSONAL CONSTRUCTION

- Formed in Italian with the impersonal pronoun si followed by the verb in the third person singular.

- If a plural noun follows the verb, then the verb is in the third person plural form.

- In compound tenses, the auxiliary in an impersonal construction is always essere, both with verbs that normally take essere as well as those that take avere.

RELATIVE PRONOUNS

- che (*that, which, who, whom*) is invariable and is never used after a preposition.

- cui (*which, whom*) is also invariable, and is always used after a preposition. Cui is also used in the expressions la ragione/il motivo per cui (*the reason why*), and il modo in cui (*the way in which*).

- chi (*he/she who, the one who, whoever*) is invariable, is only used for people, and always takes a verb in the singular. Chi is often found in proverbs and popular sayings.

COMMON ADVERBS

bene	well
male	badly
molto	very
poco	little
presto	early
tardi	late
spesso	often
insieme	together
così	so
volentieri	gladly

FORMING ADVERBS

- Many adverbs are formed by adding the suffix **-mente** to the feminine singular form of an adjective.

- If the adjective ends in **-le** or **-re**, the final **-e** is dropped before **-mente** is added.

- Some adjectives, such as **chiaro** (*clearly*), **giusto** (*right*), **forte** (*loudly*), **piano** (*slowly, softly*), **svelto** (*fast*), **vicino** (*nearby*), and **lontano** (*far*) can also be used as adverbs.

- Adverbs usually follow the verb.

- In compound tenses, however, **ancora** (*still, yet*), **già** (*already*), **mai** (*never*), **sempre** (*always*), **più** (*any more*), and **spesso** (*often*) are usually placed between the auxiliary and the past participle.

REFLEXIVE VERBS OF RECIPROCITY

• The reflexive structure is used idiomatically to express reciprocity (*one another, each other*). In these cases the subject can only be plural. As with reflexive verbs, compound tenses are formed with essere.

INDEFINITE ADJECTIVES

ogni	*each, every*
qualche	*some*
qualsiasi/qualunque	*any, any kind of*

INDEFINITE PRONOUNS

chiunque	*anyone*
niente/nulla	*nothing*
ognuno/ognuna	*everyone*
qualcosa	*something, anything*
qualcuno	*someone, anyone*
uno/una	*one*

• When an adjective follows qualcosa or niente, it is introduced by the preposition di.

• When a verb follows qualcosa or niente it is introduced by the preposition da.

INDEFINITES USED AS EITHER ADJECTIVES OR PRONOUNS

alcuni/alcune	*some, a few*
certo/-a/-i/-e	*certain, certain ones*
ciascuno/a	*each, each one*
molto/-a/-i/-e	*much, many, a lot*

nessuno/nessuna	*no, none, no one*
parecchio/-a/-i/-e	*a lot, several*
poco/-a/chi/-che	*little, few*
quanto/-a/-i/-e	*how much, how many*
tanto/-a/-i/-e	*so much, so many*
troppo/-a/-i/-e	*too much, too many*

Unit 3 Quiz

Let's put the most essential Italian words and grammar points you've learned so far to practice in a few exercises. It's important to be sure that you've mastered this material. Score yourself at the end of the review and see if you need to go back for more practice.

A. Provide the singular article for the following nouns, and then change both article and noun to the plural.

1. cinema _____

2. uovo _____

B. Change the following sentences from the plural to the singular. Change everything possible.

1. Ci sono molte chiese particolarmente belle a Firenze. _____

_____

2. Voi avete molte bambine tanto carine. _____

_____

3. I musicisti erano molto bravi. _____

_____

C. Change the following sentences to the impersonal construction, following the example:

La gente gioca molto a calcio in Italia → Si gioca molto a calcio in Italia.

1. In questo ristorante la gente mangia molto bene. _____

_____

2. Dicono che Venezia è fantastica. _____

_____

3. Per imparare uno deve studiare molto. _____

_____

D. Complete the following sentences with the appropriate relative pronoun.

1. Non conosco lo scrittore di _____ mi parli.

2. Quella signora _____ porta la giacca rossa è la madre di Giacomo.

3. _____ ha cantato quella canzone è un bravissimo cantante.

E. Translate the following sentences.

1. *He plays wonderfully.* _____

_____

2. *They speak incessantly.* _____

_____

3. *They haven't bought the car yet.* _____

_____

F. Change the following sentences into the past tense.

1. Ci salutiamo tutte le volte che ci vediamo. _____

_____

2. Loro si aiutano a studiare per l'esame. _____

_____

G. Complete with either an indefinite adjective or pronoun.

1. C'è _____ che conosce le regole del calcio tra di voi?

2. Lui non mi ha voluto dire assolutamente _____.

H. Replace the underlined expression with an indefinite pronoun.

1. A *qualche persona* piacciono le salse piccanti. _____

_____

2. Durante le feste la città è vuota, non vedi *nessuna persona* per le strade. _____

_____

ANSWER KEY
A. 1. il cinema, i cinema; 2. l'uovo, le uova
B. 1. C'è una chiesa particolarmente bella a Firenze. 2. Tu hai una bambina tanto carina.
3. Il musicista era molto bravo.
C. 1. In questo ristorante si mangia molto bene. 2. Si dice che Venezia è fantastica. 3. Per imparare
si deve studiare molto.
D. 1. di cui; 2. che; 3. Chi
E. 1. Lui suona meravigliosamente. 2. Loro parlano incessantemente. 3. Loro non hanno ancora
comprato la macchina.
F. 1. Ci siamo salutati tutte le volte che ci siamo visti. 2. Si sono aiutati a studiare per l'esame.
G. 1. qualcuno; 2. nulla/niente
H. 1. qualcuno; 2. nessuno

How Did You Do?

Give yourself a point for every correct answer, then use the following key to tell whether you're ready to move on:

0-7 points: It's probably a good idea to go back through the lesson again. You may be moving too quickly, or there may be too much "down time" between your contact with Italian. Remember that it's better to spend 30 minutes with Italian three or four times a week than it is to spend two or three hours just once a week. Find a pace that's comfortable for you, and spread your contact hours out as much as you can.

8-12 points: You would benefit from a review before moving on. Go back and spend a little more time on the specific points that gave you trouble. Re-read the Grammar Builder sections that were difficult, and do the work out one more time. Don't forget about the online supplemental practice material, either. Go to **www.livinglanguage.com/languagelab** for games and quizzes that will reinforce the material from this unit.

13-17 points: Good job! There are just a few points that you could consider reviewing before moving on. If you haven't worked with the games and quizzes on **www.livinglanguage.com/languagelab**, please give them a try.

18-20 points: Great! You're ready to move on to the next unit.

points

Unit 4:
Sports and Hobbies

What's your outlook on life? Do you like to live in the country or in the city? Do you play any sports? Do you want to express your feelings and opinions? By the end of this unit, you'll know:

☐ how to describe what you like doing in your spare time

☐ how to talk about opinions and emotions

☐ vocabulary related to sports

☐ how to talk about opinions and emotions in the past

☐ verbs that express emotion, opinion, uncertainty, and commands

☐ impersonal expressions like *it is important that ...*

☐ how to say *he wants to buy a house*

☐ how to express *to take time*

☐ how to say *I'm going dancing*

☐ formal commands

Lesson 13: Words

By the end of this lesson, you'll know:

- ☐ how to describe what you like doing in your spare time
- ☐ how to talk about opinions and emotions
- ☐ vocabulary related to sports
- ☐ how to talk about opinions and emotions in the past

Word Builder 1

▶ 13A Word Builder 1 (CD 9, Track 4)

trasferirsi	*to transfer*
(il) fine settimana	*weekend*
(il) giardino	*garden*
(l')orto	*vegetable garden*
(il) cortile	*backyard, courtyard*
(l')albero	*tree*
(il) sapore	*taste*
(le) sostanze chimiche	*chemical substances*
(la) follia	*folly*
amaramente	*bitterly*
pentirsi	*to repent; to regret*

⏸

✎ Word Practice 1

A. Translate the following words into English.

1. **(il) sapore** _____

2. **(il) giardino** _____

3. **amaramente** _____

4. **(la) follia** _____

B. Translate the following words into Italian.

1. *tree* _____

2. *vegetable garden* _____

3. *to regret* _____

4. *chemical substances* _____

ANSWER KEY
A. 1. *taste*; 2. *garden*; 3. *bitterly*; 4. *folly*
B. 1. **(l')albero**; 2. **(l')orto**; 3. **pentirsi**; 4. **(le) sostanze chimiche**

Grammar Builder 1
▶ 13B Grammar Builder 1 (CD 9, Track 5)

THE PRESENT SUBJUNCTIVE

While the indicative mood is used to express factual reality and certainty, the subjunctive mood (**il congiuntivo**) conveys uncertainty, possibility, and personal perspectives such as opinions and emotions. As we will see later in this unit, the subjunctive is primarily used in dependent clauses and is connected by **che** to an independent clause. We'll be learning the present and past tense of the subjunctive mood.

The **congiuntivo presente** is formed by adding the appropriate endings to the stem of the verb.

Regular **-are** Present Subjunctive Endings

io	-i	noi	-iamo
tu	-i	voi	-iate
lui, lei, Lei	-i	loro, Loro	-ino

Regular **-ere** and **–ire** Present Subjunctive Endings

io	-a	noi	-iamo
tu	-a	voi	-iate
lui, lei, Lei	-a	loro, Loro	-ano

Third conjugation verbs that insert **-isc-** (like **finire**) in the present indicative also insert it in the present subjunctive. Please note that the endings for the first, second, and third persons singular are identical and therefore the subject must be expressed if ambiguity arises. Also note that the **noi** form of the subjunctive, both of regular and irregular verbs, is identical to the **noi** indicative form.

PARLARE	RICEVERE	DORMIRE	FINIRE
(che) io parl-i	(che) io ricev-a	(che) io dorm-a	(che) io fin-isc-a
(che) tu parl-i	(che) tu ricev-a	(che) tu dorm-a	(che) tu fin-isc-a
(che) lui parl-i	(che) lui ricev-a	(che) lui dorm-a	(che) lui fin-isc-a
(che) lei/Lei parl-i	(che) lei/Lei ricev-a	(che) lei/Lei dorm-a	(che) lei/Lei fin-isc-a
(che) noi parl-iamo	(che) noi ricev-iamo	(che) noi dorm-iamo	(che) noi fin-iamo
(che) voi parl-iate	(che) voi ricev-iate	(che) voi dorm-iate	(che) voi fin-iate
(che) loro/Loro parl-ino	(che) loro/Loro ricev-ano	(che) loro/Loro dorm-ano	(che) loro/Loro fin-isc-ano

Note that verbs ending in **-care** or **-gare** add an **h** between the stem and the endings. Also note that verbs ending in **-iare** drop the **-i** of the stem before adding the subjunctive endings, unless the **-i** is stressed (like in *inviare*).

Voglio che i nostri bambini giochino insieme.
I want our children to play together.

Non voglio che lui paghi il conto.
I don't want him to pay the bill.

Penso che loro mangino troppo.
I think they eat too much.

Those irregular verbs that have an irregular present indicative also have an irregular present subjunctive. Here are the most common ones:

AVERE	abbia, abbiamo, abbiate, abbiano
ESSERE	sia, siamo, siate, siano
ANDARE	vada, andiamo, andiate, vadano
BERE	beva, beviamo, beviate, bevano
DARE	dia, diamo, diate, diano
DIRE	dica, diciamo, diciate, dicano
DOVERE	debba, dobbiamo, dobbiate, debbano
FARE	faccia, facciamo, facciate, facciano
PIACERE	piaccia, piacciamo, piacciate, piacciano
POTERE	possa, possiamo, possiate, possano
SAPERE	sappia, sappiamo, sappiate, sappiano
STARE	stia, stiamo, stiate, stiano
USCIRE	esca, usciamo, usciate, escano

| VENIRE | venga, veniamo, veniate, vengano |
| VOLERE | voglia, vogliamo, vogliate, vogliano |

✎ Work Out 1

Complete the following sentences with the present subjunctive of the verb in parentheses.

1. È importante che voi _____ (volere) imparare una lingua straniera.

2. Voglio che lui _____ (scrivere) una lettera a suo nonno.

3. Pensiamo che loro _____ (arrivare) domani sera.

4. Non credo che tu _____ (dire) la verità.

5. Loro desiderano che io li _____ (andare) a trovare presto.

6. Tu pensi che noi non _____ (sapere) niente.

7. Dubito che lei _____ (venire) al cinema con noi.

8. Sono felice che voi _____ (laurearsi) fra un mese.

ANSWER KEY

1. vogliate; 2. scriva; 3. arrivino; 4. dica; 5. vada; 6. sappiamo; 7. venga; 8. vi laureiate

Word Builder 2

⏵ 13C Word Builder 2 (CD 9, Track 6)

traslocare	*to move*
(il) quartiere	*neighborhood*
(il) maschio	*male*
(la) femmina	*female*

(la) palestra	*gym(nasium), health club*
(il) calcio	*soccer*
(la) pallacanestro	*basketball*
(la) palla a volo	*volleyball*
nuotare	*to swim*
correre	*to run*

✎ Word Practice 2

Match the following expressions:

1. nuotare	a. *soccer*
2. (il) maschio	b. *neighborhood*
3. (il) calcio	c. *to swim*
4. (la) palestra	d. *to run*
5. (il) quartiere	e. *male*
6. (la) palla a volo	f. *female*
7. correre	g. *volleyball*
8. (la) femmina	h. *gym*

ANSWER KEY
1. c; 2. e; 3. a; 4. h; 5. b; 6. g; 7. d; 8. f

Grammar Builder 2

▶ 13D Grammar Builder 2 (CD 9, Track 7)

THE PAST SUBJUNCTIVE

The **congiuntivo passato** (*past subjunctive*) is the equivalent of the **passato prossimo**. It is formed with the present subjunctive of **avere** and **essere** followed

by the past participle of the verb. It is used to express past actions when the verb
of the main clause is in the present, the future, or the imperative.

PARLARE	ANDARE
(che) io abbia parlato	(che) io sia andato/a
(che) tu abbia parlato	(che) tu sia andato/a
(che) lui abbia parlato	(che) lui sia andato
(che) lei abbia parlato	(che) lei sia andata
(che) Lei abbia parlato	(che) Lei sia andato/a
(che) noi abbiamo parlato	(che) noi siamo andati/e
(che) voi abbiate parlato	(che) voi siate andati/e
(che) loro/Loro abbiano parlato	(che) loro/Loro siano andati/e

Penso che loro abbiano traslocato un mese fa.
I think they moved (out) a month ago.

Ci dispiace che lui non sia uscito con noi ieri sera.
We are sorry he didn't go out with us last night.

(II)

✎ Work Out 2

Complete the following sentences with the past subjunctive of the verb in parentheses.

1. Sono contenta che loro _____ (andare) in vacanza.

2. Penso che lei _____ (arrivare) ieri sera.

3. È importante che tu _____ (studiare) per l'esame.

4. Mi dispiace che voi _____ (perdere) il lavoro.

5. Spero che lui _____ (comprare) un dolce.

ANSWER KEY
1. siano andati/e; 2. sia arrivata; 3. abbia studiato; 4. abbiate perso; 5. abbia comprato

✎ Drive It Home

A. Complete the following sentences with the present subjunctive of the verb in parentheses.

1. **Penso che lui (essere) _____ molto ricco.**

2. **Vogliono che noi (arrivare) _____ puntuali**

   all'appuntamento.

3. **Si suppone che loro (avere) _____ ragione.**

4. **Ho paura che tu non (studiare) _____ abbastanza.**

5. **Siamo contenti che vi (piacere) _____ i nostri regali.**

B. Complete the following sentences with the past subjunctive of the verb in parentheses.

1. **Crede che io (comprare) _____ troppe**

   bottiglie di vino per la cena.

2. **Ho paura che loro non (arrivare) _____ in**

   tempo per prendere il treno.

3. **Dicono che la squadra di calcio italiana (vincere) _____**

   _____ ingiustamente.

4. **Spero che Luisa (pagare) _____ i conti in tempo.**

5. **Non credo che voi (dire) _____ tutta la verità.**

ANSWER KEY

A. 1. **sia**; 2. **arriviamo**; 3. **abbiano**; 4. **studi**; 5. **piacciano**

B. 1. **abbia comprato**; 2. **siano arrivati**; 3. **abbia vinto**; 4. **abbia pagato**; 5. **abbiate detto**

How Did You Do?

Let's see how you did in this lesson. By now, you should know:

☐ how to describe what you like doing in your spare time
(Still unsure? Jump back to page 172.)

☐ how to talk about opinions and emotions (Still unsure? Jump back to page 173.)

☐ vocabulary related to sports (Still unsure? Jump back to page 176.)

☐ how to talk about opinions and emotions in the past
(Still unsure? Jump back to page 177.)

✎ Word Recall

A. Translate the following words into English.

1. **(il) calcio** _____

2. **(il) cortile** _____

3. **(la) palla a volo** _____

4. **(il) quartiere** _____

5. **(la) femmina** _____

B. Translate the following words into Italian.

1. *to swim* _____

2. *bitterly* _____

3. *taste* _____

4. *tree* _____

5. *basketball* _____

ANSWER KEY

A. 1. *soccer*; 2. *courtyard*; 3. *volleyball*; 4. *neighborhood*; 5. *female*

B. 1. **nuotare**; 2. **amaramente**; 3. **(il) sapore**; 4. **(l')albero**; 5. **(la) pallacanestro**

Lesson 14: Phrases

By the end of this lesson, you'll know:

☐ verbs that express emotion, opinion, uncertainty, and commands

☐ impersonal expressions like *it is important that ...*

Phrase Builder 1

▶ 14A Phrase Builder 1 (CD 9, Track 8)

decidere di ...	*to decide to ...*
cercare di ...	*to try to ...*
cominciare a ...	*to begin to ...*
convincere a ...	*to convince to ...*
trasferirsi in campagna	*to move to the country*
ne ha affittata una	*he rented one*
fare giardinaggio	*to do gardening*
a casa sua	*to/at his/her house*
si pentirà amaramente	*he will bitterly regret it*
prima che trovi	*before he finds*
è una follia	*it's a folly; it's crazy*

⏸

✎ Phrase Practice 1

Match the following expressions:

1. cominciare a ...   a. *to move to the country*

2. a casa sua   b. *to do gardening*

3. trasferirsi in campagna   c. *to begin to ...*

4. cercare di ...   d. *before he finds*

5. fare giardinaggio   e. *it's crazy*

6. prima che trovi   f. *at his/her house*

7. è una follia   g. *to decide to ...*

8. decidere di ...   h. *to try to ...*

ANSWER KEY
1. c; 2. f; 3. a; 4. h; 5. b; 6. d; 7. e; 8. g

Grammar Builder 1

▶ 14B Grammar Builder 1 (CD 9, Track 9)

VERBS THAT REQUIRE THE SUBJUNCTIVE

As mentioned before, the subjunctive is primarily used in dependent clauses and is connected by **che** to an independent clause. The choice of the indicative or subjunctive mood in a dependent clause is determined by the verb or the expression used in the independent clause. The following verbs require the subjunctive in a dependent clause:

• verbs that express emotions, such as **avere paura** (*to be afraid*), **essere felice/ contento** (*to be happy*), **sperare** (*to hope*);

• verbs that express opinion, such as **credere** (*to believe*), **pensare** (*to think*);

• verbs that express doubt or uncertainty, such as **dubitare** (*to doubt*);

- verbs that express wish or command, such as **ordinare** (*to order*), **comandare** (*to command*), **proibire** (*to prohibit*), **permettere** (*to allow*), **lasciare** (*to let*), **volere** (*to want*), **desiderare** (*to desire*).

Sono felice che lui non abbia traslocato.
I'm happy he didn't move (out).

Penso che gli piaccia la campagna.
I think he likes the country.

Dubito che lei voglia uscire con noi.
I doubt that she would (want to) go out with us.

Voglio che tu lo convinca a rimanere in città.
I want you to convince him to stay in the city.

By contrast, assertions expressing certainty, such as **sono sicuro che** (*I'm sure/ certain that*), **so che** (*I know that*), **è ovvio che** (*it is obvious that*), **è vero che** (*it's true that*), etc., do not require the subjunctive.

Sono sicuro che lei vuole uscire con noi.
I'm certain that she wants to go out with us.

È vero che gli piace la campagna.
It's true that he likes the country.

✎ Work Out 1

Complete the following sentences with either the present indicative or subjunctive of the verb in parentheses.

1. So che loro _____ (partire) stasera.

2. Penso che tu _____ (essere) molto stanco.

3. Dubito che lui _____ (arrivare) in orario.

4. Siamo sicuri che voi _____ (avere) molti amici.

5. Siamo felici che lei non _____ (trasferirsi).

6. Vogliono che io _____ (coltivare) un orto.

ANSWER KEY
1. partono; 2. sia; 3. arrivi; 4. avete; 5. si trasferisca; 6. coltivi

Phrase Builder 2
▷ 14C Phrase Builder 2 (CD 9, Track 10)

finire di . . .	to finish . . .
Mi dica.	Tell me.
Guardi.	Look.
Mi scusi.	Excuse me.
Ce ne sono tre.	There are three of them.
della stessa età	of the same age
fare il footing	to jog
saltare la corda	to jump rope
fare ginnastica aerobica	to do aerobics
Mi sembra eccezionale.	It sounds/looks great.

⊪

✎ Phrase Practice 2

Translate the following phrases into Italian.

1. *to do aerobics* _____

2. *Tell me (sg. fml.).* _____

3. *to finish …* _____

4. *to jog* _____

5. *of the same age* _____

6. *There are three of them.* _____

7. *Excuse me (sg. fml.).* _____

8. *It sounds great to me.* _____

ANSWER KEY
1. **fare ginnastica aerobica**; 2. **Mi dica.** 3. **finire di …** ; 4. **fare il footing**; 5. **della stessa età**; 6. **Ce ne sono tre.** 7. **Mi scusi.** 8. **Mi sembra eccezionale.**

Grammar Builder 2

▶ 14D Grammar Builder 2 (CD 9, Track 11)

IMPERSONAL EXPRESSIONS WITH THE SUBJUNCTIVE

Impersonal expressions implying doubt, necessity, desire, or emotion, also require the subjunctive: **è importante che** (*it is important that*), **è necessario che** (*it is necessary that*), **è possibile che** (*it is possible that*), **è probabile che** (*it is likely that*), **è meglio che** (*it is better that*), **è strano che** (*it is strange that*), etc.

È importante che i bambini facciano ginnastica.
It is important that children exercise.

È meglio che lui ci pensi bene prima di trasferirsi.
He better think long and hard before moving.

È strano che voi preferiate la campagna alla città.
How odd that you'd prefer the country to the city.

The subjunctive is also used after the following conjunctions: **affinché** (*in order that, so that*), **a meno che … non** (*unless*), **benché** (*although*), **a condizione che/a patto che/purché** (*provided that*), **prima che** (*before*), and **senza che** (*without*).

Dobbiamo parlargli prima che lui trovi una casa.
We must talk to him before he finds a house.

Benché lui ami la città, preferisce vivere in campagna.
Although he loves the city, he prefers to live in the country.

Andrò a casa sua a meno che lei non mi telefoni.
I'll go to her house unless she calls me.

Ⓘ

✎ Work Out 2

Translate the following sentences into Italian.

1. *I am sure she is leaving tomorrow.* _____

_____

2. *We think she is leaving today.* _____

_____

3. *It's interesting that he likes to live in the country.*_____

_____

4. *Do you think the children want to play together?* _____

_____

5. *I must call her before she goes out.* _____

_____

6. *Although sometimes he feels lonely (solo), he likes the country.* _____

_____

ANSWER KEY

1. Sono sicuro/a che lei parte domani. 2. Noi pensiamo che lei parta oggi. 3. È interessante che gli piaccia vivere in campagna. 4. Pensi che i bambini vogliano giocare insieme? 5. Devo chiamarla prima che lei esca. 6. Benché a volte si senta solo, gli piace la campagna.

✎ Drive It Home

Complete the following sentences with the appropriate tense of the verb in parentheses.

1. Penso che lui stasera (arrivare) _____ da solo.

2. Si dice che il vino (fare) _____ buon sangue.

3. Benché lui (essere) _____ stanco vuole continuare a guidare.

4. Sono certo che (preparare) _____ una cena buonissima, come sempre.

5. Dubito che loro (mangiare) _____ tutta quella pasta.

6. Sono certo che loro (bere) _____ tutto il caffè che ho fatto.

7. **Sono sicuro che finirà di leggere il libro a meno che non (lavorare)**

   _____ **tutto il giorno.**

8. **Va bene te lo do a patto che me lo (restituire)** _____ **tra una**

   settimana.

9. **Credi che lui (parlare)** _____ **anche lo spagnolo?**

10. **M'immagino che Roberto e Giorgio (dire)** _____ **spesso**

    delle bugie.

    ANSWER KEY
    1. arrivi; 2. faccia; 3. sia; 4. preparano; 5. mangino; 6. bevono; 7. lavori; 8. restituisca; 9. parli; 10. dicano

How Did You Do?

Let's see how you did in this lesson. By now, you should know:

☐ verbs that express emotion, opinion, uncertainty, and commands
(Still unsure? Jump back to page 182.)

☐ impersonal expressions like *it is important that ...*
(Still unsure? Jump back to page 185.)

✎ Word Recall

A. Translate the following phrases into English.

1. **cominciare a ...** _____

2. **trasferirsi in campagna** _____

3. **fare giardinaggio** _____

4. **a casa sua** _____

5. **prima che trovi** _____

B. Translate the following phrases into Italian.

1. *to move* _____

2. *neighborhood* _____

3. *health club* _____

4. *soccer* _____

5. *basketball* _____

ANSWER KEY
A. 1. *to begin to …* ; 2. *to move to the country*; 3. *to do gardening*; 4. *at his/her house*; 5. *before he finds*
B. 1. **traslocare**; 2. **(il) quartiere**; 3. **(la) palestra**; 4. **(il) calcio**; 5. **(la) pallacanestro**

Lesson 15: Sentences

By the end of this lesson, you'll know:

☐ how to say *he wants to buy a house*

☐ how to express *to take time*

Sentence Builder 1

▶ 15A Sentence Builder 1 (CD 9, Track 12)

Ha deciso di trasferirsi in campagna.	He decided to move to the country.
Vuole comprare una casa.	He wants to buy a house.
Penso che gli piaccia abitare in città.	I think he likes living in the city.
Credo che il suo interesse per la natura sia cominciato così.	I believe this is how his interest in nature got started.
Credo che faccia molto giardinaggio.	I think he does a lot of gardening.

Ha cominciato a coltivare un po' di verdura.	He began growing some vegetables.
Crede che la verdura sia piena di sostanze chimiche.	He believes vegetables are steeped with chemicals.
Sono sicuro che si pentirà amaramente.	I'm sure he will bitterly regret it.
Dobbiamo parlargli prima che lui trovi una casa.	We must talk to him before he finds a house.
Voglio che tu lo convinca a rimanere in città.	I want you to convince him to stay in the city.

ⓘⓘ

✎ Sentence Practice 1

Translate the following sentences into Italian.

1. *I think he likes living in the city.* _____

_____

2. *I'm sure he will bitterly regret it.* _____

_____

3. *He began growing some vegetables.* _____

_____

4. *He wants to buy a house.* _____

_____

5. *I think he does a lot of gardening.* _____

_____

6. *He decided to move to the country.* _____

_____

ANSWER KEY

1. Penso che gli piaccia abitare in città. 2. Sono sicuro che si pentirà amaramente. 3. Ha cominciato a coltivare un po' di verdura. 4. Vuole comprare una casa. 5. Credo che faccia molto giardinaggio. 6. Ha deciso di trasferirsi in campagna.

Grammar Builder 1
▶ 15B Grammar Builder 1 (CD 9, Track 13)

INFINITIVE CONSTRUCTIONS

Please note that the subjunctive is used when the subject of the independent clause is different from the subject in the dependent clause. When the subject is the same in both clauses, Italian uses an infinitive construction. Consider the examples below:

Vuole comprare una casa.
He/she wants to buy a house.

Voglio che tu lo convinca a rimanere in città.
I want you to convince him to stay in the city.

Spero di divertirmi al parco giochi.
I hope I'll have fun at the playground.

Spero che i bambini si divertano al parco giochi.
I hope the children will have fun at the playground.

Dubito di arrivare per cena.
I doubt I will get there by dinner.

Dubito che lui arrivi per cena.
I doubt he will get there by dinner.

Unit 4 Lesson 15: Sentences   191

Ti telefono prima di uscire di casa.
I'll call you before I leave the house.

Ti telefono prima che tu esca di casa.
I'll call you before you leave the house.

È importante imparare le lingue straniere.
It's important to learn foreign languages.

È importante che loro imparino le lingue straniere.
It's important that they learn foreign languages.

Ⅱ

✎ Work Out 1

Translate the following sentences into Italian.

1. *He wants to go to the mountains this summer.* _____

   _____

2. *They want me to go with them to the country.* _____

   _____

3. *I hope you'll come to my party.* _____

   _____

4. *We hope to buy a new house.* _____

   _____

5. *They are happy that you're graduating.* _____

   _____

6. *We are happy we are eating in a restaurant tonight.* _____

_____

ANSWER KEY
1. Vuole andare in montagna quest'estate. 2. Vogliono che io vada con loro in campagna. 3. Spero che tu venga alla mia festa. 4. Speriamo di comprare una casa nuova. 5. Sono felici che ti laurei. 6. Siamo felici di mangiare in un ristorante stasera.

Sentence Builder 2

▶ 15C Sentence Builder 2 (CD 9, Track 14)

Abbiamo appena finito di traslocare.	*We've just finished moving (out).*
Ci abbiamo messo una settimana.	*It took us a week.*
Credo che abbia i prezzi più bassi.	*I think it has the lowest prices.*
Ci vogliono solo pochi minuti a piedi.	*It's only a few minutes' walk.*
È necessario che i bambini facciano sport tutti i giorni.	*It's necessary that children exercise daily.*
Li voglio iscrivere in questa palestra.	*I want to enroll them at this gym.*
Voglio che i Suoi bambini conoscano i miei.	*I want your (fml.) children to meet mine.*
Li vuole mandare a casa mia domani?	*Do you want to send them to my house tomorrow?*
Sono felici di avere nuovi amici.	*They are happy to have new friends.*

⏸

✎ Sentence Practice 2

A. Translate the following sentences into English.

1. **Ci vogliono solo pochi minuti a piedi.** _____

_____

2. **Credo che abbia i prezzi più bassi.** _____

_____

3. **Li voglio iscrivere in questa palestra.** _____

_____

B. Translate the following sentences into Italian.

1. _They are happy to have new friends._ _____

_____

2. _It's necessary that children exercise daily._ _____

_____

3. _It took us a week._ _____

_____

ANSWER KEY
A. 1. _It's only a few minutes' walk._ 2. _I think it has the lowest prices._ 3. _I want to enroll them at this gym._
B. 1. **Sono felici di avere nuovi amici.** 2. **È necessario che i bambini facciano sport tutti i giorni.** 3. **Ci abbiamo messo una settimana.**

Grammar Builder 2
▶ 15D Grammar Builder 2 (CD 9, Track 15)

EXPRESSING _TO TAKE TIME_

To take (time) is rendered in Italian by two different expressions: **volerci** and **metterci**. **Volerci** is always used impersonally.

Ci vogliono solo pochi minuti a piedi.
It's only a few minutes' walk.

Expressing
to take time

         The Formal Imperative

Ci vuole molto tempo per traslocare.
It takes a long time to move.

In the compound tenses, **volerci** is conjugated with **essere**.

C'è voluto un mese per finire questo lavoro.
It took a month to finish this job.

Metterci, however, is always used with a personal subject.

(Noi) ci abbiamo messo una settimana.
It took us a week.

(Io) ci metto poco tempo a fare la spesa.
It takes me little time to shop.

In compound tenses, **metterci** is conjugated with **avere**.

Ci hanno messo tre ore ad arrivare.
It took them three hours to arrive (to get there/here).

Ⅱ

✎ Work Out 2

Complete the following sentences with the correct form of either **metterci** or **volerci**.

1. **Ieri siamo andati a Roma e** _____ **due ore.**

2. **Quanto tempo** _____ **per cucinare un arrosto?**

3. _____ **cinque ore per finire la maratona la settimana**

scorsa.

4. Io non _____ molto a pulire la casa.

5. Loro _____ sempre poco tempo a preparare un programma.

ANSWER KEY
1. ci abbiamo messo; 2. ci vuole; 3. Ci sono volute; 4. ci metto; 5. ci mettono

✎ Drive It Home

Translate the following sentences into Italian.

1. *He wants to come tomorrow at ten.* _____

   _____

2. *I hope to arrive on time.* _____

   _____

3. *We are happy to be here with you.* _____

   _____

4. *She is afraid to make too many mistakes when she speaks Italian.* _____

   _____

5. *(you) Call me before you go out of town.* _____

   _____

6. *It takes about three hours to go from Florence to Rome by car.* _____

   _____

7. *It took half an hour to finish this exercise.* _____

   _____

8. *It took them three days to finish the project.* _____

   _____

Expressing
to take time

9. *Wait for us at the station; it will take us five minutes to get there.* _____

_____

10. *It takes forever for her to get ready.* _____

_____

ANSWER KEY

1. Lui vuole venire domani alle dieci. 2. Spero di arrivare puntuale/in tempo. 3. Siamo contenti di essere qui con voi. 4. Lei ha paura di fare troppi errori quando parla italiano. 5. Chiamami prima di andare fuori città. 6. Ci vogliono circa tre ore per andare da Firenze a Roma in macchina. 7. Ci è voluta mezz'ora per finire questo esercizio. 8. Ci hanno messo tre giorni a finire il progetto. 9. Aspettateci alla stazione, ci mettiamo cinque minuti ad arrivarci. 10. Ci mette una vita a prepararsi.

How Did You Do?

Let's see how you did in this lesson. By now, you should know:

☐ how to say *he wants to buy a house* (Still unsure? Jump back to page 191.)

☐ how to express *to take time* (Still unsure? Jump back to page 194.)

✎ Word Recall

A. Translate the following sentences into English.

1. **Dobbiamo parlargli prima che lui trovi una casa.** _____

_____

2. **Ci abbiamo messo una settimana.** _____

_____

3. **Ha cominciato a coltivare un po' di verdura.** _____

_____

4. **Ci vogliono solo pochi minuti a piedi.** _____

_____

5. **Voglio che i Suoi bambini conoscano i miei.** _____

_____

B. Translate the following sentences into Italian.

1. _He believes vegetables are steeped with chemicals._ _____

_____

2. _I think he likes living in the city._ _____

_____

3. _He wants to buy a house._ _____

_____

4. _They are happy to have new friends._ _____

_____

5. _It's necessary that children exercise daily._ _____

_____

ANSWER KEY
A. 1. _We must talk to him before he finds a house._ 2. _It took us a week._ 3. _He began growing some vegetables._ 4. _It's only a few minutes' walk._ 5. _I want your children to meet mine._
B. 1. **Crede che la verdura sia piena di sostanze chimiche.** 2. **Penso che gli piaccia abitare in città.** 3. **Vuole comprare una casa.** 4. **Sono felici di avere nuovi amici.** 5. **È necessario che i bambini facciano sport tutti i giorni.**

Lesson 16: Conversations

By the end of this lesson, you'll know:

☐ how to say *I'm going dancing*

☐ formal commands

Conversation 1

▷ 16A Conversation 1 (CD 9, Track 16 - Italian; Track 17 - Italian and English)

Michele:	**Hai saputo che Vittorio ha deciso di trasferirsi in campagna?**
Enzo:	**Sì, vuole comprare una casa, ma non penso che l'abbia ancora trovata. Però ne ha affittata una per l'estate.**
Michele:	**Non capisco questa decisione, non gli piace abitare in città?**
Enzo:	**Penso che gli piaccia, qui ci sono tutte le cose che ama fare. Gli piace andare al cinema e a teatro, gli piacciono i musei e gli piace molto uscire con gli amici, mangiare al ristorante e andare in discoteca. Però l'anno scorso ha incontrato un vecchio amico che l'ha invitato a casa sua in campagna e credo che da lì sia nato questo nuovo interesse per la natura. Sai, ormai passa quasi tutti i fine settimana in campagna.**
Michele:	**Ma che cosa fa in campagna tutto quel tempo?**
Enzo:	**Credo che faccia molto giardinaggio. Ha piantato fiori attorno a tutta la casa e ha cominciato anche a coltivare un po' di verdura in un orto. Sostiene che la verdura che si compra nei negozi sia insipida e che sia piena di sostanze chimiche nocive per la salute. So che vuole anche piantare dei peschi e degli albicocchi, ma penso che aspetterà di aver la sua propria casa.**

Michele: Senti, a me pare una follia. Sono sicuro che dopo un anno di
            vita di campagna si pentirà amaramente. Dobbiamo parlargli
            prima che trovi una casa. Voglio che tu lo convinca a rimanere
            in città. Lo sai, se si trasferisce non lo vedremo più e allora con
            chi giocheremo a poker il giovedì sera?

Michele: *Did you hear that Vittorio decided to move to the country?*
Enzo: *Yes, he wants to buy a house, but I don't think he has found one yet.
            Though he rented one for the summer.*
Michele: *I don't understand his decision. Doesn't he like to live in the city?*
Enzo: *I think he does, all the things he loves to do are here. He likes to go to
            the movies and to the theater, he likes museums, and he really likes
            to go out with friends, eat in restaurants, and dance in clubs. But last
            year he met an old friend who invited him to his house in the country,
            and I believe that's when his new interest in nature started. You
            know, he now spends almost all (of his) weekends in the country.*
Michele: *But what does he do in the country all that time?*
Enzo: *I believe he does a lot of gardening. He planted flowers all around
            the house and he also began planting some vegetables in an orchard.
            He believes that the vegetables you buy in the stores are flavorless,
            and that they are full of chemicals that are harmful to health. I
            know he also wants to plant peach and apricot trees, but I think he'll
            wait until he has his own house.*
Michele: *Listen, it's crazy. I'm sure that after a year of life in the country he'll
            bitterly regret it. We must talk to him before he finds a house. I want
            you to convince him to stay in the city. You know, if he moves we're
            not going to see him any more, and who will we play poker with on
            Thursday nights?*

Expressing
to take time

The Formal Imperative

Notes:

The verb **giocare** (*to play*) always takes the preposition a before the name of the game. **Giocare a carte** (*to play cards*), **giocare a tennis** (*to play tennis*), etc. The verb **suonare** translates as *to play music/an instrument*: **Mario suona il pianoforte** (*Mario plays the piano*).

✎ Conversation Practice 1

Unscramble the following sentences:

1. **ha/in/deciso/trasferirsi/di/Vittorio/campagna/.** _____

   _____

2. **Non/abbia/che/l'/ancora/penso/trovata/.** _____

   _____

3. **Non/abitare/in/piace/gli/città/?** _____

   _____

4. **Gli/piace/gli/amici/e/gli/piacciono/molto/uscire/con/i/musei/.** _____

   _____

5. **per/la/natura/sia/che/da/lì/nato/questo/nuovo/Credo/interesse/.** _____

   _____

6. **Credo/molto/che/giardinaggio/faccia/.** _____

   _____

7. **si/Sostiene/che/compra/nei/negozi/la/verdura/che/sia/insipida/.** _____

   _____

8. **Dobbiamo/trovi/una/casa/prima/che/parlargli/.** _____

_____

ANSWER KEY

1. Vittorio ha deciso di trasferirsi in campagna. 2. Non penso che l'abbia ancora trovata. 3. Non gli piace abitare in città? 4. Gli piacciono i musei e gli piace molto uscire con gli amici. 5. Credo che da lì sia nato questo nuovo interesse per la natura. 6. Credo che faccia molto giardinaggio. 7. Sostiene che la verdura che si compra nei negozi sia insipida. 8. Dobbiamo parlargli prima che trovi una casa.

Grammar Builder 1

▶ 16B Grammar Builder 1 (CD 9, Track 18)

VERBS FOLLOWED BY VERBS IN THE INFINITIVE

As you might have already noticed, when a verb governs another verb, this second verb is always in the infinitive form in Italian.

Voglio giocare a carte.
I want to play cards.

Preferisco vivere in città.
I prefer living in the city.

Devo traslocare.
I must move (out).

Often, however, between the first and the second verb there is a preposition, usually **a** or **di**.

A few common verbs that require the preposition **a** before an infinitive are: **aiutare** (*to help*), **andare** (*to go*), **cominciare** (*to begin*), **continuare** (*to continue*), **imparare** (*to learn*), **insegnare** (*to teach*), **riuscire** (*to succeed*).

Expressing
to take time

The Formal Imperative

Io vado a ballare in discoteca.
I'm going dancing.

Vittorio ha cominciato a coltivare verdura.
Vittorio has started growing vegetables.

Loro mi aiutano a piantare fiori.
They help me plant flowers.

Among those verbs that require the preposition **di** before an infinitive are:
cercare (*to try*), **decidere** (*to decide*), **dimenticare** (*to forget*), **finire** (*to finish*),
promettere (*to promise*), **ricordare** (*to remember*), **smettere** (*to quit, to stop*),
sperare (*to hope*).

Ⅱ

✎ Work Out 1

Complete the following sentences with **a**, **di**, or leave an empty space, appropriately.

1. **Desidero** _____ **comprare una casa al mare.**

2. **Speriamo** _____ **andarlo a trovare in campagna.**

3. **Cominciano** _____ **lavorare alle nove e finiscono** _____ **lavorare alle sei.**

4. **Loro mi insegnano** _____ **giocare a golf.**

5. **Lui ha deciso** _____ **andare in vacanza in Italia.**

6. **Imparate** _____ **parlare l'italiano.**

ANSWER KEY
1. ----; 2. di; 3. a, di; 4. a; 5. di; 6. a

ⓐ Conversation 2

▶ Track: Lesson 16 Conversation 2 (CD 9, Track 19 - Italian; Track 20 - Italian and English)

Signora Fucini: Buon giorno, mi chiamo Laura Fucini. Finalmente io e mio marito abbiamo appena finito di traslocare nell'appartamento di fronte al Suo. Ci abbiamo messo un'intera settimana!

Signor Dondi: Ah, piacere signora, sono Giovanni Dondi. Benvenuti nel nostro palazzo.

Signora Fucini: Grazie mille. Mi dica, visto che questo è un nuovo quartiere per noi, saprebbe indicarmi un buon negozio di alimentari?

Signor Dondi: Guardi, ce ne sono tre, tutti molto buoni. Io credo però che Pollini abbia i prezzi più bassi e la frutta e la verdura più fresche. È qui vicino, in via Arno, ci vogliono solo pochi minuti a piedi.

Signora Fucini: Mi scusi se Le faccio un'altra domanda. Lei ha bambini?

Signor Dondi: Sì, ne ho due, un maschio e una femmina di sei e nove anni.

Signora Fucini: Davvero? Anch'io ne ho due della stessa età. I suoi dove vanno a giocare di solito?

Signor Dondi: C'è un parco giochi qui vicino e quando posso li porto lì. Visto che è necessario per i bambini fare moto tutti i giorni, li ho iscritti in una palestra dove il pomeriggio si tengono classi per i bambini.

Signora Fucini: Guardi, anch'io ritengo sia molto importante che i bambini facciano ginnastica. Quali altre attività sono offerte in questa palestra?

Signor Dondi: Possono giocare a calcio, a pallacanestro o a pallavolo. Hanno anche una piscina e due pomeriggi alla settimana possono anche nuotare. E poi corrono, saltano la corda e fanno anche ginnastica aerobica. C'è un'ampia varietà di scelta.

Signora Fucini: Mi sembra eccezionale, anch'io li voglio iscrivere a questa palestra. Voglio anche che i nostri bambini si conoscano, che abbiano la possibilità diventare amici e di giocare insieme. Li vuole mandare a casa mia domani pomeriggio?

Signor Dondi: Certamente, saranno molto contenti di avere nuovi amici nel palazzo!

Signora Fucini: Good morning, my name is Laura Fucini. My husband and I have finally just finished moving into the apartment across from yours. It took us a whole week!

Signor Dondi: Ah, nice to meet you, Madam, I'm Giovanni Dondi, welcome to our building.

Signora Fucini: Thank you so much. As we are new to the neighborhood, could you please tell us where we can find a good grocery store?

Signor Dondi: Look, there are three very good ones in the area. But I think Pollini has the lowest prices and the freshest fruits and vegetables. It's nearby, on Arno Street, it's only a few minutes' walk from here.

Signora Fucini: Excuse me if I ask yet another question. Do you have any children?

Signor Dondi: Yes, I have two of them, a boy and a girl; they're six and nine.

Signora Fucini: Really? I have two of the same age. Where do they usually play?

Signor Dond: There's a playground nearby, when I can I take them there. But since it's necessary that children move every day, I enrolled them in a gym where they have classes for children in the afternoon.

Signora Fucini: Look, I also believe that it's important that children exercise. What other activities are available at this gym?

Signor Dondi: They can play soccer, basketball, and volleyball. They also have a swimming pool and they swim two afternoons a week. And then they run, jump rope, and they also do aerobic exercise. There's a wide variety of choices.

Signora Fucini: It seems great; I want to enroll them at this gym as well. I also
                    want your children to meet mine, so they can become friends and
                    play together. Do you want to send them to my house tomorrow
                    afternoon?
Signor Dondi: Sure, they'll be very happy to have new friends in the building!

Notes:

There are two verbs that indicate *to move* in Italian, **traslocare** and **trasferirsi**.
They are sometimes interchangeable, however **traslocare**, and also **fare il
trasloco**, indicate the actual moving of furniture, whereas **trasferirsi** has a more
generic meaning.

✎ Conversation Practice 2

Fill in the blanks in the following sentences with the missing words in the word
bank. If you're unsure of the answer, listen to the conversation on your audio
one more time.

**li voglio, messo, si tengono, abbia, ci vogliono, facciano, ne ho due, conoscano,
a pallacanestro, saprebbe**

1. Ci abbiamo _____ un'intera settimana!

2. _____ indicarmi un buon negozio di alimentari?

3. Io credo però che Pollini _____ i prezzi più bassi

4. _____ solo pochi minuti a piedi.

5. Sì, _____, un maschio e una femmina.

6. Il pomeriggio _____ classi per i bambini.

7. **Ritengo sia molto importante che i bambini** _____ **ginnastica.**

8. **Possono giocare a calcio,** _____ **o a pallavolo.**

9. **Anch'io** _____ **iscrivere a questa palestra.**

10. **Voglio che i nostri bambini si** _____ **.**

ANSWER KEY
1. messo; 2. Saprebbe; 3. abbia; 4. Ci vogliono; 5. ne ho due; 6. si tengono; 7. facciano;
8. a pallacanestro; 9. li voglio; 10. conoscano

Grammar Builder 2
▷ 16D Grammar Builder 2 (CD 9, Track 21)

THE FORMAL IMPERATIVE

In Lesson 6 we studied the informal forms of command. The forms of the formal imperative are the same as the **Lei** form of the present subjunctive. Thus, verbs that have irregular forms in the subjunctive will also have irregular forms of the formal imperative.

PARLARE	SCRIVERE	SENTIRE	FINIRE
Parli!	Scriva!	Senta!	Finisca!

Guardi, ci sono tre negozi.
Actually, there are three stores.

Signora, scriva il suo nome per favore.
Madam, please write your name/sign your name here.

The negative formal imperative is formed by placing **non** in front of the imperative.

Per favore, non fumi in quest'ufficio.
Please, don't smoke in this office.

Direct and indirect object pronouns, as well as reflexive pronouns, always precede
the formal imperative.

Mi scusi, posso farLe una domanda?
Excuse me, may I ask you a question?

Mi dica, ha bambini?
Tell me, do you have children?

(II)

✎ Work Out 2

Change the following informal sentence into formal ones.

1. **Dimmi quando arrivi domani.** _____

   _____

2. **Non parlare così velocemente.** _____

   _____

3. **Ascolta, devo dirti una cosa importante.** _____

   _____

4. **Parlami del film che hai visto ieri.** _____

   _____

5. **Non vestirti in modo sportivo: sarà una festa elegante.** _____

   _____

6. **Fammi un favore!** _____

   _____

ANSWER KEY

1. Mi dica quando arriva domani. 2. Non parli così velocemente. 3. Ascolti, devo dirLe una cosa importante. 4. Mi parli del film che ha visto ieri. 5. Non si vesta in modo sportivo: sarà una festa elegante. 6. Mi faccia un favore.

✎ Drive It Home

A. Complete the following sentences with a, di, or leave an empty space, appropriately.

1. Desidero _____ comprare una macchina sportiva.

2. A che ora finisci _____ lavorare domani?

3. Ho cominciato _____ leggere il libro che mi hai dato.

4. Pensi _____ venire stasera alla festa di Ugo?

5. Preferisco _____ andare al cinema in compagnia.

B. Fill in the blanks with the appropriate formal imperative forms.

1. (aspettare) _____, non (andare) _____ ancora via.

2. (guardare) _____, se non Le piace non lo (comprare) _____.

3. Mi (dare) _____ la Sua valigia.

4. (provare) _____ a telefonare più tardi, forse lo trova.

5. (seguire) _____ il mio consiglio, (assaggiare) _____ questo vino.

ANSWER KEY

A. 1. ----; 2. di; 3. a; 4. di; 5. ----
B. 1. Aspetti, vada; 2. Guardi, compri; 3. dia; 4. Provi; 5. Segua, assaggi

How Did You Do?

Let's see how you did in this lesson. By now, you should know:

- ☐ how to say *I'm going dancing* (Still unsure? Jump back to page 202.)
- ☐ formal commands (Still unsure? Jump back to page 207.)

✎ Word Recall

Complete the following sentences translating the words and expressions
suggested in parentheses.

1. (*Did you know*) _____ che Vittorio ha deciso

   di trasferirsi in campagna?

2. (*I don't understand*) _____ questa decisione.

3. (*He likes*) _____ i musei e (*he likes*) _____

   molto uscire con gli amici.

4. L'anno scorso (*he met*) _____ un vecchio amico.

5. Dobbiamo parlargli (*before he finds*) _____ una casa.

6. Abbiamo appena (*finished moving*) _____

   _____ nell'appartamento di fronte al Suo.

7. (*Look*) _____, ce ne sono tre, tutti molto buoni.

8. I suoi bambini (*where do they play*) _____

   _____ di solito?

9. **Ritengo sia molto importante che i bambini** *(exercise)* _____

_____.

10. **Saranno molto contenti** *(to have)* _____ **nuovi amici nel palazzo.**

ANSWER KEY

1. Hai saputo; 2. Non capisco; 3. Gli piacciono, gli piace; 4. ha incontrato; 5. prima che trovi; 6. finito di traslocare; 7. Guardi; 8. dove vanno a giocare; 9. facciano ginnastica; 10. di avere

Don't forget to practice and reinforce what you've learned by visiting **www.livinglanguage.com/ languagelab** for flashcards, games, and quizzes!

Unit 4 Essentials

Vocabulary Essentials

Test your knowledge of the key material in this unit by filling in the blanks in the following charts. Once you've completed these pages, you'll have tested your retention, and you'll have your own reference for the most essential vocabulary.

WORDS RELATED TO HOBBIES

	weekend
	garden
	vegetable garden
	back yard, courtyard
	tree
	taste
	folly

[pg. 172]

SPORTS

	soccer
	basketball
	volleyball
	to swim
	to run
	gym(nasium), health club

[pg. 177]

EXPRESSIONS

	to decide to …
	to try to …
	to begin to …
	to convince to …
	to/at his/her house
	it's a folly; it's crazy
	it sounds/looks great

[pg. 181]

ACTIVITIES

	to do gardening
	to jog
	to jump rope
	to do aerobics

[pg. 181, 184]

VERBS

	to transfer
	to repent, regret
	to move

[pg. 172, 176]

Don't forget: if you're having a hard time remembering this vocabulary, check out the supplemental flashcards for this unit online, at **www.livinglanguage. com/languagelab**.

Grammar Essentials

Here is a reference of the key grammar that was covered in Unit 4. Make sure you understand the summary and can use all of the grammar in it.

THE PRESENT SUBJUNCTIVE

Formed by adding the appropriate endings to the stem of the verb.

Regular -are Present Subjunctive Endings

io	-i	noi	-iamo
tu	-i	voi	-iate
lui/lei/Lei	-i	loro/Loro	-ino

Regular -ere and –ire Present Subjunctive Endings

io	-a	noi	-iamo
tu	-a	voi	-iate
lui, lei, Lei	-a	loro, Loro	-ano

Note:

- third conjugation verbs that insert -isc- (like finire) in the present indicative also insert it in the present subjunctive.

- verbs ending in -care or -gare add an h between the stem and the endings.

- verbs ending in -iare drop the -i of the stem before adding the subjunctive endings, unless the -i is stressed (as in inviare).

THE PAST SUBJUNCTIVE

- Formed with the present subjunctive of avere and essere followed by the past participle of the verb.

VERBS THAT REQUIRE THE SUBJUNCTIVE

- verbs that express emotions, such as **avere paura** (*to be afraid*), **essere felice/contento** (*to be happy*), **sperare** (*to hope*);

- verbs that express opinion, such as **credere** (*to believe*), **pensare** (*to think*);

- verbs that express doubt or uncertainty, such as **dubitare** (*to doubt*);

- verbs that express wish or command, such as **ordinare** (*to order*), **comandare** (*to command*), **proibire** (*to prohibit*), **permettere** (*to allow*), **lasciare** (*to let*), **volere** (*to want*), **desiderare** (*to desire*).

- Note that assertions expressing certainty, such as **sono sicuro che** (*I'm sure/certain that*), **so che** (*I know that*), **è ovvio che** (*it is obvious that*), **è vero che** (*it's true that*), etc., do not require the subjunctive.

IMPERSONAL EXPRESSIONS WITH THE SUBJUNCTIVE

è importante che	*it is important that*
è necessario che	*it is necessary that*
è possibile che	*it is possible that*
è probabile che	*it is likely that*
è meglio che	*it is better that*
è strano che	*it is strange that*
affinché	*in order that, so that*
a meno che … non	*unless*
benché	*although*
a condizione che/a patto che/purché	*provided that*
prima che	*before*
senza che	*without*

EXPRESSING *TO TAKE TIME*

- *To take (time)* is rendered by two different expressions: **volerci** and **metterci**.

- in the compound tenses, **volerci** is conjugated with **essere**.

- **metterci**, however, is always used with a personal subject.

- in compound tenses, **metterci** is conjugated with **avere**.

THE FORMAL IMPERATIVE

- The forms of the formal imperative are the same as the **Lei** (sg.) and **Loro** (pl.) form of the present subjunctive.

PARLARE *(TO SPEAK)*	
Parli!	*Speak!*
Parlino!	*Speak! (pl.)*

SCRIVERE *(TO WRITE)*	
Scriva!	*Write!*
Scrivano!	*Write! (pl.)*

SENTIRE *(TO FEEL, TO HEAR)*	
Senta!	*Listen!*
Sentano!	*Listen! (pl.)*

SENTIRE *(TO FINISH)*	
Finisca!	*Finish!*
Finiscano!	*Finish! (pl.)*

- The negative formal imperative is formed by placing **non** in front of the imperative.

- Direct and indirect object pronouns, as well as reflexive pronouns, always precede the formal imperative.

VERBS IN THE PRESENT SUBJUNCTIVE

PARLARE (TO SPEAK)			
(che) io parli	*I speak*	(che) noi parliamo	*we speak*
(che) tu parli	*you speak*	(che) voi parliate	*you speak*
(che) lui/lei/Lei parli	*he/she speaks, you (fml.) speak*	(che) loro/Loro parlino	*they speak, you (fml. pl.) speak*

RICEVERE (TO RECEIVE)			
(che) io riceva	*I receive*	(che) noi riceviamo	*we receive*
(che) tu riceva	*you receive*	(che) voi riceviate	*you receive*
(che) lui/lei/Lei riceva	*he/she receives, you (fml.) receive*	(che) loro/Loro ricevano	*they receive, you (fml. pl.) receive*

DORMIRE (TO SLEEP)			
(che) io dorma	*I sleep*	(che) noi dormiamo	*we sleep*
(che) tu dorma	*you sleep*	(che) voi dormiate	*you sleep*
(che) lui/lei/Lei dorma	*he/she sleeps, you (fml.) sleep*	(che) loro/Loro dormano	*they sleep, you (fml. pl.) sleep*

FINIRE (TO FINISH)			
(che) io finisca	*I finish*	(che) noi finiamo	*we finish*
(che) tu finisca	*you finish*	(che) voi finiate	*you finish*
(che) lui/lei/Lei finisca	*he/she finishes, you (fml.) finish*	(che) loro/Loro finiscano	*they finish, you (fml. pl.) finish*

IRREGULAR VERBS IN THE PRESENT SUBJUNCTIVE

AVERE (TO HAVE)

(che) io abbia	*I have*	(che) noi abbiamo	*we have*
(che) tu abbia	*you have*	(che) voi abbiate	*you have*
(che) lui/lei/Lei abbia	*he/she has, you (fml.) have*	(che) loro/Loro abbiano	*they have, you (fml. pl.) have*

ESSERE (TO BE)

(che) io sia	*I am*	(che) noi siamo	*we are*
(che) tu sia	*you are*	(che) voi siate	*you are*
(che) lui/lei/Lei sia	*he/she is, you (fml.) are*	(che) loro/Loro siano	*they are, you (fml. pl.) are*

ANDARE (TO GO)

(che) io vada	*I go*	(che) noi andiamo	*we go*
(che) tu vada	*you go*	(che) voi andiate	*you go*
(che) lui/lei/Lei vada	*he/she goes, you (fml.) go*	(che) loro/Loro vadano	*they go, you (fml. pl.) go*

BERE (TO DRINK)

(che) io beva	*I drink*	(che) noi beviamo	*we drink*
(che) tu beva	*you drink*	(che) voi beviate	*you drink*
(che) lui/lei/Lei beva	*he/she drinks, you (fml.) drink*	(che) loro/Loro bevano	*they drink, you (fml. pl.) drink*

DARE (TO GIVE)

(che) io dia	*I give*	(che) noi diamo	*we give*
(che) tu dia	*you give*	(che) voi diate	*you give*
(che) lui/lei/Lei dia	*he/she gives, you (fml.) give*	(che) loro/Loro diano	*they give, you (fml. pl.) give*

DIRE (TO SAY)

(che) io dica	*I say*	(che) noi diciamo	*we say*
(che) tu dica	*you say*	(che) voi diciate	*you say*
(che) lui/lei/Lei dica	*he/she says, you (fml.) say*	(che) loro/Loro dicano	*they say, you (fml. pl.) say*

DOVERE (MUST)

(che) io debba	*I must*	(che) noi dobbiamo	*we must*
(che) tu debba	*you must*	(che) voi dobbiate	*you must*
(che) lui/lei/Lei debba	*he/she must, you (fml.) must*	(che) loro/Loro debbano	*they must, you (fml. pl.) must*

FARE (TO DO)

(che) io faccia	*I do*	(che) noi facciamo	*we do*
(che) tu faccia	*you do*	(che) voi facciate	*you do*
(che) lui/lei/Lei faccia	*he/she does, you (fml.) do*	(che) loro/Loro facciano	*they do, you (fml. pl.) do*

PIACERE (TO LIKE)

(che) mi piaccia/ piacciano	*I like*	(che) ci piaccia/ piacciano	*we like*
(che) ti piaccia/ piacciano	*you like*	(che) vi piaccia/ piacciano	*you like*
(che) gli/le/Le piaccia/piacciano	*he/she likes, you (fml.) like*	(che) gli piaccia/ piacciano; (che) piaccia/ piacciano Loro	*they like, you (fml. pl.) like*

POTERE (CAN)

(che) io possa	*I can*	(che) noi possiamo	*we can*
(che) tu possa	*you can*	(che) voi possiate	*you can*
(che) lui/lei/Lei possa	*he/she can, you (fml.) can*	(che) loro/Loro possano	*they can, you (fml. pl.) can*

SAPERE (TO KNOW)

(che) io sappia	*I know*	(che) noi sappiamo	*we know*
(che) tu sappia	*you know*	(che) voi sappiate	*you know*
(che) lui/lei/Lei sappia	*he/she knows, you (fml.) know*	(che) loro/Loro sappiano	*they know, you (fml. pl.) know*

STARE (TO STAY, TO REMAIN, TO BE)

(che) io stia	*I stay, remain, am*	(che) noi stiamo	*we stay, remain, are*
(che) tu stia	*you stay, remain, are*	(che) voi stiate	*you stay, remain, are*
(che) lui/lei/Lei stia	*he/she stays, remains, is; you (fml.) stay, remain, are*	(che) loro/Loro stiano	*they stay, remain, are; you (fml. pl.) stay, remain, are*

USCIRE (TO GO OUT, TO LEAVE)

(che) io esca	*I go out, leave*	(che) noi usciamo	*we go out, leave*
(che) tu esca	*you go out, leave*	(che) voi usciate	*you go out, leave*
(che) lui/lei/Lei esca	*he/she goes out, leaves; you (fml.) go out, leave*	(che) loro/Loro escano	*they go out, leave; you (fml. pl.) go out, leave*

VENIRE *(TO COME)*			
(che) io venga	*I come*	(che) noi veniamo	*we come*
(che) tu venga	*you come*	(che) voi veniate	*you come*
(che) lui/lei/Lei venga	*he/she comes, you (fml.) come*	(che) loro/Loro vengano	*they come, you (fml. pl.) come*

VOLERE *(TO WANT)*			
(che) io voglia	*I want*	(che) noi vogliamo	*we want*
(che) tu voglia	*you want*	(che) voi vogliate	*you want*
(che) lui/lei/Lei voglia	*he/she wants, you (fml.) want*	(che) loro/Loro vogliano	*they want, you (fml. pl.) want*

VERBS IN THE PAST SUBJUNCTIVE

PARLARE *(TO SPEAK)*			
(che) io abbia parlato	*I spoke*	(che) noi abbiamo parlato	*we spoke*
(che) tu abbia parlato	*you spoke*	(che) voi abbiate parlato	*you spoke*
(che) lui/lei/Lei abbia parlato	*he/she spoke, you (fml.) spoke*	(che) loro/Loro abbiano parlato	*they spoke, you (fml. pl.) spoke*

ANDARE *(TO GO)*			
(che) io sia andato/a	*I went*	(che) noi siamo andati/e	*we went*
(che) tu sia andato/a	*you went*	(che) voi siate andati/e	*you went*
(che) lui/lei/Lei sia andato/a	*he/she went, you (fml.) went*	(che) loro/Loro siano andati/e	*they went, you (fml. pl.) went*

Unit 4 Quiz

Let's put the most essential Italian words and grammar points you've learned so far to practice in a few exercises. It's important to be sure that you've mastered this material before you move on. Score yourself at the end of the review and see if you need to go back for more practice.

A. Complete the following sentences with the present subjunctive of the verb in parentheses.

1. È importante che noi _____ (lavarsi) sempre i denti dopo cena.

2. Voglio che lui _____ (telefonare) a sua madre più spesso.

3. Spero che loro _____ (venire) con me al cinema.

4. Non credono che io _____ (lavorare) abbastanza.

B. Complete the following sentences with the past subjunctive of the verb in parentheses.

1. Mi dispiace che loro _____ (perdere) il treno.

2. Penso che lei _____ (cantare) molto bene ieri sera.

3. Sono felice che tu _____ (trovare) un buon lavoro.

C. Complete the following sentences with either the present indicative or subjunctive of the verb in parentheses.

1. Sono sicuro che _____ (chiamarsi) Francesco.

2. Vuole che noi _____ (andare) in vacanza insieme.

3. Dubiti che io _____ (dire) la verità?

D. Translate the following sentences into Italian.

1. *I am sure she is Italian.* _____

_____

2. *We think they are leaving tomorrow.* _____

_____

E. Translate the following sentences into Italian.

1. *He wants to learn to drive.* _____

_____

2. *They want me to learn to drive.* _____

_____

F. Complete the following sentences with the correct form of either **metterci** or **volerci**.

1. Quanto tempo _____ per cuocere la pasta?

2. Io _____ cinque minuti a prepararmi.

G. Complete the following sentences with **a** or **di**, appropriately.

1. Ieri ho cominciato _____ studiare all'una e ho finito _____ fare i

   compiti alle tre.

2. Quando hai deciso _____ imparare l'italiano?

H. Change the following informal sentences into formal ones.

1. Per favore, dimmi come andare alla stazione. _____

   _____

2. Non preoccuparti, ci penso io. _____

   _____

How Did You Do?

Give yourself a point for every correct answer, then use the following key to tell whether you're ready to move on:

0-7 points: It's probably a good idea to go back through the lesson again. You may be moving too quickly, or there may be too much "down time" between your contact with Italian. Remember that it's better to spend 30 minutes with Italian three or four times a week than it is to spend two or three hours just once a week. Find a pace that's comfortable for you, and spread your contact hours out as much as you can.

8-12 points: You would benefit from a review before moving on. Go back and spend a little more time on the specific points that gave you trouble. Re-read the Grammar Builder sections that were difficult, and do the work out one more time. Don't forget about the online supplemental practice material, either. Go to **www. livinglanguage.com/languagelab** for games and quizzes that will reinforce the material from this unit.

13-17 points: Good job! There are just a few points that you could consider reviewing before moving on. If you haven't worked with the games and quizzes on **www.livinglanguage.com/languagelab**, please give them a try.

18-20 points: Great! Your Italian has come a long way! Even though you've reached the end of this course, there's no reason to stop learning.

points

Consider some of these activities to keep your Italian active, and to continue learning.

- ☐ Watch Italian language movies.
- ☐ Download a few Italian songs and pay attention to the lyrics.
- ☐ Bookmark an online Italian newspaper or magazine. Read a little bit every day.
- ☐ Buy a book in Italian and try to read every day.
- ☐ Check out chatrooms or other online communities in Italian.
- ☐ Use your imagination, and tailor your exposure to Italian to your interests. Enjoy!

Pronunciation Guide

Italian pronunciation

Many Italian sounds are like English sounds, though the differences are enough that you need to familiarize yourself with them in order to make yourself understood properly in the Italian language. Some key things to remember:

1. Each vowel is pronounced clearly and crisply.

2. A single consonant is pronounced with the following vowel.

3. Some vowels bear an accent mark, sometimes used to show the accentuated syllable (**la città**, *the city*), and sometimes merely to distinguish words (**e**, *and*; **è**, *is*). An acute accent, on the other hand, gives a more closed pronunciation (**perché**, *why*).

4. When the accent is on the letter **e**, it gives it a more open pronunciation (**caffè**, *coffee*).

5. The apostrophe is used to mark elision, the omission of a vowel. For example, when the word **dove** (*where*) is combined with **è** (*is*), the **e** in **dove** is dropped: **Dov'è?** (*Where is?*).

The rest is a matter of listening and repeating, which you should do with each word in this section as you start to learn how the Italian language sounds.

VOWELS

Now that you've looked at the difference between Italian and English on a broad scale, let's get down to the specifics by looking at individual sounds, starting with Italian vowels.

LETTER	PRONUNCIATION	EXAMPLES
a	*ah* in *father*	a, amico, la, lago, pane, parlare
e	*e* in *bent*	era, essere, pera, padre, carne, treno, tre, estate, se
i	*i* in *police, machine, marine*	misura, sì, amica, oggi, piccolo, figlio
o	*o* in *no*	no, poi, ora, sono, corpo, con, otto, come, forma, voce
u	*oo* in *noon*	uno, una, tu, ultimo

There are also several diphthongs in Italian, vowel-and-vowel combinations which create a new sound.

LETTER	PRONUNCIATION	EXAMPLES
ai	*i* in *ripe*	guai
au	*ow* in *now*	auto
ei	*ay* in *say*	sei
eu	*ay* in *say* + *oo* in *noon*	neutro
ia	*ya* in *yarn*	italiano
ie	*ye* in *yet*	miele
io	*yo* in *yodel*	campione
iu	*you*	fiume
oi	*oy* in *boy*	poi

LETTER	PRONUNCIATION	EXAMPLES
ua	*wa* in *wand*	quando
ue	*we* in *wet*	questo
uo	*wa* in *war*	suono
ui	*wee* in *sweet*	guido

1. CONSONANTS

Next, let's take a look at Italian consonants. The consonants b, d, f, k, l, m, n, p, q, t, and v are all pronounced as they are in English. The rest differ slightly, as you'll see below.

LETTER	PRONUNCIATION	EXAMPLES
c	before e or i, *ch* in *church*	cena, cibo
c	before a, o, and u, *k* in *bake*	caffè, conto, cupola
g	before e or i, *j* in *joy*	gente, gita
g	before a, o, or u, *g* in *gold*	gala, gondola, gusto
h	silent	hotel
r	trilled	rumore
s	generally, *s* in *set*	pasta
s	between two vowels, or before b, d, g, l, m, n, r, or v, *z* in *zero*	sbaglio
z	generally, *ts* in *pits*	zucchero, grazie
z	sometimes, *ds* in *toads*	zingaro, zanzara

2. SPECIAL ITALIAN SOUNDS

There are several sound combinations in Italian that appear quite often as exceptions to the above rules, so study them carefully.

CLUSTER	PRONUNCIATION	EXAMPLES
ch	before e or i, *c* in *can*	amiche, chilo

CLUSTER	PRONUNCIATION	EXAMPLES
gh	*g* in *get*	spaghetti, ghiotto
	gh in *ghost*	funghi
gl	before a vowel + consonant, *gl* in *globe*	globo, negligente
gli	*lli* in *scallion*	gli
glia	*lli* in *scallion* + *ah*	famiglia
glie	*lli* in *scallion* + *eh*	moglie
glio	*lli* in *scallion* + *oh*	aglio
gn	*ny* in *canyon*	Bologna
sc	before e or i, *sh* in *fish*	pesce, sci
sc	before a, o, or u, *sc* in *scout*	scala, disco
sch	before e or i, *sk* in *sky*	pesche, fischi

Grammar Summary

1. ARTICLES

a. Definite

	MASCULINE	FEMININE
Singular	il (in front of a consonant) l' (in front of a vowel) lo (in front of s + consonant, z-, ps-, or gn-)	la (in front of a consonant) l' (in front of a vowel)
Plural	i (in front of consonants) gli (in front of s + consonant, z-, ps-, gn-, or vowels)	le (in front of consonants or vowels)

b. Indefinite

	MASCULINE	FEMININE
Singular	un (in front of a consonant or vowel) uno (in front of s + consonant, z-, ps-, gn-)	una (in front of a consonant) un' (in front of a vowel)

2. PLURALS OF NOUNS AND ADJECTIVES

GENDER	SINGULAR ENDING	PLURAL ENDING
Masculine	-o	-i
Masculine/Feminine	-e	-i
Feminine	-a	-e

Some exceptions:

a. A few nouns ending in -o are feminine.

b. Some masculine nouns ending in -o have two plurals, with different meanings for each.

c. Masculine nouns ending in -a form their plural in –i.

SPECIAL CASES

1. Nouns ending in -ca or -ga insert h in the plural in order to keep the "k" and "g" sound in the plural.

2. Nouns ending in -cia or -gia (with unaccented i) form their plural in -ce or -ge if the c or g is double or is preceded by another consonant. Nouns ending in -cia or -gia form their plural in -cie or -gie if c or g is preceded by a vowel or if the i is accented.

3. Nouns ending in -io (without an accent on the i) have a single i in the plural. If the i is accented, the plural has ii.

4. Nouns ending in -co or -go form their plural in -chi or -ghi if the accent falls on the syllable before the last. If the accent falls on the third-to-last syllable, the plural is in -ci or -gi.

5. Nouns in the singular with the accent on the last vowel do not change in the plural.

6. There is no special plural form for:

- Nouns with a written accent on the last vowel.

- Nouns ending in i in the singular, and almost all the nouns in ie.

- Nouns ending in a consonant.

3. THE PARTITIVE

a. di + a form of the definite article il, lo, la, l', i, le, gli
b. qualche (only with singular nouns)
c. alcuni, alcune (only in the plural)
d. un po' di

4. COMPARISON

Equality	(così) ... come	as ... as
Equality	tanto ... quanto	as much/as many as
Superiority	più ... di or che	More ... than
Inferiority	meno ... di or che	less/fewer ... than

5. RELATIVE SUPERLATIVE

a. The relative superlative (expressed in English using *the most/the least/the .
. . -est of/in*) is formed by placing the appropriate definite article before più or meno followed by the adjective. *Of/in* is translated with di, whether by itself or combined with the definite article.

b. If a clause follows the superlative, the verb is often in the subjunctive form.

c. With the superlative of adverbs, the definite article is often omitted, unless *possibile* is added to the adverb.

6. ABSOLUTE SUPERLATIVE

a. The absolute superlative is formed by dropping the last vowel of the adjective and adding -issimo, -issima, -issimi, -issime.

b. By putting the words molto, troppo, or assai in front of the adjectives.

c. By using a second adjective of almost the same meaning, or by repeating the adjective.

d. By using stra-, arci-, sopra-, super-, extra-.

7. IRREGULAR COMPARATIVES AND SUPERLATIVES

ADJECTIVE	COMPARATIVE	SUPERLATIVE
good: buono(a)	*better:* più buono(a) migliore	*the best:* il più buono buonissimo(a) ottimo(a) il/la migliore
bad: cattivo(a)	*worse:* peggiore più cattivo(a) peggio	*the worst:* il/la più cattivo(a) cattivissimo(a) pessimo(a) il/la peggiore
big/great: grande	*bigger/greater:* maggiore più grande	*the biggest/greatest:* il/la più grande grandissimo(a) massimo(a) il/la maggiore
small/little: piccolo(a)	*smaller/lesser:* minore più piccolo(a)	*the smallest:* il/la più piccolo(a) piccolissimo(a) minimo(a) il/la minore

ADVERB	COMPARATIVE	SUPERLATIVE
well: bene	*better:* meglio (il migliore)	*the best:* il meglio
badly: male	*worse:* peggio (il peggiore)	*the worst:* il peggio

8. DIMINUTIVES AND AUGMENTATIVES

a. The endings -ino, -ina, -ello, -ella, -etto, -etta, -uccio, -uccia imply smallness.

b. The endings -one, -ona, -otta imply largeness or hyperbole.

c. The endings -uccia, -uccio indicate endearment.

d. The endings -accio, -accia, -astro, -astra, -azzo, -azza indicate depreciation.

9. DEMONSTRATIVES

questo, -a, -i, -e	*this, these*
quello, -a, -i, -e	*that, those*

There are also the masculine forms quel, quell', quei, quegli. Here is how they are used:

a. If the article il is used before the noun, use quel.

b. If the article l' is used before the noun, then use quell'.

c. If i is used before the noun, use quei.

d. If gli is used before the noun, use quegli.

Note that the same rules apply to bel, bell', bei, begli, from bello, -a, -i, -e (*beautiful*).

10. POSSESSIVE ADJECTIVES

	MASCULINE SINGULAR	MASCULINE PLURAL	FEMININE SINGULAR	FEMININE PLURAL
my	il mio	i miei	la mia	le mie
your	il tuo	i tuoi	la tua	le tue
his, her, its	il suo	i suoi	la sua	le sue
your (fml.)	il Suo	i Suoi	la Sua	le Sue
our	il nostro	i nostri	la nostra	le nostre
your	il vostro	i vostri	la vostra	le vostre
their	il loro	i loro	la loro	le loro
your (fml. pl.)	il Loro	i Loro	la Loro	le Loro

11. INDEFINITE ADJECTIVES AND PRONOUNS

some	qualche *(sg.)*, alcuni *(pl.)*
any	qualunque, qualsiasi *(no pl.)*
each, every	ogni *(no pl.)*, ciascun, ciascuno, ciascuna *(no pl.)*
other, more	altro, altra, altri, altre
no, no one, none of	nessuno, nessun, nessuna *(no pl.)*

12. INDEFINITE PRONOUNS

some	alcuni
someone, somebody	qualcuno
anybody, anyone	chiunque
each one, each person	ognuno
everybody, everyone	tutti *(pl.)*
each, each one	ciascuno
everything	tutto
the other, the others, else (in interrogative or negative sentences), anything else (in interrogative or negative sentences)	l'altro, l'altra, gli altri, le altre, altro
another one	un altro
nothing	niente, nulla
nobody, no one	nessuno *(no pl.)*

13. RELATIVE PRONOUNS

chi	*who*
che	*who, whom, that, which*
cui	*whom, which*

a cui	to whom, to which
di cui	of whom, of which
in cui	in which

a. **che**: For masculine, feminine, singular, plural; for persons, animals, things. Not used if there is a preposition.

b. **cui**: Masculine, feminine, singular, plural; for persons, animals, things; used instead of **che** when there is a preposition.

c. **il quale**, **la quale**, **i quali**, **le quali**: For persons, animals, things, with the same English meanings as **che**; can be used with or without prepositions. When used with prepositions, the contracted forms are used, e.g., **alla quale**, **dei quali**, etc.

14. PRONOUNS

	SUBJECT	DIRECT OBJECT	INDIRECT OBJECT	WITH PREPOSITION	REFLEXIVE
1st sg.	io	mi	mi	me	mi
2nd sg.	tu	ti	ti	te	ti
3rd m. sg.	lui	lo	gli	lui	si
3rd f. sg.	lei	la	le	lei	si
2nd sg. fml.	Lei	La	Le	Lei	Si
1st pl.	noi	ci	ci	noi	ci
2nd pl.	voi	vi	vi	voi	vi
3rd pl.	loro	li/le	gli/loro	loro	si
2nd pl. fml.	Loro	Li/Le	Gli/Loro	Loro	Si

15. DOUBLE OBJECT PRONOUNS

INDIRECT OBJECT	+ LO	+ LA	+ LI	+ LE	+ NE
mi	me lo	me la	me li	me le	me ne
ti	te lo	te la	te li	te le	te ne
gli/le/ Le	glielo	gliela	glieli	gliele	gliene
ci	ce lo	ce la	ce li	ce le	ce ne
vi	ve lo	ve la	ve li	ve le	ve ne
gli	glielo/ Glielo	gliela/ Gliela	glieli/Glieli	gliele/ Gliele	gliene/ Gliene
loro/ loro	lo … loro/Loro	la … loro/Loro	li … loro/Loro	le … loro/Loro	ne … loro/Loro

16. ADVERBS

a. Many adverbs end in -mente.

b. Adjectives ending in -le or -re drop the final e before adding -mente if the l or r is preceded by a vowel.

c. Adverbs may have a comparative and superlative form.

17. PREPOSITIONS

di	of
a	at, to
da	from
in	in
con	with
su	above
per	through, by means of, on
tra, fra	between, among

Prepositions + Definite Articles

	DI	A	SUL	CON
il	del	al	sul	col
lo	dello	allo	sullo	-
la	della	alla	sulla	-
l'	dell'	all'	sull'	-
i	dei	ai	sui	coi
gli	degli	agli	sugli	-
le	delle	alle	sulle	-

18. NEGATION

a. **Non** (*not*) comes before the verb.

b. Note that **non** can be combined with negative pronouns in the same sentence (double negative).

c. If the negative pronoun begins the sentence, **non** is not used.

19. QUESTION WORDS

Perché?	*Why?*
Come?	*How?*
Quando?	*When?*
Dove?	*Where?*
Quanto/quanta?	*How much?*
Quanti/quante?	*How many?*

20. THE SUBJUNCTIVE

The subjunctive mood expresses doubt, uncertainty, hope, fear, desire, supposition, possibility, probability, or granting. It is mostly found in clauses dependent upon another verb.

The subjunctive is used:

a. after verbs expressing hope, wish, desire, command, doubt.

b. after verbs expressing an opinion (penso, credo).

c. after expressions made with a form of essere and an adjective or an adverb (è necessario, è facile, è possibile), or some impersonal expressions like bisogna, importa, etc.

d. after conjunctions such as sebbene, quantunque, per quanto, benché, affinché, prima che (subjunctive to express a possibility; indicative to express a fact).

21. "IF" CLAUSES

An "*if*" clause can express:

a. REALITY. In this case, the indicative present and future is used.

b. POSSIBILITY. The imperfect subjunctive and the conditional present are used to express possibility in the present. The past perfect subjunctive and the past conditional are used to express a possibility in the past.

c. IMPOSSIBILITY or COUNTERFACTUALITY. Use the same construction as in (b); the only difference is that we know that the condition cannot be fulfilled.

amare
to love, to like

io	noi
tu	voi
lui/lei/Lei	loro/Loro

Present		Imperative	
amo	amiamo		Amiamo!
ami	amate	Ama!	Amate!
ama	amano	Ami!	Amino!

Past		Imperfect	
ho amato	abbiamo amato	amavo	amavamo
hai amato	avete amato	amavi	amavate
ha amato	hanno amato	amava	amavano

Future		Conditional	
amerò	ameremo	amerei	ameremmo
amerai	amerete	ameresti	amereste
amerà	ameranno	amerebbe	amerebbero

Future Perfect		Past Conditional	
avrò amato	avremo amato	avrei amato	avremmo amato
avrai amato	avrete amato	avresti amato	avreste amato
avrà amato	avranno amato	avrebbe amato	avrebbero amato

Past Perfect		Subjunctive	
avevo amato	avevamo amato	ami	amiamo
avevi amato	avevate amato	ami	amiate
aveva amato	avevano amato	ami	amino

temere
to fear

io	noi
tu	voi
lui/lei/ Lei	loro/Loro

Present		Imperative	
temo	temiamo		Temiamo!
temi	temete	Temi!	Temete!
teme	temono	Tema!	Temano!

Past		Imperfect	
ho temuto	abbiamo temuto	temevo	temevamo
hai temuto	avete temuto	temevi	temevate
ha temuto	hanno temuto	temeva	temevano

Future		Conditional	
temerò	temeremo	temerei	temeremmo
temerai	temerete	temeresti	temereste
temerà	temeranno	temerebbe	temerebbero

Future Perfect		Past Conditional	
avrò temuto	avremo temuto	avrei temuto	avremmo temuto
avrai temuto	avrete temuto	avresti temuto	avreste temuto
avrà temuto	avranno temuto	avrebbe temuto	avrebbero temuto

Past Perfect		Subjunctive	
avevo temuto	avevamo temuto	tema	temiamo
avevi temuto	avevate temuto	tema	temiate
aveva temuto	avevano temuto	tema	temano

sentire
to hear

io	noi
tu	voi
lui/lei/ Lei	loro/Loro

Present		Imperative	
sento	sentiamo		Sentiamo!
senti	sentite	Senti!	Sentite!
sente	sentono	Senta!	Sentano!

Past		Imperfect	
ho sentito	abbiamo sentito	sentivo	sentivamo
hai sentito	avete sentito	sentivi	sentivate
ha sentito	hanno sentito	sentiva	sentivano

Future		Conditional	
sentirò	sentiremo	sentirei	sentiremmo
sentirai	sentirete	sentiresti	sentireste
sentirà	sentiranno	sentirebbe	sentirebbero

Future Perfect		Past Conditional	
avrò sentito	avremo sentito	avrei sentito	avremmo sentito
avrai sentito	avrete sentito	avresti sentito	avreste sentito
avrà sentito	avranno sentito	avrebbe sentito	avrebbero sentito

Past Perfect		Subjunctive	
avevo sentito	avevamo sentito	senta	sentiamo
avevi sentito	avevate sentito	senta	sentiate
aveva sentito	avevano sentito	senta	sentano

capire
to understand

io	noi
tu	voi
lui/lei/ Lei	loro/Loro

Present		Imperative	
capisco	capiamo		Capiamo!
capisci	capite	Capisci!	Capite!
capisce	capiscono	Capisca!	Capiscano!

Past		Imperfect	
ho capito	abbiamo capito	capivo	capivamo
hai capito	avete capito	capivi	capivate
ha capito	hanno capito	capiva	capivano

Future		Conditional	
capirò	capiremo	capirei	capiremmo
capirai	capirete	capiresti	capireste
capirà	capiranno	capirebbe	capirebbero

Future Perfect		Past Conditional	
avrò capito	avremo capito	avrei capito	avremmo capito
avrai capito	avrete capito	avresti capito	avreste capito
avrà capito	avranno capito	avrebbe capito	avrebbero capito

Past Perfect		Subjunctive	
avevo capito	avevamo capito	capisca	capiamo
avevi capito	avevate capito	capisca	capiate
aveva capito	avevano capito	capisca	capiscano

Advanced Italian

essere
to be

io	noi
tu	voi
lui/lei/Lei	loro/Loro

Present		Imperative	
sono	siamo		Siamo!
sei	siete	Sii!	Siate!
è	sono	Sia!	Siano!

Past		Imperfect	
sono stato/a	siamo stati/e	ero	eravamo
sei stato/a	siete stati/e	eri	eravate
è stato/a	sono stati/e	era	erano

Future		Conditional	
sarò	saremo	sarei	saremmo
sarai	sarete	saresti	sareste
sarà	saranno	sarebbe	sarebbero

Future Perfect		Past Conditional	
sarò stato/a	saremo stati/e	sarei stato/a	saremmo stati/e
sarai stato/a	sarete stati/e	saresti stato/a	sareste stati/e
sarà stato/a	saranno stati/e	sarebbe stato/a	sarebbero stati/e

Past Perfect		Subjunctive	
ero stato/a	eravamo stati/e	sia	siamo
eri stato/a	eravate stati/e	sia	siate
era stato/a	erano stati/e	sia	siano

avere
to have

io	noi
tu	voi
lui/lei/Lei	loro/Loro

Present		Imperative	
ho	abbiamo		Abbiamo!
hai	avete	Abbi!	Abbiate!
ha	hanno	Abbia!	Abbiano!

Past		Imperfect	
ho avuto	abbiamo avuto	avevo	avevamo
hai avuto	avete avuto	avevi	avevate
ha avuto	hanno avuto	aveva	avevano

Future		Conditional	
avrò	avremo	avrei	avremmo
avrai	avrete	avresti	avreste
avrà	avranno	avrebbe	avrebbero

Future Perfect		Past Conditional	
avrò avuto	avremo avuto	avrei avuto	avremmo avuto
avrai avuto	avrete avuto	avresti avuto	avreste avuto
avrà avuto	avranno avuto	avrebbe avuto	avrebbero avuto

Past Perfect		Subjunctive	
avevo avuto	avevamo avuto	abbia	abbiamo
avevi avuto	avevate avuto	abbia	abbiate
aveva avuto	avevano avuto	abbia	abbiano

andare
to go

io	noi
tu	voi
lui/lei/Lei	loro/Loro

Present		Imperative	
vado	andiamo		Andiamo!
vai	andate	Va!/Va'!/Vai!	Andate!
va	vanno	Vada!	Vadano!

Past		Imperfect	
sono andato/a	siamo andati/e	andavo	andavamo
sei andato/a	siete andati/e	andavi	andavate
è andato/a	sono andati/e	andava	andavano

Future		Conditional	
andrò	andremo	andrei	andremmo
andrai	andrete	andresti	andreste
andrà	andranno	andrebbe	andrebbero

Future Perfect		Past Conditional	
sarò andato/a	saremo andati/e	sarei andato/a	saremmo andati/e
sarai andato/a	sarete andati/e	saresti andato/a	sareste andati/e
sarà andato/a	saranno andati/e	sarebbe andato/a	sarebbero andati/e

Past Perfect		Subjunctive	
ero andato/a	eravamo andati/e	vada	andiamo
eri andato/a	eravate andati/e	vada	andiate
era andato/a	erano andati/e	vada	vadano

bere
to drink

io	noi
tu	voi
lui/lei/ Lei	loro/Loro

Present		Imperative	
bevo	beviamo		Beviamo!
bevi	bevete	Bevi!	Bevete!
beve	bevono	Beva!	Bevano!

Past		Imperfect	
ho bevuto	abbiamo bevuto	bevevo	bevevamo
hai bevuto	avete bevuto	bevevi	bevevate
ha bevuto	hanno bevuto	beveva	bevevano

Future		Conditional	
berrò	berremo	berrei	berremmo
berrai	berrete	berresti	berreste
berrà	berranno	berrebbe	berrebbero

Future Perfect		Past Conditional	
avrò bevuto	avremo bevuto	avrei bevuto	avremmo bevuto
avrai bevuto	avrete bevuto	avresti bevuto	avreste bevuto
avrà bevuto	avranno bevuto	avrebbe bevuto	avrebbero bevuto

Past Perfect		Subjunctive	
avevo bevuto	avevamo bevuto	beva	beviamo
avevi bevuto	avevate bevuto	beva	beviate
aveva bevuto	avevano bevuto	beva	bevano

dare
to give

io	noi
tu	voi
lui/lei/Lei	loro/Loro

Present		Imperative	
do	diamo		Diamo!
dai	date	Dai!/Dà!/Da'!	Date!
dà	danno	Dia!	Diano!

Past		Imperfect	
ho dato	abbiamo dato	davo	davamo
hai dato	avete dato	davi	davate
ha dato	hanno dato	dava	davano

Future		Conditional	
darò	daremo	darei	daremmo
darai	darete	daresti	dareste
darà	daranno	darebbe	darebbero

Future Perfect		Past Conditional	
avrò dato	avremo dato	avrei dato	avremmo dato
avrai dato	avrete dato	avresti dato	avreste dato
avrà dato	avranno dato	avrebbe dato	avrebbero dato

Past Perfect		Subjunctive	
avevo dato	avevamo dato	dia	diamo
avevi dato	avevate dato	dia	diate
aveva dato	avevano dato	dia	diano

dire
to say

io	noi
tu	voi
lui/lei/ Lei	loro/Loro

Present		Imperative	
dico	diciamo		Diciamo!
dici	dite	Di'!/Dì!	Dite!
dice	dicono	Dica!	Dicano!

Past		Imperfect	
ho detto	abbiamo detto	dicevo	dicevamo
hai detto	avete detto	dicevi	dicevate
ha detto	hanno detto	diceva	dicevano

Future		Conditional	
dirò	diremo	direi	diremmo
dirai	direte	diresti	direste
dirà	diranno	direbbe	direbbero

Future Perfect		Past Conditional	
avrò detto	avremo detto	avrei detto	avremmo detto
avrai detto	avrete detto	avresti detto	avreste detto
avrà detto	avranno detto	avrebbe detto	avrebbero detto

Past Perfect		Subjunctive	
avevo detto	avevamo detto	dica	diciamo
avevi detto	avevate detto	dica	diciate
aveva detto	avevano detto	dica	dicano

dovere
to owe, to be obliged, to have to

io	noi
tu	voi
lui/lei/ Lei	loro/Loro

Present		Imperative	
devo (debbo)	dobbiamo		Dobbiamo!
devi	dovete	Devi!	Dovete!
deve	devono (debbono)	Debba!	Debbano!

Past		Imperfect	
ho dovuto	abbiamo dovuto	dovevo	dovevamo
hai dovuto	avete dovuto	dovevi	dovevate
ha dovuto	hanno dovuto	doveva	dovevano

Future		Conditional	
dovrò	dovremo	dovrei	dovremmo
dovrai	dovrete	dovresti	dovreste
dovrà	dovranno	dovrebbe	dovrebbero

Future Perfect		Past Conditional	
avrò dovuto	avremo dovuto	avrei dovuto	avremmo dovuto
avrai dovuto	avrete dovuto	avresti dovuto	avreste dovuto
avrà dovuto	avranno dovuto	avrebbe dovuto	avrebbero dovuto

Past Perfect		Subjunctive	
avevo dovuto	avevamo dovuto	debba	dobbiamo
avevi dovuto	avevate dovuto	debba	dobbiate
aveva dovuto	avevano dovuto	debba	debbano

fare
to do

io	noi
tu	voi
lui/lei/ Lei	loro/Loro

Present		Imperative	
faccio	facciamo		Facciamo!
fai	fate	Fa!/Fai!/Fa'!	Fate!
fa	fanno	Faccia!	Facciano!

Past		Imperfect	
ho fatto	abbiamo fatto	facevo	facevamo
hai fatto	avete fatto	facevi	facevate
ha fatto	hanno fatto	faceva	facevano

Future		Conditional	
farò	faremo	farei	faremmo
farai	farete	faresti	fareste
farà	faranno	farebbe	farebbero

Future Perfect		Past Conditional	
avrò fatto	avremo fatto	avrei fatto	avremmo fatto
avrai fatto	avrete fatto	avresti fatto	avreste fatto
avrà fatto	avranno fatto	avrebbe fatto	avrebbero fatto

Past Perfect		Subjunctive	
avevo fatto	avevamo fatto	faccia	facciamo
avevi fatto	avevate fatto	faccia	facciate
aveva fatto	avevano fatto	faccia	facciano

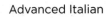

potere
to be able, can

io	noi
tu	voi
lui/lei/ Lei	loro/Loro

Present		Imperative	
posso	possiamo		Possiamo!
puoi	potete	Puoi!	Possiate!
può	possono	Possa!	Possano!

Past		Imperfect	
ho potuto	abbiamo potuto	potevo	potevamo
hai potuto	avete potuto	potevi	potevate
ha potuto	hanno potuto	poteva	potevano

Future		Conditional	
potrò	potremo	potrei	potremmo
potrai	potrete	potresti	potreste
potrà	potranno	potrebbe	potrebbero

Future Perfect		Past Conditional	
avrò potuto	avremo potuto	avrei potuto	avremmo potuto
avrai potuto	avrete potuto	avresti potuto	avreste potuto
avrà potuto	avranno potuto	avrebbe potuto	avrebbero potuto

Past Perfect		Subjunctive	
avevo potuto	avevamo potuto	possa	possiamo
avevi potuto	avevate potuto	possa	possiate
aveva potuto	avevano potuto	possa	possano

rimanere
to stay

io	noi
tu	voi
lui/lei/ Lei	loro/Loro

Present		Imperative	
rimango	rimaniamo		Rimaniamo!
rimani	rimanete	Rimani!	Rimanete!
rimane	rimangono	Rimanga!	Rimangano!

Past		Imperfect	
sono rimasto/a	siamo rimasti/e	rimanevo	rimanevamo
sei rimasto/a	siete rimasti/e	rimanevi	rimanevate
è rimasto/a	sono rimasti/e	rimaneva	rimanevano

Future		Conditional	
rimarrò	rimarremo	rimarrei	rimarremmo
rimarrai	rimarrete	rimarresti	rimarreste
rimarrà	rimarranno	rimarrebbe	rimarrebbero

Future Perfect		Past Conditional	
sarò rimasto/a	saremo rimasti/e	sarei rimasto/a	saremmo rimasti/e
sarai rimasto/a	sarete rimasti/e	saresti rimasto/a	sareste rimasti/e
sarà rimasto/a	saranno rimasti/e	sarebbe rimasto/a	sarebbero rimasti/e

Past Perfect		Subjunctive	
ero rimasto/a	eravamo rimasti/e	rimanga	rimaniamo
eri rimasto/a	eravate rimasti/e	rimanga	rimaniate
era rimasto/a	erano rimasti/e	rimanga	rimangano

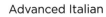

sapere
to know

io	noi
tu	voi
lui/lei/ Lei	loro/Loro

Present		Imperative	
so	sappiamo		Sappiamo!
sai	sapete	Sappi!	Sappiate!
sa	sanno	Sappia!	Sappiano!

Past		Imperfect	
ho saputo	abbiamo saputo	sapevo	sapevamo
hai saputo	avete saputo	sapevi	sapevate
ha saputo	hanno saputo	sapeva	sapevano

Future		Conditional	
saprò	sapremo	saprei	sapremmo
saprai	saprete	sapresti	sapreste
saprà	sapranno	saprebbe	saprebbero

Future Perfect		Past Conditional	
avrò saputo	avremo saputo	avrei saputo	avremmo saputo
avrai saputo	avrete saputo	avresti saputo	avreste saputo
avrà saputo	avranno saputo	avrebbe saputo	avrebbero saputo

Past Perfect		Subjunctive	
avevo saputo	avevamo saputo	sappia	sappiamo
avevi saputo	avevate saputo	sappia	sappiate
aveva saputo	avevano saputo	sappia	sappiano

scegliere
to choose

io	noi
tu	voi
lui/lei/ Lei	loro/Loro

Present		Imperative	
scelgo	scegliamo		Scegliamo!
scegli	scegliete	Scegli!	Scegliete!
sceglie	scelgono	Scelga!	Scelgano!

Past		Imperfect	
ho scelto	abbiamo scelto	sceglievo	sceglievamo
hai scelto	avete scelto	sceglievi	sceglievate
ha scelto	hanno scelto	sceglieva	sceglievano

Future		Conditional	
sceglierò	sceglieremo	sceglierei	sceglieremmo
sceglierai	sceglierete	sceglieresti	scegliereste
sceglierà	sceglieranno	sceglierebbe	sceglierebbero

Future Perfect		Past Conditional	
avrò scelto	avremo scelto	avrei scelto	avremmo scelto
avrai scelto	avrete scelto	avresti scelto	avreste scelto
avrà scelto	avranno scelto	avrebbe scelto	avrebbero scelto

Past Perfect		Subjunctive	
avevo scelto	avevamo scelto	scelga	scegliamo
avevi scelto	avevate scelto	scelga	scegliate
aveva scelto	avevano scelto	scelga	scelgano

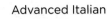

uscire
to go out

io	noi
tu	voi
lui/lei/ Lei	loro/Loro

Present		Imperative	
esco	usciamo		Usciamo!
esci	uscite	Esci!	Uscite!
esce	escono	Esca!	Escano!

Past		Imperfect	
sono uscito/a	siamo usciti/e	uscivo	uscivamo
sei uscito/a	siete usciti/e	uscivi	uscivate
è uscito/a	sono usciti/e	usciva	uscivano

Future		Conditional	
uscirò	usciremo	uscirei	usciremmo
uscirai	uscirete	usciresti	uscireste
uscirà	usciranno	uscirebbe	uscirebbero

Future Perfect		Past Conditional	
sarò uscito/a	saremo usciti/e	sarei uscito/a	saremmo usciti/e
sarai uscito/a	sarete usciti/e	saresti uscito/a	sareste usciti/e
sarà uscito/a	saranno usciti/e	sarebbe uscito/a	sarebbero usciti/e

Past Perfect		Subjunctive	
ero uscito/a	eravamo usciti/e	esca	usciamo
eri uscito/a	eravate usciti/e	esca	usciate
era uscito/a	erano usciti/e	esca	escano

vedere
to see

io	noi
tu	voi
lui/lei/ Lei	loro/Loro

Present		Imperative	
vedo	vediamo		Vediamo!
vedi	vedete	Vedi!/Ve'!	Vedete!
vede	vedono	Veda!	Vedano!

Past		Imperfect	
ho visto	abbiamo visto	vedevo	vedevamo
hai visto	avete visto	vedevi	vedevate
ha visto	hanno visto	vedeva	vedevano

Future		Conditional	
vedrò	vedremo	vedrei	vedremmo
vedrai	vedrete	vedresti	vedreste
vedrà	vedranno	vedrebbe	vedrebbero

Future Perfect		Past Conditional	
avrò visto	avremo visto	avrei visto	avremmo visto
avrai visto	avrete visto	avresti visto	avreste visto
avrà visto	avranno visto	avrebbe visto	avrebbero visto

Past Perfect		Subjunctive	
avevo visto	avevamo visto	veda	vediamo
avevi visto	avevate visto	veda	vediate
aveva visto	avevano visto	veda	vedano

venire
to come

io	noi
tu	voi
lui/lei/ Lei	loro/Loro

Present		Imperative	
vengo	veniamo		Veniamo!
vieni	venite	Vieni!	Venite!
viene	vengono	Venga!	Vengano!

Past		Imperfect	
sono venuto/a	siamo venuti/e	venivo	venivamo
sei venuto/a	siete venuti/e	venivi	venivate
è venuto/a	sono venuti/e	veniva	venivano

Future		Conditional	
verrò	verremo	verrei	verremmo
verrai	verrete	verresti	verreste
verrà	verranno	verrebbe	verrebbero

Future Perfect		Past Conditional	
sarò venuto/a	saremo venuti/e	sarei venuto/a	saremmo venuti/e
sarai venuto/a	sarete venuti/e	saresti venuto/a	sareste venuti/e
sarà venuto/a	saranno venuti/e	sarebbe venuto/a	sarebbero venuti/e

Past Perfect		Subjunctive	
ero venuto/a	eravamo venuti/e	venga	veniamo
eri venuto/a	eravate venuti/e	venga	veniate
era venuto/a	erano venuti/e	venga	vengano

volere
to want

io	noi
tu	voi
lui/lei/ Lei	loro/Loro

Present		Imperative	
voglio	vogliamo		vogliamo!
vuoi	volete	vogli!	vogliate!
vuole	vogliono	voglia!	vogliano!

Past		Imperfect	
ho voluto	abbiamo voluto	volevo	volevamo
hai voluto	avete voluto	volevi	volevate
ha voluto	hanno voluto	voleva	volevano

Future		Conditional	
vorrò	vorremo	vorrei	vorremmo
vorrai	vorrete	vorresti	vorreste
vorrà	vorranno	vorrebbe	vorrebbero

Future Perfect		Past Conditional	
avrò voluto	avremo voluto	avrei voluto	avremmo voluto
avrai voluto	avrete voluto	avresti voluto	avreste voluto
avrà voluto	avranno voluto	avrebbe voluto	avrebbero voluto

Past Perfect		Subjunctive	
avevo voluto	avevamo voluto	voglia	vogliamo
avevi voluto	avevate voluto	voglia	vogliate
aveva voluto	avevano voluto	voglia	vogliano

Advanced Italian

Glossary

Note that the following abbreviations will be used in this glossary: (m.) = masculine, (f.) = feminine, (inv.) = invariable, (sg.) = singular, (pl.) = plural, (fml.) = formal/polite, (infml.) = informal/familiar. If a word has two grammatical genders, (m./f.) or (f./m.) is used.

Italian-English

A

a *to, at, in, by*
  a + definite article *in the style of*
  A dopo. *See you later.*
  a tempo pieno *full-time*
  A presto. *See you soon.*
  a proposito *by the way*
  a proposito di ... *speaking of ...*
  a volte *sometimes*
abbastanza *fairly, enough*
abbigliamento (m.) *clothing*
  negozio (m.) di abbigliamento *clothing store*
abbondante *abundant, plentiful*
  cena (f.) abbondante *large dinner*
abbracciarsi *to hug*
abitabile *habitable*
  cucina (f.) abitabile *eat-in kitchen*
abitare *to live*
abito (m.) *suit (men's), dress (women's)*
  abito da uomo *men's suit*
accessorio (m.) *accessory*
accettare *to accept*
accettazione (f.) *reception desk*
accomodante *accommodating*
accompagnare *to accompany*
accordo (m.) *agreement*
  essere d'accordo *to agree*
  d'accordo *agreed, O.K.*
acqua (f.) *water*
  acqua minerale *mineral water*
  acqua minerale naturale *still mineral water*
  acqua minerale frizzante *sparkling mineral water*
adatto *appropriate*
addormentarsi *to fall asleep*

adesso *now*
adolescente (m./f.) *teenager*
adorabile *adorable*
adulto/a (m./f.) *adult*
aereo (m.) *airplane*
  in aereo *by plane*
aerobico *aerobic*
  fare ginnastica aerobica *to do aerobics*
aeroporto (m.) *airport*
affari (m. pl.) *business*
  uomo (m.) d'affari *businessman*
  donna (f.) d'affari *businesswoman*
affatto *completely*
  non ... affatto *not ... at all*
affermare *to claim*
affettare *to slice*
affettato (m.) *sliced cold meat*
  affettati misti *mixed cold cuts*
affinché *in order that, so that*
affittare *to rent*
affollato *crowded*
affrettato *fast, rushed*
affumicato *smoked*
agenzia (f.) *agency*
aggettivo (m.) *adjective*
aggiungere *to add*
agitarsi *to get nervous*
agosto (m.) *August*
aiutare *to help*
  aiutare a ... *to help ... ing*
aiutarsi *to help each other*
aiuto (m.) *help*
albergo (m.) *hotel*
albero (m.) *tree*
albicocca (f.) *apricot*
albicocco (m.) *apricot tree*
alcuni/e *a few, some*
alimentari (m. pl.) *groceries*

negozio (m.) di alimentari *grocery store*
alla brace *grilled/barbecued*
 carne alla brace *grilled/barbecued meat*
allegare *to attach*
 allegare un file *to attach a file*
 allegare un documento *to attach a document*
allegato (m.) *attachment*
allenatore/trice (m./f.) *coach*
alloggio (m.) *accommodation, apartment*
allora *then, well then, so*
alluce (m.) *big toe*
almeno *at least*
alpino *alpine*
 sci (m.) alpino *alpine skiing*
alternare *to alternate*
alto *tall*
altro *other*
 un altro/un'altra *another*
 tutti gli altri *everyone else*
alzarsi *to get up*
amaramente *bitterly*
amare *to love*
 Ti amo. *I love you.*
amaro *sour, bitter*
ambientazione (f.) *settings*
americano *American*
 futbol (m.) americano *American football*
amicizia (f.) *friendship*
 fare amicizia *to make friends*
amico (m.)/amici (m. pl.) *friend*
ammalato *ill, sick*
amore (m.) *love*
 storie (f. pl.) d'amore *love stories*
ampio *spacious, wide*
ananas (m. sg./pl.) *pineapple*
anche *also, too*
ancora *again, still, yet*
andare *to go*
 andare a ... *to go ... ing*
 andare a trovare *to go visit*
 andare in barca a vela *to sail*
 andare in bicicletta *to ride a bike*
 Andiamoci. *Let's go there.*
 Come va? *How's it going?*
 Va meglio. *It's better.*
 Va' avanti. *Go ahead.*
 Vacci. *Go there.*
anello (m.) *ring*

animale (m.) *animal*
anniversario (m.) *anniversary*
 Buon anniversario. *Happy anniversary.*
anno (m.) *year*
 anno scorso *last year*
 Ho ... anni. *I am ... years old.*
 Quanti anni hai? *How old are you?* (infml.)
 tutti gli anni *every year*
annoiarsi *to get bored*
anticipo (m.) *advance*
 essere in anticipo *to be early*
antico *ancient*
antipasto (m.) *appetizer*
antipatico *unfriendly*
antistress (m. sg./pl.) *anti-stress*
anzi *on the contrary*
aperitivo (m.) *aperitif*
aperto *open*
 all'aperto *outdoors*
apparecchiare *to set (a table)*
appartamento (m.) *apartment*
appena *just*
appetito (m.) *appetite*
 Buon appetito. *Enjoy your meal.*
apprendere *to learn*
appuntamento (m.) *appointment*
aprile (m.) *April*
aprire *to open*
 aprire un documento *to open a document*
 aprire un file *to open a file*
arabo *Arab*
aragosta (f.) *lobster*
arancia (f.) *orange (fruit)*
arancione (inv.) *orange (color)*
archeologico (m.)/archeologici (m. pl.) *archeological*
architetto (m.) *architect*
aria (f.) *air*
 aria condizionata *air conditioning*
armadietto (m.) *medicine cabinet*
armadio (m.) *closet, wardrobe*
aroma (m.) *aroma*
arrivare *to arrive*
Arrivederci. *Good-bye* (infml.)
 ArrivederLa. *Good-bye* (sg. fml.)
arrosto *roast*
arte (f.) *art*
 arte moderna *modern art*

articolo (m.) *article*
artista (m./f.) *artist*
asciugamano (m.) *towel*
ascoltare *to listen to*
aspettare *to wait for*
asse (f.) *board*
  asse da stiro *ironing board*
assistente (m./f.) *assistant*
assolutamente *absolutely*
assorbire *to absorb*
astronauta (m./f.) *astronaut*
atleta (m./f.) *athlete*
attaccare *to attach*
attento *attentive, careful*
  Sta' attento! *Pay attention!/Be careful!/Watch out!*
attenzione (f.) *attention*
  fare attenzione *to pay attention*
attico (m.)/attici (m. pl.) *penthouse*
attività (f.)/attività (f. pl.) *activity*
attore (m.) *actor*
attorno *around*
  attorno a … *around …*
attrice (f.) *actress*
attuale *current*
autobus (m.) *bus*
automobile (f.) *car*
autore/trice (m./f.) *author*
autunno (m.) *fall*
  in/d'autunno *in the fall*
avanti *forward, before, ahead*
  Va' avanti. *Go ahead.*
avere *to have*
  avere bisogno di … *to need …*
  avere caldo *to be hot*
  avere freddo *to be cold*
  avere in comune *to share*
  avere fretta *to be in a hurry*
  avere la febbre *to have a fever*
  avere male a … *to have a pain in …*
  avere paura (di) *to be afraid (of)*
  avere ragione *to be right*
  avere sete *to be thirsty*
  avere sonno *to be sleepy*
  avere tempo *to have time*
  avere torto *to be wrong*
  avere un dolore a … *to have a pain in …*
  avere voglia di … *to feel like …*

  Ho … anni. *I am … years old.*
  Quanti anni hai? *How old are you?* (infml.)
avocado (m. sg./pl.) *avocado*
avvocato (m.) *lawyer*
azione (f.) *action*
  film (m. pl.) d'azione *action movies*

B

baciarsi *to kiss*
bagno (m.) *bathroom*
  costume (m.) da bagno *bathing trunks, bathing suit*
  fare il bagno *to take a bath*
  vasca (f.) (da bagno) *bath tub*
bagnoschiuma (m.) *bath gel*
ballare *to dance*
ballo (m.) *dance*
bambino/a (m./f.) *baby, child (from 0 to 10 years old)*
banana (f.) *banana*
banca (f.) *bank*
banchiere/a (m./f.) *banker*
bar (m.) *café*
barba (f.) *beard*
  crema (f.) da barba *shaving cream*
  farsi la barba *to shave*
barca (f.) *boat*
  andare in barca a vela *to sail*
barocco (m.) *baroque*
barzelletta (f.) *joke*
baseball (m.) *baseball*
basilico (m.) *basil*
basket (m.) *basketball*
basso *short, low*
bastare *to be enough*
  Basta così! *That's enough!*
beato *lucky*
  Beati voi. *Lucky you.* (pl.)
  Beato te! *Lucky you!* (sg. infml.)
Beh … *Well …*
beige (inv.) *beige*
bello *beautiful*
  bellissimo *very beautiful*
  Che bello! *How nice!/How beautiful!*
  Che bel piatto! *What a beautiful dish!*
  Fa bello. *It's beautiful. (weather)*
  fare bella figura *to make a good impression*
benché *although*

benda (f.) *bandage*

bene *well*

  (Sto) bene, grazie. *Fine, thanks.*

  Benissimo! *Wonderful!/Very well!*

  Molto bene, grazie. *Very well, thanks.*

  Va bene. *All right.*

  Bentornato. *Welcome back.*

benvenuto *welcome*

bere *to drink*

  qualcosa da bere *something to drink*

bevanda (f.) *drink*

bianco *white*

  vino (m.) bianco *white wine*

bibita (f.) *soft drink, soda*

biblioteca (f.) *library*

bicchiere (m.) *glass*

bichini (m.) *bikini*

bici (f. sg./pl.) *bike*

bicicletta (f.) *bicycle*

  andare in bicicletta *to ride a bike*

biglietto (m.) *ticket*

biliardo (m.) *pool, billiards*

biologia (f.) *biology*

birra (f.) *beer*

bisogno (m.) *need*

  avere bisogno di … *to need …*

  essere nel bisogno *to need*

bistecca (f.) *beefsteak*

blu (inv.) *blue*

blue jeans (m. pl.) *jeans*

bocca (f.) *mouth*

  In bocca al lupo! *Break a leg! (lit. In the mouth of the wolf!)*

bocciare *to reject*

  essere bocciato *to fail (an exam)*

bollire *to boil*

bollitore (m.) *tea kettle*

borotalco (m.) *powder (talcum)*

borsa (f.) *bag, purse*

bosco (m.) *wood*

botte (f.) *cask*

bottiglia (f.) *bottle*

boutique (f.) *boutique*

braccialetto (m.) *bracelet*

braccio (m.) *arm*

  braccia (f. pl.) *arms*

braciola (f.) *chop*

  braciola di maiale *pork chop*

bravo *skillful, talented, nice*

broccolo (m.) *broccoli*

bruschetta (f.) *bruschetta*

brutto *ugly*

  Fa brutto. *It's bad. (weather)*

bucato (m.) *laundry*

  detersivo (m.) per il bucato *laundry detergent*

  fare il bucato *to do the laundry*

bugia (f.) *lie*

buono/buon (before masculine nouns except when they begin with the letter s followed by a consonant, or with the letter z) *good*

  Buon anniversario. *Happy anniversary.*

  Buon appetito. *Enjoy your meal.*

  Buon compleanno. *Happy birthday.*

  Buon giorno. *Good morning.*

  Buon Natale. *Merry Christmas.*

  Buon pomeriggio. *Good afternoon. (from 1 p.m. to 6 p.m.)*

  Buon riposo. *Have a good rest.*

  Buon viaggio. *Have a good trip.*

  Buona cena. *Enjoy your dinner./Have a good dinner.*

  Buona fortuna. *Good luck.*

  Buona giornata. *Have a good day.*

  Buona notte. *Good night.*

  Buona passeggiata. *Enjoy your walk./Have a good walk.*

  Buona sera. *Good evening.*

  Buona serata. *Have a good evening.*

  Buone feste. *Happy holidays.*

burro (m.) *butter*

business (m. sg./pl.) *business*

C

C'è … *There is …*

  C'è il sole. *It's sunny.*

  C'è nebbia. *It's foggy.*

  C'è un temporale. *It's stormy.*

  C'è vento. *It's windy.*

cachemire (m.) *cashmere*

  di cachemire *made out of cashmere*

cadere *to fall*

caffè (m. sg./pl.) *coffee, coffee shop*

caffetteria (f.) *coffee shop*

caffettiera (f.) *coffee maker (stovetop)*

calcio (m.) *soccer*

caldo (m.) *heat*

avere caldo *to be hot*
Fa caldo. *It's hot.*
calpestare *to tread on*
calze (f. pl.) *socks*
cambiare *to change*
  cambiare canale *to flip channels*
camera (f.) *room, bedroom, cabinet*
  camera da letto *bedroom*
  camera doppia *double room*
    (two twin-size beds)
  camera matrimoniale *double room*
    (one queen-size bed)
  camera singola *single room (one twin bed)*
cameriera (f.) *waitress*
cameriere (m.) *waiter*
camicetta (f.) *blouse*
camicia (f.) *shirt*
camminare *to walk*
  camminare in montagna *to go hiking*
campagna (f.) *countryside, country*
  in campagna *to the country*
campeggio (m.) *camping*
  fare il campeggio *to go camping*
campione/essa (m./f.) *champion*
campo (m.) *field*
canale (m.) *channel*
  cambiare canale *to flip channels*
cancellare *to delete*
candeggina (f.) *bleach*
canottiera (f.) *undershirt*
cantare *to sing*
canzone (f.) *song*
capacità (f. sg./pl.) *ability*
capelli (m. pl.) *hair*
capire *to understand*
capo/a (m./f.) *boss*
cappello (m.) *hat*
cappotto (m.) *coat (to the knees or longer)*
cappuccino (m.) *cappuccino*
carino *cute, pretty*
carne (f.) *meat*
  carne alla brace *grilled/barbecued meat*
caro *expensive*
carota (f.) *carrot*
carta (f.) *paper, card*
  carta di credito *credit card*
  carta igienica *toilet paper*
  giocare a carte *to play cards*

cartella (f.) *file*
cartina (f.) *map*
casa (f.) *house, home*
  a casa *at home*
  in giro per la casa *around the house*
casalinga (f.) *stay-at-home mom*
casalingo (m.) *stay-at-home dad*
caso (m.) *chance, case*
  in ogni caso *in any event*
  per caso *by any chance*
cassetto (m.) *drawer*
cattivo *naughty*
caviglia (f.) *ankle*
cavo (m.) *cable*
  cavo adsi *cable (dsl)*
cd rom (m.) *CD-ROM*
celebrare *to celebrate*
celibe (m.) *single (man)*
cellulare (m.) *cell phone*
cena (f.) *dinner*
Buona cena. *Enjoy your dinner./Have a good*
  dinner.
centimetro (m.) *centimeter*
cento *hundred*
centro (m.) *center*
  centro acquisti, centro
    commerciale *shopping mall*
  centro informazioni *information center*
  in centro *downtown, to/in the city*
cercare *to look for*
  cercare di … *to try to …*
cerimonia (f.) *ceremony*
cerotto (m.) *bandage*
certamente *certainly*
certo *some, a few*
certo/a (m./f.) *certain, certain ones*
cervello (m.) *brain*
cetriolo (m.) *cucumber*
chatroom (f.) *chatroom*
che *what* (question); *what, how* (exclamation);
  who, whom, which, that (relative pronoun); *that*
  (conjunction); *than* (comparative)
Che bello! *How nice!/How beautiful!*
Che cosa? *What?*
Che ora è?/Che ore sono? *What time is it?*
Che tempo fa? *What's the weather like?*
meno … che *less … than*
Non c'è di che. *Don't mention it.*

più … che *more/-er … than*
sia … che *as/so … as, both … and*
chi *who* (question); *he/she who, the one who,*
   whoever (relative pronoun)
   Di chi è … ? *Whose … is it ?*
   Di chi sono … ? *Whose … are they?*
chiamare *to call, to telephone*
chiamarsi *to be named*
   Mi chiamo … *My name is …*
   Si chiama … *His/Her name is …*
chiaro (adjective) *clear*
chiaro (adverb), chiaramente *clearly*
chiedere *to ask, to ask for*
   chiedere (un) consiglio *to ask for advice*
chiesa (f.) *church*
chilo (m.) *kilo*
chilometro *kilometer*
chimica (f.) *chemistry*
chimico (m. pl *chimici*) *chemical*
chitarra (f.) *guitar*
chiudere *to close*
   chiudere un documento/file *to close a*
      document/file
chiunque *anyone*
ci *us* (direct object pronoun); *to us* (indirect object
   pronoun); *here, there; about/of/on it*
   Andiamoci. *Let's go there.*
   Arrivederci. *Good-bye* (infml.)
   C'è … *There is …*
   Ci penserò. *I'll think about it.*
   Ci sono … *There are …*
   Rieccoci! *Here we are again!*
Ciao. *Hi./Hello./Good-bye.*
   Ciao ciao! *Bye-bye!*
ciascuno *each*
ciascuno/a (m./f.) *each one*
cibo (m.) *food*
ciclismo (m.) *biking*
cielo (m.) *sky*
ciglio (m.) *eyelash*
   ciglia (f. pl.) *eyelashes*
Cina (f.) *China*
cinema (m. sg./pl.) *movie theater*
cinese (m.) *Chinese (language)*
   parlare cinese *to speak Chinese*
cinquanta *fifty*
cinque *five*
   tra cinque minuti *in five minutes*

cintura (f.) *belt*
ciotola (f.) *bowl*
cipolla (f.) *onion*
circa *about*
circo (m.) *circus*
città (f. sg./pl.) *city*
   città natale *hometown*
   fuori città *out of town*
   in giro per la città *around town*
cittadina (f.) *town*
cittadinanza (f.) *citizenship*
civile *civil*
   stato (m.) civile *marital status*
classe (f.) *classroom, class*
classico (m.)/classici (m. pl.) *classical*
   musica (f.) classica *classical music*
cliente (m./f.) *customer*
clima (m.) *climate*
club (m. sg./pl.) *club*
colazione (f.) *breakfast*
   fare colazione *to have breakfast*
collana (f.) *necklace*
collega (m./f.) *colleague*
collina (f.) *hill*
collo (m.) *neck*
colloquio (m.) *talk, conversation, interview*
   colloquio di lavoro *job interview*
colonia (f.) *cologne*
coltello (m.) *knife*
coltivare *to grow*
comandare *to command*
come *how, as*
   Com'è? *How is … ?*
   Come mi sta? *How do I look?*
   Come sono? *How are … ?*
   Come sta? *How are you doing* (fml.)?
   Come stai? *How are you doing* (infml.)?
   Come va? *How's it going?*
   così … come *as/so … as*
   Ma come! *How's it possible!/How can this be!*
cominciare *to begin*
cominciare a … *to begin to …*
commedia (f.) *comedy*
commerciante (m./f.) *vendor*
commercio (m.) *business, commerce*
comodo *comfortable*
compagnia (f.) *company*
competenza (f.) *competence*

compiere *to complete*
compleanno (m.) *birthday*
  Buon compleanno. *Happy birthday.*
complimento (m.) *compliment*
  Complimenti! *Congratulations!*
comprare *to buy*
computer (m., pl.) *computer*
comune (m.) *common*
  avere in comune *to share*
comunità (f. sg./pl.) *community*
comunque *in any case*
con *with*
  con talento *talented*
concerto (m.) *concert*
condividere *to share*
condizionato *conditionin*
  aria (f.) condizionata *air conditioned*
condizione (f.) *condition, situation*
  a condizione che … *provided that …*
condominio (m.)/condomini (m. pl.) *apartment building*
confessare *to confess*
congiuntivo (m.) *subjunctive mood (grammar)*
  congiuntivo presente *present subjunctive*
conoscere *to know (a person), to meet (a person for the first time)*
conoscersi *to know each other*
consiglio (m.) *advice*
  chiedere (un) consiglio *to ask for advice*
contadino/a (m./f.) *farmer*
contare *to count*
contemporaneo *contemporary*
  romanzi (m. pl.) contemporanei *contemporary novels*
contento *happy*
  contento di … *happy to …*
continuare *to continue*
  orario (m.) continuato *open all day*
conto (m.) *check, bill*
contorno (m.) *side dish*
  di/per contorno *as a side dish*
controllare *to check*
convincere *to convince*
  convincere a … *to convince to …*
convinto *convinced*
coordinare *to coordinate*
coppia (f.) *couple*
corda (f.) *rope*

saltare la corda *to jump rope*
correre *to run*
corso (m.) *course*
cortile (m.) *back yard, courtyard*
corto *short*
cosa (f.) *thing*
  Che cosa? *What?*
  cose da fare *things to do*
  mille cose *tons of things, a thousand things*
  Tu cosa prendi? *What are you having?*
così *so*
  Basta così! *That's enough!*
  così … come *as/so … as*
  Così, così. *So so./Not bad.*
costa (f.) *coast, rib*
  di velluto a coste *made out of corduroy*
  velluto a coste *corduroy*
costare *to cost*
  Quanto costa? *How much does it cost?*
costo (m.) *cost*
  a tutti i costi *at all costs*
costoso *expensive*
costume (m.) *costume*
  costume da bagno *bathing trunks, bathing suit*
cotone (m.) *cotton*
cottura (f.) *cooking*
cravatta (f.) *tie*
credenza (f.) *cupboard*
credere *to believe*
  Non credo. *I don't think so.*
credito (m.) *credit*
  carta (f.) di credito *credit card*
crema (f.) *cream*
  crema da barba *shaving cream*
crescere *to grow, to raise*
croce (f.) *tail (of coin)*
  fare testa o croce *to flip a coin*
cucchiaio (m.) *spoon*
cucina (f.) *kitchen*
  cucina a gas *stove*
  cucina abitabile *eat-in kitchen*
  cucina elettrica *stove*
cucinare *to cook*
cugino/a (m./f.) *cousin*
cui *which, whom* (relative pronoun)
  il modo in cui … *the way in which …*
  la ragione/il motivo per cui … *the reason*

why …

cultura (f.) *culture*

cuocere *to cook*

cuore (m.) *heart*

curare *to treat, to cure*

cuscino (m.) *pillow*

D

da *from, to, at, for, since*

  dal lunedì al venerdì *from Monday to Friday*

  dalle … alle … *from … to … (time periods)*

  dalle undici meno un quarto alle tre *from 10:45 a.m. to 3:00 p.m.*

dare *to give*

  dare una festa *to have a party*

data (f.) *date, day*

dati (m. pl.) *data*

  dati anagrafici *personal information*

davanti *in front*

  davanti a … *in front of …*

davvero *really*

debole *weak*

decidere *to decide*

  decidere di … *to decide to …*

decimo *tenth*

decollare *to take off*

delizioso *delicious*

denaro (m.) *money*

dente (m.) *tooth*

dentista (m./f.) *dentist*

deodorante (m.) *deodorant*

depresso *depressed*

descrivere *to describe*

deserto (m.) *desert*

desiderare *to want, to desire*

destra (f.)

  (a) destra *right, on the right, to the right*

determinare *to determine*

detersivo (m.) *detergent*

  detersivo per il bucato *laundry detergent*

  detersivo per i piatti *dishwashing detergent*

di *of, from, than*

  di + definite article *some, any*

  Di chi è … ? *Whose … is it?*

  Di chi sono … ? *Whose … are they?*

  Di dov'è? *Where are you from? (sg. fml.)/Where is he/she from?*

  Di dove sei? *Where are you from? (infml.)*

di legno *wooden*

di lei *her*

di lui *his*

di mattina *in the morning, from 4 to 11 a.m.*

di notte *at night, from midnight to 3 a.m*

di pomeriggio *in the afternoon, from 1 to 5 p.m.*

di sera *in the evening, from 6 to 11 p.m.*

di solito *usually*

È di … *It belongs to …*

È ora di … *It's time to …*

meno … di *less … than*

più … di *more/-er … than*

Sono di … *I'm from …*

dicembre (m.) *December*

diciannove *nineteen*

diciassette *seventeen*

diciotto *eighteen*

dieci *ten*

dietro *behind* (adv.)

differenza (f.) *difference*

difficile *difficult*

dimagrire *to lose weight*

dimenticare

  dimenticare di … *to forget, to forget to … (do something)*

diploma (m.) *diploma*

dire *to say, to tell*

  Non c'è di che. *Don't mention it.*

direttore (m.) *director*

diritto *straight*

  sempre diritto *straight ahead*

discorso (m.) *speech, talk*

discoteca (f.) *disco, club*

disoccupato/a (m./f.) *unemployed*

dispiacere *to displease, to upset*

  Mi dispiace. *I'm sorry.*

disponibile *available*

disponibilità (f.) *availability*

distruggere *to destroy*

dito (m.) *finger*

  dita (f. pl.) *fingers*

divano (m.) *sofa, couch*

diventare *to become*

diverso *different*

divertente *amusing, funny*

divertirsi *to have fun, to enjoy oneself*

divorziarsi *to get a divorce*

divorziarsi da … *to divorce … (someone)*
doccia (f.) *shower*
  fare la doccia *to take a shower*
docciaschiuma (m.) *bath gel*
documentario (m.) *documentary*
documento (m.) *document, file*
  allegare un documento *to attach a file*
  aprire un documento *to open a file*
  chiudere un documento *to close a file*
  inviare un documento *to send a file*
  salvare un documento *to save a file*
dodici *twelve*
dolce *sweet*
dolce (m.) *dessert*
dollaro (m.) *dollar*
  un milione di dollari *a million dollars*
dolore (m.) *pain*
  avere un dolore a … *to have a pain in …*
domanda (f.) *question*
  fare una domanda *to ask a question*
domani *tomorrow*
domenica (f.) *Sunday*
donna (f.) *woman*
  donna d'affari *businesswoman*
  donna poliziotto *police woman*
dopo *after*
  A dopo. *See you later.*
doppio *double*
  camera (f.) **doppia** *double room (two twin-size beds)*
dormire *to sleep*
  farsi una bella dormita *to take a nice long nap*
dottore/essa (m./f.) *doctor*
dove *where*
  Di dov'è? *Where are you from?* (sg. fml.)/*Where is he/she from?*
  Di dove sei? *Where are you from?* (infml.)
  Dov'è … ? *Where is … ?*
  Dove sono … ? *Where are … ?*
dovere *must, to have to*
dovuto *due*
  dovuto a … *due to …*
dramma (m.) *drama*
dubitare *to doubt*
due *two*
  due ore e mezzo *two and a half hours*
  duemila *two thousand*
  Sono le due. *It's two (o'clock).*

dunque *therefore*
durare *to last*
dvd (m.) *DVD player*

E

e/ed (before a vowel) *and*
  … e Lei? *… and you?* (sg. fml.)
  … e tu? *… and you?* (infml.)
eccellente *excellent*
eccetto *except*
eccezionale *exceptional*
ecco *here*
  Ecco … *Here is …*
economia (f.) *economics*
edificio (m.) *building*
elegante *elegant*
elegantemente *elegantly*
elementare *elementary*
  la prima elementare *the first grade at elementary school*
elettricista (m.) *electrician*
elettrico *electric*
  cucina (f.) **elettrica** *electric stove*
elettrocardiogramma (m.) *electrocardiogram*
elettronica (f.) *electronics*
  negozio (m.) **di elettronica** *electronics store*
eliminare *to delete*
email (f.)/**mail (inv.)** *e-mail*
  mandare un'email/una mail *to send an e-mail*
enorme *enormous*
entrambi/e *both (of them)*
entrare *to come in*
entusiasticamente *enthusiastically*
erba (f.) *grass*
erboristeria (f.) *herbalist's shop*
ereditare *to inherit*
esagerare *to exaggerate, to go too far*
esagerato *exaggerated*
esame (m.) *exam*
escursione (f.) *hike, excursion*
  fare un'escursione *to go hiking*
esistere *to exist*
esperienza (f.) *experience*
esperto/a (m./f.) *expert*
essere *to be*
  C'è … *There is …*
  C'è il sole. *It's sunny.*

C'è nebbia. *It's foggy.*
C'è un temporale. *It's stormy.*
C'è vento. *It's windy.*
Ci sono … *There are …*
Di chi è … ? *Whose … is it ?*
Di chi sono … ? *Whose … are they?*
È di … *It belongs to …*
È l'una di notte. *It's 1:00 a.m.*
È nuvoloso. *It's cloudy.*
È ora di … *It's time to …*
essere bocciato *to fail*
essere d'accordo *to agree*
essere impauriti *to be afraid of*
essere in anticipo *to be early*
essere in cerca di … *to be looking for …*
essere in orario *to be on time*
essere in ritardo *to be late*
essere in sovrappeso *to be overweight*
essere nel bisogno *to need*
essere puntuale *to be on time*
essere promosso *to pass*
Sono di … *I'm from …*
estate (f.) *summer*
 d'estate *in the summer*
estero *foreign*
 all'estero *abroad*
 viaggiare all'estero *to travel abroad*
età (f./f/ pl.) *age*
euro (m. sg./pl.) *euro*
Europa (f.) *Europe*
europeo *European*
extra (inv.) *extra*

F

fa *ago*
 due giorni fa *two days ago*
 un mese fa *a month ago*
fabbrica (f.) *factory*
faccia (f.) *face*
facile *easy*
falegname (m.) *carpenter*
falso *false*
fame (f.) *hunger*
 avere fame *to be hungry*
famiglia (f.) *family*
 famiglia numerosa *large family*
famoso *famous*
fantastico (m.)/fantastici (m. pl.) *fantastic*

fare *to do, to make, to be*
 Che tempo fa? *What's the weather like?*
 Fa bello. *It's beautiful. (weather)*
 Fa brutto *It's bad. (weather)*
 Fa caldo. *It's hot.*
 Fa freddo. *It's cold.*
 Fammi vedere. *Let me see.*
 fare amicizia *to make friends*
 fare attenzione *to pay attention*
 fare bella figura *to make a good impression*
 fare colazione *to have breakfast*
 fare giardinaggio *to do gardening*
 fare ginnastica *to exercise*
 fare ginnastica aerobica *to do aerobics*
 fare il bagno *to take a bath*
 fare il bucato *to do the laundry*
 fare il campeggio *to go camping*
 fare il footing *to jog*
 fare il trasloco *to move (to a new house)*
 fare la doccia *to take a shower*
 fare il bucato *to do the laundry*
 fare la spesa/le spese *to go shopping, to do grocery shopping*
 fare le valige *to pack (a suitcase)*
 fare pari *to draw, to tie*
 fare paura *to be scary*
 fare rumore *to make noise*
 fare spese *to shop*
 fare sport *to practice sports*
 fare testa o croce *to flip a coin*
 fare un'escursione *to go hiking*
 fare un giro *to go for a walk/ride*
 fare un giro a piedi *to go for a walk*
 fare un pisolino *to take a nap*
 fare un viaggio *to take a trip*
 fare una domanda *to ask a question*
 fare una foto/fotografia *to take a picture*
 fare una gita *to take a trip*
 fare una passeggiata *to take a walk*
 fare una pausa *to take a break*
 fare una vacanza *to go on a vacation*
 fare vedere *to show*
farmacia (f.) *drugstore, pharmacy*
farsi *to get, to become*
 farsi la barba *to shave*
 farsi una bella dormita *to take a nice long nap*
 farsi una bella mangiata *to have a nice big meal*

fatto (m.) *fact*
fattore (m.) *factor*
favola (f.) *fairy tale*
favore (m.) *favor*
  Per favore. *Please.*
fax (m. sg./pl.) *fax machine*
febbraio (m.) *February*
febbre (f.) *fever*
  avere la febbre *to have a fever*
fegato (m.) *liver*
felice *happy*
femmina (f.) *female*
ferie (f. pl.) *vacation*
  in ferie *on vacation*
fermarsi *to stop*
ferro (m.) *iron (metal)*
  ferro da stiro *iron (appliance)*
festa (f.) *party, holiday*
  Buone feste. *Happy holidays.*
  dare una festa *to have a party*
fettina (f.) *thin slice*
fettuccine (f. pl.) *fettuccine*
fiaba (f.) *fairy tale*
fianco (m.) *hip*
fidanzato *engaged*
fidanzato/a (m./f.) *fiancé(e)*
fiera (f.) *trade fair*
figlia (f.) *daughter*
  figlia di mia moglie (di mio
    marito) *stepdaughter*
figlio (m.) *son*
  figlio di mia moglie (di mio marito) *stepson*
figura (f.) *figure, illustration*
  fare bella figura *to make a good impression*
file (m.) *file*
  allegare un file *to attach a file*
  aprire un file *to open a file*
  chiudere un file *to close a file*
  inviare un file *to send a file*
film (m. sg./pl.) *movie, film*
  film d'azione *action movies*
finalista (m./f.) *finalist*
finalmente *finally*
finché *until*
fine settimana (m. sg./pl.) *weekend*
finestra (f.) *window*
finire *to finish*
  finire di ... *to finish ... ing*

per finire *to end/finish*
fino (a) *up to, until, till*
  fino a tardi *until late*
  fino in fondo *until the end*
fiore (m.) *flower*
Firenze (f.) *Florence*
fisso *fixed, permanent*
  lavoro (m.) fisso *steady job*
fiume (m.) *river*
follia (f.) *folly*
fondo *bottom*
  di fondo *long distance*
  fino in fondo *until the end*
  in fondo a ... *the bottom/end of ...*
  sci (m.) di fondo *cross-country skiing*
footing (m.) *jogging*
  fare il footing *to jog*
foresta (f.) *forest*
forma (f.) *form, shape*
  in ottima forma *in great shape*
formaggio (m.) *cheese*
formazione (f.) *training, education*
forno (m.) *oven*
  forno a microonde *microwave oven*
  maiale (m.) al forno *roast pork*
forse *maybe, perhaps*
forte (adjective) *strong*
forte (adverb) *loudly*
fortuna (f.) *luck*
  Buona fortuna. *Good luck.*
fortunato *lucky*
foto (f. sg./pl.) *photograph*
  fare una foto *to take a picture*
fotografia (f.) *photograph, photography*
  fare una fotografia *to take a picture*
foulard (m.) *scarf (square)*
fra *between, among, in*
  fra ... e ... *between ... and ...*
  fra mezz'ora *in half an hour*
  fra tre quarti d'ora *in forty-five minutes*
fragola (f.) *strawberry*
francamente *frankly*
francese *French*
fratello (m.) *brother*
frattempo *meantime*
  nel frattempo *in the meantime*
freddo (m.) *cold*
  avere freddo *to be cold*

Glossary   271

Fa freddo. *It's cold.*
frequentare *to attend*
fresco *fresh*
fretta (f.) *hurry*
  avere fretta *to be in a hurry*
  in fretta *in a hurry, quickly*
frigorifero (m.) (frigo) *refrigerator*
fronte (f.) *forehead*
  di fronte *opposite*
  di fronte a …   *facing … , in front of …*
frullatore (m.) *blender*
frutta (f.) *fruit*
  frutta fresca *fresh fruit*
fucsia (inv.) *fuchsia*
fulmine (m.) *lightning*
fungo (m.) *mushroom*
fuori *outside*
  fuori città *out of town*
futbol (m.) *football*
  futbol americano *American football*

G

gabinetto *toilet*
galleria (f.) *gallery*
gamba (f.) *leg*
  in gamba *talented* (colloquial)
gamberetto (m.) *shrimp*
gambero (m.) *shrimp, crawfish*
gara (f.) *event*
garage (m. sg./pl.) *garage*
gas (m. sg./pl.) *gas*
  cucina (f.) a gas *gas stove*
gelato (m.) *ice cream*
generale *general*
genetico (m.)/genetici (m. pl.) *genetic*
genitore (m.)/genitrice (f.)/genitori (pl.) *parent*
gennaio (m.) *January*
gente (f.) *people*
gentile *kind*
Germania (f.) *Germany*
ghiaccio (m.) *ice*
hockey (m.) su ghiaccio *ice hockey*
già *already*
giacca (f.) *jacket*
giaccone (m.) *coat (above the knees)*
giallo *yellow*
giardinaggio (m.) *gardening*
fare giardinaggio *to do gardening*

giardino (m.) *garden*
ginnastica (f.) *gymnastics*
  fare ginnastica *to exercise*
  fare ginnastica aerobica *to do aerobics*
  scarpe (f. pl.) da ginnastica *sneakers*
ginocchio (m.) *knee*
  ginocchia (f. pl.)/ginocchi (m. pl.) *knees*
giocare *to play*
  giocare a carte *to play cards*
  giocare a tennis *to play tennis*
giocatore/trice (m./f.) *player*
giornale (m.) *newspaper*
giornale radio (m.) *news (on the radio)*
giornalista (m./f.) *journalist*
giornata (f.) *day*
  Buona giornata. *Have a good day.*
  giornata piena *full/busy day*
giorno (m.) *day*
  Buon giorno. *Good morning.*
  due giorni fa *two days ago*
  fra qualche giorno *in a few days*
  pochi giorni *a few days*
  tutti i giorni *every day*
giovane *young*
giovedì (m. sg./pl.) *Thursday*
girare *to turn*
giro (m.) *circle, tour*
  fare un giro *to go for a walk/ride*
  fare un giro a piedi *to go for a walk*
  in giro per la casa *around the home*
  in giro per la città *around town*
gita (f.) *day trip, short trip*
  fare una gita *to take a trip*
giugno (m.) *June*
giusto (adjective) *right, correct*
giusto (adverb) *exactly, correctly*
gli *the* (m. pl.) *(in front of s + consonant, z, ps, gn, in front of vowels); to him, to it, to them* (indirect object pronoun)
gnomo (m.) *gnome*
gomito (m.) *elbow*
gonna (f.) *skirt*
grado (m.) *degree*
grande *big*
  grande magazzino (m.) *department store*
grandinare *to hail*
  Grandina. *It's hailing.*
grasso (adjective) *fat*

grasso (m.) *fat*
grattugiare *to grate*
grave *serious*
Grazie. *Thank you.*
  Grazie mille. *Thanks a lot.*
  Molto bene, grazie. *Very well, thanks.*
Grecia (f.) *Greece*
greco *Greek*
grigio *gray*
griglia (f.) *grill*
  pesce (m.) alla griglia *grilled fish*
grosso *large, thick*
gruppo (m.) *group, band (music)*
  gruppi (pl.) inglesi *British bands*
guadagnare *to earn*
guancia (f.) *cheek*
guanti (m. pl.) *gloves*
guardare *to watch, to look at*
  guardare la tivù/tele/televisione *to watch television*
  guardare lo sport in/alla televisione *to watch sports on TV*
guida (f.) *guide*
guidare *to drive*

H

hobby (m./m. pl) *hobby*
hockey (m.) *hockey*
  hockey su ghiaccio *ice hockey*
hotel (m. sg./pl.) *hotel*

I

i *the* (m. pl.) (in front of consonants)
idea (f.) *idea*
  nessuna idea *no idea*
idraulico/a (m./f.) *plumber*
ieri *yesterday*
  ieri sera *last night*
igienico *hygienic*
  carta (f.) igienica *toilet paper*
il *the* (m. sg.) (in front of a consonant)
immaginare *to imagine*
imparare *to learn*
impaurire *to scare*
  essere impauriti da *to be afraid of*
impegnato *busy*
impegno (m.) *obligation, engagement*
imperfetto (m.) *imperfect*

impiegato/a (m./f.) *employee, clerk*
importante *important*
imprenditore (m.) *businessman*
imprenditrice (f.) *businesswoman*
improvvisamente *suddenly*
in *in, at, to, on, by*
  in centro *downtown, to/in the city*
  in gamba *talented* (colloquial)
  in giro per la casa *around the home*
  in giro per la città *around town*
  in vacanza *on vacation*
incontrare *to meet (a person casually)*
incontrarsi *to meet each other*
incrocio (m.) *intersection*
indagine (f.) *study, research*
indeciso *undecided*
indicare *to show, to indicate*
indirizzo (m.) *address*
indossare *to wear*
infarto (m.) *heart attack*
infatti *in fact*
infermiere/a (m./f.) *nurse*
influenza (f.) *influence*
informatica (f.) *computer science*
informatico (adjective) *computer*
ingegnere (m.) *engineer*
inglese *English*
  gruppi (m. pl.) inglesi *British bands (music)*
inglese (m.) *English (language)*
ingrassare *to gain weight*
ingrediente (m.) *ingredient*
ingresso (m.) *hall*
innamorato *in love*
inoltrare *to forward*
inoltre *besides, moreover*
insalata (f.) *salad*
  insalata mista *mixed salad*
insegnante (m./f.) *teacher*
insegnare *to teach*
insieme *together*
  insieme a te *(together) with you*
insistere *to insist*
insonnolito *sleepy*
intellettivo *intellectual*
  quoziente (m.) intellettivo *intelligence quotient (IQ)*
intelligente *intelligent*
interessante *interesting*

interessantissimo *very interesting*
interessare *to interest*
interesse (m.) *interest*
internet (m.) *internet*
intero *whole, entire*
interrompere *to interrupt*
intervallo (m.) *intermission*
intervista (f.) *interview*
  interviste (pl.) alla televisione *talk show*
intestino (m.) *intestine*
intorno *around*
  intorno a mezzanotte *around midnight*
  intorno al mondo *around the world*
invecchiare *to grow old*
invece *instead*
invernale (adjective) *winter*
inverno (m.) *winter*
  d'inverno *in winter*
inviare *to send*
  inviare un file/documento *to send a file/ document*
invitare *to invite*
io *I*
iscrivere *to enroll*
isola (f.) *island*
istituto (m.) *institute*
  istituto tecnico *professional school*
istruzione (f.) *education*
Italia (f.) *Italy*
italiano *Italian*

L

l' *the* (m. sg./f. sg.) (in front of a vowel)
la *the* (f. sg.) (in front of a consonant); *her, it* (direct object pronoun)
La *you* (sg. fml.) (direct object pronoun)
lago (m.) *lake*
  al lago *at the lake*
lampada (f.) *lamp*
lampeggiare *to flash*
lampione (m.) *lamp post*
lampo (m.) *lightning*
lana (f.) *wool*
lasagne (f. pl.) *lasagna*
lasciare *to leave, to let*
latinoamericano *Latin American*
latte (m.) *milk*
lattina (f.) *can*

lattuga (f.) *lettuce*
laurea (f.) *degree, university degree*
laurearsi *to graduate*
lavabiancheria (f.) *washing machine*
lavabo (m.) *sink (wash basin)*
lavanderia (f.) *laundry*
lavandino (m.) *sink (kitchen)*
lavapiatti (f.) *dishwasher*
lavare *to wash*
lavare i piatti *to do the dishes*
lavarsi *to wash oneself*
lavastoviglie (f.) *dishwasher*
lavatrice (f.) *washing machine*
lavorare *to work*
lavoro (m.) *job, work*
  Che lavoro fai? *What do you do?*
  colloquio (m.) di lavoro *job interview*
  lavoro fisso *steady job*
  lavoro part-time *part-time job*
  lavoro temporaneo *summer job*
  per lavoro *on business*
le *the* (f. pl.) (in front of consonants and vowels); *them* (f.) (direct object pronoun); *to her, to it* (indirect object pronoun)
Le *to you* (sg. fml.) (indirect object pronoun)
leggere *to read*
leggero *light*
legno (m.) *wood*
di legno *wooden*
lei *she* (subject pronoun); *her, it* (direct object, disjunctive pronoun)
  a lei *to her, to it* (indirect object, disjunctive pronoun)
Lei *you* (sg. fml.) (subject pronoun); *you* (sg. fml.) (direct object, disjunctive pronoun)
  a Lei *to you* (sg. fml.) (indirect object, disjunctive pronoun)
lentamente *slowly*
lenzuolo (m.) *bed sheet*
  lenzuola (f. pl.) *bed sheets*
lettera (f.) *letter*
letteratura (f.) *literature*
letto (m.) *bed*
  camera (f.) da letto *bedroom*
  letto matrimoniale *double bed*
  stanza (f.) da letto *bedroom*
lettore (m.) *reader, player*
  lettore cd *CD-ROM drive*

lettore cd-rom *CD-ROM drive*
lettore di cd *CD player*
lezione (f.) *lesson*
li *them* (m.) (direct object pronoun)
lì *there*
 lì vicino *near there*
libero *free*
 tempo (m.) libero *free time*
libreria (f.) *bookstore, bookcase (in a house or office)*
libro (m.) *book*
 libro (di testo) *textbook*
liceo (m.) *high school*
lingua (f.) *language, tongue*
 lingua straniera *foreign language*
lino (m.) *linen*
 di lino *made out of linen*
lista (f.) *list*
 lista dei vini *wine list*
litro (m.) *liter*
livello (m.) *level*
lo *the* (m. sg.) (in front of s + consonant, z, ps, gn); *him, it* (direct object pronoun)
 Lo so. *I know.*
 Non lo so. *I don't know.*
lontano (adjective) *distant*
lontano (adverb) *far*
loro *they* (subject pronoun); *them* (direct object, disjunctive pronoun)
 a loro *to them* (indirect object, disjunctive pronoun)
Loro *you* (pl. fml.) (subject pronoun)
loro (inv.) *their*
lotteria (f.) *lottery*
luglio (m.) *July*
lui *he* (subject pronoun); *him, it* (direct object, disjunctive pronoun)
 a lui *to him, to it* (indirect object, disjunctive pronoun)
luna (f.) *moon*
lunedì (m. sg./pl.) *Monday*
 il lunedì *on Mondays*
lungo (adjective) *long*
lungo (preposition) *along*
luogo (m.) *place*
lupo (m.) *wolf*
 In bocca al lupo! *Break a leg! (lit. In the mouth of the wolf!)*

Crepi il lupo. *Thank you. (In response to In bocca al lupo! Lit. May the wolf die.)*

M

ma *but*
 Ma come! *How's it possible!/How can this be!*
macchina (f.) *car, machine*
 in macchina *by car*
 macchina del caffè *espresso machine*
 macchina fotografica *camera*
macelleria (f.) *butcher shop*
madre (f.) *mother*
 marito (m.) di mia madre *stepfather*
maestro/a (m./f.) *teacher (nursery school and elementary school)*
magari *I wish, perhaps*
magazzino (m.) *warehouse*
 grande magazzino *department store*
maggio (m.) *May*
maggiore *older, elder*
maglietta (f.) *T-shirt*
maglioncino (m.) *light sweater*
maglione (m.) *sweater*
Magro *thin*
mai *ever, never (in negative sentences)*
 Mai ! *Never!*
 mai più *never again*
maiale (m.) *pork*
 braciola (f.) di maiale *pork chop*
 maiale al forno *roast pork*
malato *sick*
malattia (f.) *disease*
male *badly*
 avere male a ... *to have a pain in ...*
 Fa male. *It hurts.*
mamma (f.) *mom*
manca (f.) *left (hand)*
 Manca un quarto alle quattro. *It's 3:45.*
mancia (f.) *tip*
mancino *left-handed*
mandare *to send*
 mandare un'email *to send an e-mail*
mangiare *to eat*
 farsi una bella mangiata *to have a nice big meal*
mano (f.)/mani (f. pl.) *hand*
manzo (m.) *beef*
mappa (f.) *map*

maratona (f.) *marathon*
marciapiede (m.) *sidewalk*
mare (m.) *sea, seaside*
  al mare *at the beach*
marito (m.) *husband*
  figlia (f.) di mia moglie (di mio
    marito) *stepdaughter*
  figlio (m.) di mia moglie (di mio
    marito) *stepson*
  marito di mia madre *stepfather*
marrone *brown*
martedì (m. sg./pl.) *Tuesday*
marzo (m.) *March*
maschio (m.) *male*
matematica (f.) *math*
materia (f.) *subject*
matrimoniale *matrimonial*
  camera (f.) matrimoniale *double room (one
    queen-size bed)*
  letto (m.) matrimoniale *double bed*
matrimonio (m.) *wedding*
mattina (f.) *morning*
  di mattina *in the morning, from 4 to 11 a.m.*
  Sono le undici e un quarto di mattina.
    It's 11:15 a.m.
  tutte le mattine *every morning*
maturità (f.) *high school degree*
me *me* (direct object, disjunctive pronoun)
  a me *to me* (indirect object, disjunctive pronoun)
meccanico (m.)/meccanici (m. pl.) *mechanic*
media (f.) *average*
medicina (f.) *medicine*
medico (m.) *medical doctor*
meglio (adverb) *better, the best*
  Va meglio. *It's better.*
meglio (inv.) *better*
mela (f.) *apple*
melanzana (f.) *eggplant*
melone (m.) *melon*
memoria (f.) *memory*
meno *less*
  a meno che ... non *unless ...*
  meno ... di/che *less ... than*
  Sono le quattro meno un quarto. *It's 3:45.*
mento (m.) *chin*
mentre *while*
menù (m.) *menu*
meraviglioso *wonderful, marvelous*

mercato (m.) *market*
mercoledì (m. sg./pl.) *Wednesday*
mescolare *to mix*
mese (m.) *month*
  mese prossimo *next month*
  un mese fa *a month ago*
messaggio (m.) *message*
  messaggio immediato *instant message*
messinscena (f.) *production (theater)*
mettersi *to put on*
  Si mette ... *He/She wears/puts on ...*
metrò (m. in Milan/f. in Rome) *subway, metro*
metro (m.) *meter*
mettere *to put*
  mettere in ordine *to put things away*
  metterci *to take (time)*
mezzanotte (f.) *midnight*
  È mezzanotte. *It's midnight.*
  intorno a mezzanotte *around midnight*
mezzo *half, half hour*
  alle sette e mezza *at seven thirty (7:30)*
  due ore e mezzo *two and a half hours*
  fra mezz'ora *in half an hour*
  mezze stagioni *half seasons (spring and fall)*
mezzo (m.) *means*
  mezzo di trasporto *means of transportation*
mezzogiorno (m.) *noon*
  È mezzogiorno. *It's noon.*
mi *me* (direct object pronoun); *to me* (indirect
  object pronoun)
  Mi chiamo ... *My name is ...*
  Mi dispiace. *I'm sorry.*
  Mi piace/piacciono ... (sg./pl.) *I like ...*
microonda (f.) *microwave*
  forno (m.) a microonde *microwave oven*
miele (m.) *honey*
migliore (adjective) *better, the best*
Milano (f.) *Milan*
miliardo (m.)/miliardi (m. pl.) *billion*
milione (m.)/milioni (m. pl.) *million*
  un milione di dollari *a million dollars*
mille (m.)/mila (m. pl.) *thousand*
  duemila *two thousand*
  Grazie mille. *Thanks a lot.*
  mille cose (f. pl.) *tons of things,
    a thousand things*
minerale *mineral*
  acqua (f.) minerale *mineral water*

acqua minerale naturale *still mineral water*
acqua minerale frizzante *sparkling*
  mineral water
minestra (f.) *soup*
minore *younger*
minuto (m.) *minute*
  tra cinque minuti *in five minutes*
mio *my*
  figlia (f.) di mia moglie (di mio
    marito) *stepdaughter*
  figlio (m.) di mia moglie (di mio
    marito) *stepson*
  marito (m.) di mia madre *stepfather*
  (la mia) ragazza (f.) *(my) girlfriend*
  (il mio) ragazzo (m.) *(my) boyfriend*
  moglie (f.) di mio padre *stepmother*
  Piacere mio. *Pleased to meet you, too.*
misto *mixed*
  affettati (m. pl.) misti *mixed cold cuts*
  insalata (f.) mista *mixed salad*
misura (f.) *size (shirts)*
misurare *to measure*
mobili (m. pl.) *furniture*
moda (f.) *fashion*
  sfilata (f.) di moda *fashion show*
modello/a (m./f.) *model (fashion)*
modem (m.) *modem*
moderno *modern*
  arte moderna *modern art*
modo (m.) *way, manner*
  il modo in cui ... *the way in which ...*
moglie (f.) *wife*
molto (adjective) *much, many, a lot of*
  molto tempo *long time*
molto (adverb) *very*
  Molto bene, grazie. *Very well, thanks.*
  Molto piacere! *Very pleased to meet you!*
molto/a (m./f.) (noun) *much, many, a lot*
momento (m.) *moment*
  in questo momento *right now*
  Un momento. *Wait a second.*
mondo (m.) *world*
  del mondo *in the world*
  intorno al mondo *around the world*
monitor (m.) *monitor, screen*
montagna (f.) *mountain*
  camminare in montagna *to go hiking*
  in montagna *to the mountains*

monumento (m.) *monument*
moquette (f.) *carpet (wall-to-wall)*
morire *to die*
moschea (f.) *mosque*
mostra (f.) *exhibition*
mostrare *to show*
motivo (m.) *reason*
  il motivo per cui ... *the reason why ...*
moto (f. sg./pl.) *motorbike*
motocicletta (f.) *motorbike*
mouse (m.) (computer) *mouse*
municipio (m.) *city hall, municipal building*
muovere *to move*
muratore/trice (m./f.) *construction worker*
muro (m.) *wall*
muscolo (m.) *muscle*
museo (m.) *museum*
musica (f.) *music*
  musica classica *classical music*
  musica pop *pop music*
musicista (m./f.) *musician*
mutande (f. pl.) *boxers*
mutandine (f. pl.) *underpants (women's)*

N

Napoli (f.) *Naples*
nascere *to be born*
nascita (f.) *birth*
naso (m.) *nose*
natale *native*
  città (f.) natale *hometown*
Natale (m.) *Christmas*
  Buon Natale. *Merry Christmas.*
natura (f.) *nature*
naturale *natural*
  acqua (f.) minerale naturale *still mineral water*
ne *about it/them, of it/them*
  Ce ne sono tre. *There are three of them.*
neanche *not even*
nebbia (f.) *fog*
  C'è nebbia. *It's foggy.*
necessario *necessary*
negozio (m.) *store*
  negozio di abbigliamento *clothing store*
  negozio di alimentari *grocery store*
  negozio di elettronica *electronics store*
  negozio di scarpe *shoe store*
nemmeno *not even*

nero *black*

nervoso *nervous*

nessuno *no*

  nessuna idea *no idea*

nessuno/a (m./f.) *none, nobody*

neve (f.) *snow*

nevicare *to snow*

  Nevica. *It's snowing.*

niente *nothing*

  niente di buono da mangiare *nothing good to eat*

nipote (m./f.) *nephew, niece, grandson, granddaughter*

no *no*

nocivo *harmful*

noi *we* (subject pronoun); *us* (direct object, disjunctive pronoun)

  a noi *to us* (indirect object, disjunctive pronoun)

noioso *boring*

nome (m.) *name*

non *not*

  Non c'è di che. *Don't mention it.*

  Non lo so. *I don't know.*

nonna (f.) *grandmother*

nonno (m.) *grandfather*

nono *ninth*

normale *normal*

normalmente *normally*

norvegese (m./f.) *Norwegian*

nostro *our*

notare *to notice*

notizie (f. pl.) *news*

notte (f.) *night*

  Buona notte. *Good night.*

  di notte *at night, from midnight to 3 a.m.*

  È l'una di notte. *It's 1:00 a.m.*

novanta *ninety*

nove *nine*

novembre (m.) *November*

nubile (f.) *single (woman)*

nulla *nothing*

numero (m.) *number, size (shoes)*

numeroso *numerous, large (family)*

  famiglia (f.) numerosa *large family*

nuotare *to swim*

nuoto (m.) *swimming*

nuovo *new*

  di nuovo *again*

nuvola (f.) *cloud*

nuvoloso *cloudy*

  È nuvoloso. *It's cloudy.*

O

O *or*

occhiali (m. pl.) *eyeglasses*

  occhiali da sole *sunglasses*

occhio (m.) *eye*

occupato *busy*

oceano (m.) *ocean*

offrire *to offer*

oggi *today*

ogni *each, every*

  in ogni caso *in any event*

  ogni volta *every time*

ognuno/a (m./f.) *everyone*

olio (m.) *oil*

oliva (f.) *olive*

ombrello (m.) *umbrella*

omeopatia (f.) *homeopathy*

omeopatico (m.)/omeopatici (m. pl.) *homeopathic*

opera (f.) *work, opera*

  opere d'arte *works of art*

operaio/a (m./f.) *worker*

opuscolo (m.) *brochure*

ora (f.) *hour*

  Che ora è?/Che ore sono? *What time is it?*

  due ore e mezzo *two and a half hours*

  È ora di … *It's time to …*

  fra mezz'ora *in half an hour*

orario (m.) *time*

  essere in orario *to be on time*

  orario continuato *open all day*

  orario ridotto *shorter working hours*

ordinare *to order*

ordine (m.) *order*

  mettere in ordine *to put things away*

orecchini (m. pl.) *earrings*

orecchio (m.) *ear*

  orecchi (m. pl.)/orecchie (f. pl.) *ears*

organizzare *to organize*

  viaggio (m.) organizzato *guided tour*

ormai *by now, almost*

orologio (m.) *watch*

orto (m.) *vegetable garden, orchard*

ospedale (m.) *hospital*

ospite (m./f.) *guest (male and female)*
osso (m.) *bone*
  ossa (f. pl.) *bones*
ossobuco (m.) *osso buco*
ostello (m.) *youth hostel*
ottanta *eighty*
ottavo *eighth*
ottimo *excellent*
  in ottima forma *in great shape*
otto *eight*
ottobre (m.) *October*
ovvio *obvious*

P

padre (m.) *father*
  moglie (f.) di mio padre *stepmother*
paese (m.) *town (small), village*
paesino (m.) *village (small)*
pagare *to pay*
  pagare il conto (dell'hotel) *to check out*
pagina (f.) *page*
  pagina web *webpage*
paio (m.) *pair*
  paio di scarpe *pair of shoes*
palazzina (f.) *(4-5 story) apartment building*
palazzo (m.) *palace, mansion, apartment building*
palestra (f.) *gym(nasium), health club*
palla (f.) *ball*
  palla a volo *volleyball*
pallacanestro (f.) *basketball*
pallone (m.) *ball*
pancetta (f.) *bacon*
pancia (f.) *stomach (below the waist), belly*
pane (m.) *bread*
panino (m.) *sandwich*
panorama (m.) *panorama*
pantaloni (m. pl.) *pants*
papà (m.) *dad*
parcheggiare *to park*
parco (m.) *park*
  parco giochi *playground*
parecchio (adjective) *a lot of, several*
parecchio/a (m./f.) (noun) *a lot, several*
parente (m./f.) *relative*
parete (f.) *wall*
pari (inv.) *equal, same*
  fare pari *to draw, to tie*

Parigi (f.) *Paris*
parlare *to speak*
  parlare cinese *to speak Chinese*
parmigiano (m.) *Parmesan cheese*
parolaccia (f.) *bad word*
parte (f.) *part*
partecipare *to participate*
partire *to leave*
  a partire da ... *starting from ...*
partita (f.) *game*
part-time *part-time*
  lavoro (m.) part-time *part-time job*
passaporto (m.) *passport*
passare *to pass*
passato (m.) *past (tense)*
  passato prossimo *present perfect (grammar)*
passeggiata (f.) *walk*
  Buona passeggiata. *Enjoy your walk./Have a good walk.*
  fare una passeggiata *to take a walk*
passione (f.) *passion*
  passione per ... *passion for ...*
pasta (f.) *pasta*
pasticceria (f.) *bakery*
patata (f.) *potato*
patto (m.) *condition*
  a patto che ... *provided that ...*
paura (f.) *fear*
  avere paura (di) *to be afraid (of)*
  fare paura *to be scary*
pausa (f.) *break*
  fare una pausa *to take a break*
pavimento (m.) *floor (inside a house or apartment)*
paziente (m./f.) *patient*
pazienza (f.) *patience*
peccato (m.) *sin*
  Peccato! *Too bad!*
pediatra (m./f.) *pediatrician*
pelle (f.) *skin, leather*
  di pelle *made out of leather*
penne (f. pl.) *penne (pasta)*
pensare *to think*
  pensare a ... *to think about ... (something/somebody)*
  pensare di ... *to think about ... (doing somehing)*
pensionato/a (m./f.) *retired*

pentirsi *to repent, to regret*
pentola (f.) *pan, pot*
pepe (m.) *pepper (spice)*
peperone (m.) *pepper (vegetable)*
per *for, through, by*
  detersivo (m.) per i piatti *dishwashing detergent*
  detersivo (m.) per il bucato *laundry detergent*
  in giro per la casa *around the house*
  in giro per la città *around town*
  passione per … *passion for …*
  per caso *by any chance*
  per contorno *as a side dish*
  Per favore. *Please.*
  per lavoro *on business*
  per le sette *by seven (o'clock)*
  pronto per … *ready to …*
pera (f.) *pear*
perché *why, because*
perdere *to lose*
  perdere tempo *to waste time*
perfetto *perfect*
pericoloso *dangerous*
periferia (f.) *suburbs*
periferico *suburban*
periodo (m.) *period*
  in questo periodo *in this period, currently*
permettere *to allow*
permettersi *to allow, to afford*
però *however, but*
persona (f.) *person*
  di persona *in person*
  persona sportiva *athletic person*
  persone (pl.) *people*
pesca (f.) *peach*
pesce (m.) *fish*
  pesce alla griglia *grilled fish*
petto (m.) *chest*
pezzo (m.) *piece*
piacere *to be pleasing (to someone)*
  Mi piace/piacciono … (sg./pl.) *I like …*
  Piacere. *Pleased to meet you.*
  Piacere mio. *Pleased to meet you, too.*
  Molto piacere! *Very pleased to meet you!*
piacevole *pleasant*
pianeta (m.) *planet*
pianista (m./f.) *pianist*
piano (adjective) *smooth, simple*

piano (adverb) *slowly, softly*
piano (m.) *floor*
  piano terra *ground floor*
  primo piano *first floor (second floor in the U.S.)*
pianoforte (m.) *piano*
  suonare il pianoforte *to play the piano*
pianta (f.) *plant*
piantare *to plant*
pianterreno *ground floor*
piantina (f.) *map*
piatto (m.) *plate, dish*
  detersivo (m.) per i piatti *dishwashing detergent*
  lavare i piatti *to do the dishes*
  primo (piatto) *first course*
  secondo (piatto) *main course*
piazza (f.) *square*
piccolo *small*
piede (m.) *foot*
  a piedi *on foot*
  fare un giro a piedi *to go for a walk*
pieno *full*
  a pieno tempo *full-time*
  giornata (f.) piena *full day*
pietra (f.) *stone*
pigiama (m.) *pajamas*
pioggia (f.) *rain*
piovere *to rain*
  Piove. *It's raining.*
pisolino (m.) *nap*
  fare un pisolino *to take a nap*
più *more*
  mai più *never again*
  non … più *no longer, no more*
  più … di/che *more/-er … than*
piuttosto *rather*
plastica (f.) *plastic*
  di plastica *made from plastic*
plurale (m.) *plural*
poco (adjective) *little, few*
  pochi giorni *a few days*
poco/a (m./f.) (noun) *little, few*
  un poco/un po' *a little*
poema (m.) *poem*
poi *then*
  E poi? *And then?*
poker (m. sg./pl.) *poker*

poliziotto (m.) *policeman*
pollice (m.) *thumb*
pollo (m.) *chicken*
polmone (m.) *lung*
polso (m.) *wrist*
pomeriggio (m.) *afternoon*
  Buon pomeriggio. *Good afternoon. (from 1 p.m. to 6 p.m.)*
  di pomeriggio *in the afternoon*
pomodoro (m.) *tomato*
pop (inv.) *pop*
  musica (f.) *pop* *pop music*
porta (f.) *door*
portare *to carry, to take, to wear*
porto (m.) *harbor*
posate (f. pl.) *silverware*
possessivo *possessive*
possibile *possible*
posta (f.) *mail*
  posta elettronica *e-mail*
postale (adjective) *mail*
  ufficio postale *post office*
posto (m.) *place*
potere *can, to be able to*
  Posso … ? *May I … ?/Can I … ?*
pranzo (m.) *lunch*
  sala (f.) da pranzo *dining room*
praticare *to play*
  praticare uno sport *to play a sport*
prato (m.) *meadow*
preferire *to prefer*
Prego. *You're welcome.*
prendere *to take, to have (food and drink)*
  Tu cosa prendi? *What are you having?*
prenotare *to reserve*
prenotazione (f.) *reservation*
preoccupare *to worry*
  Sono preoccupato. *I'm worried.*
preparare *to prepare*
prepararsi *to get ready*
preposizione (f.) *preposition*
presentare *to present, to introduce*
presentazione (f.) *introduction*
presente (adjective) *present*
  congiuntivo (m.) presente *present subjunctive*
pressione (f.) *pressure*
presso *at, with*
presto *soon, early*

A presto. *See you soon.*
prezzo (m.) *price*
prima *sooner, in advance*
  prima che … , prima di … *before …*
  prima di tutto *first of all*
primavera (f.) *spring*
  in primavera *in the spring*
primo *first*
  per primo *as first course*
  primo (piatto) (m.) *first course*
  primo piano *first floor (second floor in the U.S.)*
primogenito/a (m./f.) *first-born*
privato *private*
probabile *likely*
probabilmente *probably*
problema (m.) *problem*
prodotto (m.) *product*
professionale *professional*
professore/essa (m./f.) *professor*
profondamente *deep*
profumo (m.) *perfume*
progettare *to plan*
programma (m.) *program*
proibire *to prohibit*
promettere *to promise*
  promettere di … *to promise to … (do something)*
promuovere *to promote*
  essere promosso *to pass (an exam)*
pronome (m.) *pronoun*
pronto *ready, fast*
  pronto per … *ready to …*
  pronto soccorso (m.) *emergency room*
proposito (m.) *intention*
  a proposito *by the way*
proprio *exactly, just, really*
prossimo *next, close*
  mese (m.) prossimo *next month*
  passato (m.) prossimo *present perfect (grammar)*
  prossima settimana (f.) *next week*
  trapassato (m.) prossimo *past perfect (grammar)*
provare *to try, to try on*
provincia (f.) *province*
psichiatra (m./f.) *psychiatrist*
psicologo (m./f.) *psychologist*

pubblicare *to publish*
pulire *to clean*
pulirsi *to clean oneself*
pulito *clean*
pullman (m.) *tour bus*
puntuale *punctual*
 essere puntuale *to be on time*
purché *provided that*
purtroppo *unfortunately*

Q

quaderno (m.) *notebook*
quadro (m.) *painting, picture*
qualche *a few, some*
 fra qualche giorno *in a few days*
 qualche volta *sometimes*
qualcosa *something, anything*
 qualcosa da bere *something to drink*
 qualcosa di bello da fare *anything
 interesting/cool to do*
qualcuno *someone, anyone*
quale *which*
qualsiasi *any*
qualunque *any*
quando *when*
quanto *how many, how much*
 Da quanto tempo ... ? *How long has it been
 since ... ?*
 Quanti anni hai? *How old are you?*
 Quanto costa? *How much does it cost?*
 tanto ... quanto *as much/many ... as*
quaranta *forty*
 Sono le tre e quarantacinque. *It's 3:45.*
quartiere (m.) *neighborhood*
quarto *fourth*
quarto (m.) *quarter*
 fra tre quarti d'ora *in forty-five minutes*
 Manca un quarto alle quattro. *It's 3:45.*
 Sono le quattro meno un quarto. *It's 3:45.*
 Sono le tre e tre quarti. *It's 3:45.*
 Sono le undici e un quarto di mattina. *It's
 11:15 a.m.*
quasi *almost*
quattordici *fourteen*
quattro *four*
 Manca un quarto alle quattro. *It's 3:45.*
 Sono le quattro. *It's four (o'clock).*
 Sono le quattro meno un quarto. *It's 3:45.*

quello *that*
questo *this*
 in questo momento *right now*
 in questo periodo *in this period, currently*
 questa sera *this evening*
 questa settimana *this week*
qui *here*
 qui vicino *nearby*
quindi *therefore, so*
quindici *fifteen*
 Sono le tre e quindici. *It's 3:15.*
quinto *fifth*
quotidiano *daily*
 vita (f.) quotidiana *everyday life*
quoziente (m.) *quotient*
 quoziente intellettivo *intelligence quotient
 (IQ)*

R

raccogliere *to pick up*
raccontare *to tell*
radersi *to shave*
ragazza (f.) *girl (from 14 to 35 years old)*
 la mia ragazza (f.) *my girlfriend*
ragazzina (f.) *girl (from 11 to 13 years old)*
ragazzino (m.) *boy (from 11 to 13 years old)*
ragazzo (m.) *boy (from 14 to 35 years old)*
 il mio ragazzo *my boyfriend*
raggiungere *to reach*
ragione (f.) *reason*
 avere ragione *to be right*
 la ragione per cui ... *the reason why ...*
ragù (m. sg./pl.) *meat sauce*
raramente *rarely*
rasoio (m.) *razor*
ravioli (m. pl.) *ravioli*
reception (f. sg./pl.) *reception desk*
regalo (m.) *gift*
reggiseno (m.) *bra*
regista (m./f.) *movie director*
registrarsi (all'hotel) *to check in*
regolarmente *regularly*
rene (m.) *kidney*
residenza (f.) *residence*
respirare *to breathe*
restare *to stay*
ricco *rich*
ricercatore/trice (m./f.) *researcher, scientist*

ricetta (f.) *recipe*

ricevere *to receive*

ricordare *to remember*

  ricordarsi di … *to remember to … (do something)*

ridotto *reduced*

  orario (m.) ridotto *shorter working hours*

riecco *here again*

  Rieccoci ! *Here we are again !*

riempirsi *to fill*

  riempirsi di … *to fill up with …*

rilassarsi *to relax*

rimanere *to remain*

rinascimentale (adjective) *Renaissance*

Rinascimento (m.) *Renaissance*

riposo (m.) *rest*

  Buon riposo. *Have a good rest.*

riso (m.) *rice*

rispettivamente *respectively*

rispondere *to reply*

rispondere (a) *to answer*

  rispondere al telefono *to answer the phone*

ristorante (m.) *restaurant*

ritardo (m.) *delay*

  essere in ritardo *to be late*

ritornare *to return, to go back*

riunione (f.) *meeting*

  sala (f.) delle riunioni *meeting room*

riuscire *to manage, to be able*

  riuscire a … *to manage to … , to be able to …*

rivista (f.) *magazine, journal*

roba (f.) *stuff*

  un sacco di roba *a bunch/lot of stuff*

roccia (f.) *rock*

Roma (f.) *Rome*

romantico (m.)/ romantici (m. pl.) *romantic*

romanzo (m.) *novel*

  romanzi (m. pl.) contemporanei *contemporary novels*

rompere *to break*

rosa (inv.) *pink*

rosolare *to sauté, to brown*

rosso *red*

  vino (m.) rosso *red wine*

rumore (m.) *noise*

  fare rumore *to make noise*

rumoroso *noisy*

rurale *rural*

S

sabato (m.) *Saturday*

sabbia (f.) *sand*

sacco (m.) *bag*

  un sacco di … *a lot of …*

  un sacco di roba *a bunch/lot of stuff*

sala (f.) *room*

  sala da pranzo *dining room*

  sala delle riunioni *meeting room*

salario (m.) *salary*

salato *expensive*

sale (m.) *salt*

salone (m.) *living room*

saltare *to jump*

  saltare la corda *to jump rope*

salutarsi *to greet each other*

salute (f.) *health*

saluto (m.) *greeting*

salvare *to save*

  salvare un documento *to save a document*

Salve. *Hello.*

sangue (m.) *blood*

sano *healthy*

sapere *to know (a fact), to know how*

  Lo so. *I know.*

  Non lo so. *I don't know.*

saponetta (f.) *soap (bar)*

sapore (m.) *taste, flavor*

Sardegna (f.) *Sardinia*

sbattere *to beat*

sbucciare *to peel*

scaffale (m.) *shelf*

  scaffale (dei libri) *book shelf*

scala (f.) *stairs, staircase*

scarpe (f. pl.) *shoes*

  negozio (m.) di scarpe *shoe store*

  paio (m.) di scarpe *pair of shoes*

  scarpe da ginnastica *sneakers*

  scarpe da tennis *tennis shoes, sneakers*

scatola (f.) *box, carton*

scegliere *to choose*

scelta (f.) *choice*

scheda (f.) *report card*

schedario (m.) *file cabinet*

schermo (m.) *monitor, screen*

schiena (f.) *back*

sci (m.)/sci (m., pl.) *skiing*

sci alpino *alpine skiing*
sci di fondo *cross-country skiing*
sciare *to ski*
sciarpa (f.) *scarf (long)*
scodella (f.) *bowl (small, for one person)*
scolare *to drain*
scolastico (m.)/scolastici (m. pl.) *scholastic*
scopa (f.) *broom*
scorso *last*
  anno (m.) scorso *last year*
  settimana (f.) scorsa *last week*
scrittore/trice (m./f.) *writer*
scrivania (f.) *desk*
scrivere *to write*
scultura (f.) *sculpture*
scuola (f.) *school*
  scuola superiore *high school*
scusare *to excuse*
  Scusa. *Excuse me.* (infml.)
  (Mi) scusi. *Excuse me.* (sg. fml.)
  Scusami. *I'm sorry.*
se *if*
sé *himself, herself, itself, oneself*
secco *dry*
secondo *second*
  di secondo *as main course*
  secondo (piatto) (m.) *main course*
  secondo (preposition) *according to*
secondogenito/a (m./f.) *second-born*
sedere (m.) *behind*
sedia (f.) *chair*
sedici *sixteen*
segretario/a (m./f.) *secretary*
seguire *to follow*
sei *six*
selvaggio *wild*
semaforo (m.) *street light, traffic light*
sembrare *to seem*
seminterrato (m.) *basement*
sempre *always*
  sempre diritto *straight ahead*
seno (m.) *breast*
sentire *to hear*
sentirsi *to feel*
Mi sento bene. *I am well.*
  sentirsi di … *to feel like …*
senza *without*
  senza che … *without …*

sera (f.) *evening*
  Buona sera. *Good evening. (from 6 to 11 p.m.)*
  di sera *in the evening*
  ieri sera *last night*
  questa sera *this evening*
  vestito (m.) da sera *evening gown*
serata (f.) *evening*
  Buona serata. *Have a good evening.*
servire *to serve*
servizio (m.) *bathroom*
sessanta *sixty*
sesto *sixth*
seta (f.) *silk*
  di seta *made of silk*
sete (f.) *thirst*
  avere sete *to be thirsty*
settanta *seventy*
sette *seven*
  alle sette e mezza *at seven thirty (7:30)*
  per le sette *by seven (o'clock)*
  Siamo in sette. *There are seven of us.*
settembre (m.) *September*
settimana (f.) *week*
  due volte alla settimana *twice a week*
  fine settimana (m. sg./pl.) *weekend*
  prossima settimana *next week*
  questa settimana *this week*
  settimana scorsa *last week*
settimo *seventh*
sfilata (f.) *parade, march*
  sfilata di moda *fashion show*
shampo (m.) *shampoo*
si *one, they, people (impersonal pronoun)*
sì *yes*
sia … che *as/so … as, both … and*
Sicilia (f.) *Sicily*
sicuro *sure*
signora (f.) *Mrs., lady*
signore (m.) *Mr., gentleman*
silenzioso *silent*
simile *similar*
simpatico *friendly, nice*
sindaco (m.) *mayor*
sinfonia (f.) *symphony*
singolo *single*
  camera (f.) singola *single room (one twin bed)*
sinistra (f.) *left*
  (a) sinistra *on the left, to the left*

sintomo (m.) *symptom*
sistema (m.) *system*
sito (m.) *site*
sito web *website*
slip (m. pl.) *underpants (men's)*
smettere *to quit, to stop*
smettere di ... *to quit/stop ... ing*
smog (m.) *smog*
sneakers (m. pl.) *sneakers*
soccorso (m.) *aid, rescue*
pronto soccorso *emergency room*
sociale *social*
soddisfatto *satisfied*
sofà (m.) *sofa, couch*
soffitto (m.) *ceiling*
soggiorno (m.) *living room*
soldi (m. pl.) *money*
sole (m.) *sun*
C'è il sole. *It's sunny.*
solito *usual*
del solito *than usual*
di solito *usually*
solo *alone, lonely, only, just*
soltanto *only*
sonno (m.) *sleep*
avere sonno *to be sleepy*
sopracciglio (m.) *eyebrow*
sopracciglia (f. pl.) *eyebrows*
soprattutto *above all*
sorella (f.) *sister*
sorprendere *to surprise*
sorpresa (f.) *surprise*
Che sorpresa! *What a surprise!*
sostanza (f.) *substance*
sostituto/a (m./f.) *substitute*
sottile *thin*
sotto *under*
sottopiano (m.) *basement*
sovrappeso (m. sg./pl.) *overweight*
essere in sovrappeso *to be overweight*
spaghetti (m. pl.) *spaghetti*
spalla (f.) *shoulder*
spazioso *spacious*
specchio (m.) *mirror*
spedire *to send*
spendere *to spend*
sperare *to hope*
sperare di ... *to hope to ...*

spesa (f.) *shopping*
fare la spesa/le spese *to go shopping, to do grocery shopping*
fare spese *to shop*
spesso *often*
spettacolo (m.) *performance, play (theater)*
spezzatino (m.) *stew*
spiaggia (f.) *beach*
splendere *to shine*
sporco *dirty*
sport (m. sg./pl.) *sport*
guardare lo sport in/alla televisione *to watch sports on TV*
fare sport *to practice sports*
praticare uno sport *to play a sport*
sportivo *athletic, casual*
persona (f.) sportiva *athletic person*
sposarsi *to get married*
Si sposa. *He/She is getting married.*
sposarsi con ... *to marry ... (someone)*
sposato *married*
spumante (m.) *sparkling wine*
spuntino (m.) *snack*
squadra (f.) *team*
squisito *exquisite, delicious*
stadio (m.) *stadium*
staff (m.) *staff*
stage (m. sg./pl.) *internship*
stagione (f.) *season*
mezze stagioni *half seasons (spring and fall)*
stagno (m.) *pond*
stampante (f.) *printer*
stanco *tired*
stanza (f.) *room, chatroom*
stanza da letto *bedroom*
stare *to stay, to be feeling, to be*
Come mi sta? *How do I look?*
Come sta? *How are you doing* (sg. fml.)?/*How is he?*
Come stai? *How are you doing* (infml.)?
stare per ... *to be about to ...*
stasera *this evening, tonight*
stato (m.) *state*
stato civile *marital status*
stazione (f.) *station*
stazione (dei treni) *train station*
stella (f.) *star*
stereo (m. sg./pl.) *stereo*

stesso *same*
  allo stesso tempo *at the same time*
stimolante *exciting*
stomaco (m.) *stomach (above the waist)*
storia (f.) *story, history*
  storie (pl.) d'amore *love stories*
strada (f.) *street, road*
straniero *foreign*
  lingua (f.) straniera *foreign language*
  turisti (m./f. pl.) stranieri *foreign tourists*
strano *strange*
stressante *stressful*
stressato *stressed, under stress*
studente/essa (m./f.) *student*
  studente universitario *university student*
studiare *to study*
studio (m.) *study, office*
su *on, upon, over, about*
subito *immediately*
succedere *to happen*
succo (m.) *juice*
suo *his, her, its*
Suo *your* (sg. fml.)
suocera (f.) *mother-in-law*
suocero (m.) *father-in-law*
suonare *to play (an instrument), to ring (a bell)*
  suonare il pianoforte *to play the piano*
superiore *superior, higher*
  scuola (f.) superiore *high school*
supermercato (m.) *supermarket*
svegliarsi *to wake up*
svelto *fast*

T

taglia (f.) *size (dresses, pants)*
tagliare *to cut, to slice*
tagliatelle (f. pl.) *tagliatelle (pasta)*
tailleur (m. sg./pl.) *suit (women's)*
  tailleur pantalone *pant suit*
tanto (adjective) *so much, so many, a lot of*
  tanto ... quanto *as much/many ... as*
tanto (adverb) *so, so much, very*
  Tanto vale ... *(One) might as well ...*
tanto/a (m./f.) (noun) *so much, so many*
tappetino (m.) *mouse pad*
tappeto (m.) *carpet, rug*
tardi *late*
  fino a tardi *until late*

tassista (m./f.) *taxi driver*
tastiera (f.) *keyboard*
tavolo (m.) *table*
taxi (m.) *taxi*
tazza (f.) *cup*
te *you* (sg. infml.) (direct object, disjunctive pronoun)
  a te *to you* (sg. infml.) (indirect object, disjunctive pronoun)
tè (m.) *tea*
teatro (m.) *theater*
tecnico *technical*
  istituto (m.) tecnico *professional school*
teenager (m./f. sg./pl.) *teenager*
tele (f.) *television*
  guardare la tele *to watch television*
telefonare *to telephone*
telefonarsi *to call each other*
telefonino (m.) *cell phone*
telefono (m.) *telephone*
  rispondere al telefono *to answer the phone*
telegiornale (m.) *news (on TV)*
telegramma (m.) *telegram*
televisione (f.) *television*
  guardare la televisione *to watch television*
  guardare lo sport in/alla televisione *to watch sports on TV*
  interviste (f. pl.) alla televisione *talk show*
televisore (m.) *television*
temperatura (f.) *temperature*
tempio (m.) *temple*
tempo (m.) *time, weather*
  a tempo pieno *full-time*
  avere tempo *to have time*
  Che tempo fa? *What's the weather like?*
  Da quanto tempo ... ? *How long has it been since ... ?*
  molto tempo *long time*
  perdere tempo *to waste time*
  tempo libero *free time*
temporale (m.) *storm*
  C'è un temporale. *It's stormy.*
temporaneo *temporary*
  lavoro (m.) temporaneo *summer job*
tenda (f.) *curtain*
tendere *to have a tendency*
tendine (m.) *tendon*
tennis (m. sg./pl.) *tennis*
  giocare a tennis *to play tennis*

scarpe (f. pl.) da tennis *tennis shoes, sneakers*
televisivo (adjective) *television*
trasmissione (f.) televisiva *television program*
terme (f. pl.) *spa*
terra (f.) *land*
terra (inv.) *ground*
piano (m.) terra *ground floor*
terribile *terrible*
terrina (f.) *bowl*
terzo *third*
terzogenito/a *third-born*
tesi (f.)/tesi (f., pl.) *thesis*
test (m.) *test*
testa (f.) *head*
  fare testa o croce *to flip a coin*
TG (m.) *news (on TV)*
ti *you* (sg. infml.) (direct object pronoun); *to you* (sg. infml.) (indirect object pronoun)
tipo (m.) *type, kind*
tirare *to draw*
  Tira vento. *It's windy.*
titolo (m.) *title*
tivù (f.) *television*
  guardare la tivù *to watch television*
tornare *to return, to go back*
torre (f.) *tower*
torta (f.) *cake*
tortellini (m. pl.) *tortellini*
torto (m.) *fault*
  avere torto *to be wrong*
tra *between, among, in*
  tra … e … *between … and …*
  tra cinque minuti *in five minutes*
tradizionale *traditional*
traffico (m.) *traffic*
tranquillizzare *to calm down*
trapassato (m.) prossimo *past perfect*
trasferirsi *to move, to transfer*
traslocare *to move (to a new house)*
trasloco (m.) *move, removal*
  fare il trasloco *to move (to a new house)*
trasmissione (f.) *program*
  trasmissione televisiva *television program*
trasparente *transparent*
trasporto (m.) *transportation*
  mezzo (m.) di trasporto *means of transportation*
trattoria (f.) *family style restaurant*

tre *three*
  fra tre quarti d'ora *in forty-five minutes*
  Sono le tre. *It's three (o'clock).*
  Sono le tre e quarantacinque. *It's 3:45.*
  Sono le tre e tre quarti. *It's 3:45.*
tredici *thirteen*
treno (m.) *train*
  in treno *train station*
  stazione (f.) (dei treni) *by train*
trenta *thirty*
  Sono le tre e trenta. *It's 3:30.*
triste *sad*
troppo *too (much/many)*
troppo/a (m./f.) *too much, too many*
trovare *to find*
  andare a trovare *to go visit*
  venire a trovare *to come visit*
tu *you* (sg. infml.) (subject pronoun)
tuo *your* (sg. infml.)
tuonare *to thunder*
tuono (m.) *thunder*
tuorlo (m.) *yolk*
turista (m./f.) *tourist*
  turisti (pl.) stranieri *foreign tourists*
tutto *all*
  a tutti i costi *at all costs*
  di tutti *of all*
  prima di tutto *first of all*
  tutte le mattine *every morning*
  tutti gli altri *everyone else*
  tutti gli anni *every year*
  tutti i giorni *every day*

U

ubriaco *drunk*
ufficio (m.) *office*
  in ufficio *in the office*
  ufficio postale *post office*
ultimo *last, final*
un (m.)/uno (m. in front of s + consonant, z, ps, gn)/una (f.)/un' (m./f. in front of a vowel) *a, one*
  È l'una di notte. *It's 1:00 a.m.*
undicesimo *eleventh*
undici *eleven*
  Sono le undici e un quarto di mattina. *It's 11:15 a.m.*
università (f. sg./pl.) *university*
universitario (adjective) *university*

studente (m.) universitario *university student*
uno *one*
uomo (m.)/uomini (m. pl.) *man*
  abito da uomo *men's suit*
  uomo d'affari *businessman*
uovo (m.) *egg*
  uova (f. pl.) *eggs*
uragano (m.) *hurricane*
urbano *urban*
usare *to use*
uscire *to go out*
utile *useful*
  Posso esserLe utile? *How can I help you?/Can
   I assist you?* (sg. fml.)
uva (f.) *grapes*
  un grappolo d'uva *a bunch of grapes*

V

vacanza (f.) *vacation, holiday*
  fare una vacanza *to go on vacation*
  in vacanza *on vacation*
vagamente *vaguely*
valere *to be worth*
  Tanto vale … *(One) might as well …*
valigia (f.) *suitcase*
  fare le valige/valigie *to pack*
varietà (f.) *variety*
  varietà di scelta *variety of choices*
vasca (f.) *tub*
  vasca (da bagno) *bath tub*
vecchio *old*
vedere *to see, to meet (a person)*
  Fammi vedere. *Let me see.*
  fare vedere *to show*
  visto che … *given that … /since …*
vedersi *to see each other*
vela (f.) *sail*
  andare in barca a vela *to sail*
vela (f.) *sailing*
velluto (m.) *velvet*
  di velluto a coste *made out of corduroy*
  velluto a coste *corduroy*
veloce *fast, quick*
velocemente *quickly*
venditore (m.) *salesman*
venditrice (f.) *saleswoman*
venerdì (m. sg./pl.) *Friday*
Venezia (f.) *Venice*

venire *to come*
  venire a trovare *to come visit*
venti *twenty*
ventidue *twenty-two*
ventilatore (m.) *fan*
ventiquattro *twenty-four*
ventitré *twenty-three*
vento (m.) *wind*
  C'è vento. *It's windy.*
  Tira vento. *It's windy.*
ventre (m.) *stomach (below the waist)*
ventuno *twenty-one*
veramente *actually, really*
verde *green*
verdura (f.) *vegetable*
vergine (f.) *virgin*
verità (f. sg./pl.) *truth*
vero *true, right*
versare *to pour*
versione (f.) *version*
vestirsi *to get dressed*
vestito (m.) *dress*
  vestito da sera *evening gown*
veterinario/a (m./f.) *veterinarian*
vi *you* (pl.) (direct object pronoun); *to you* (pl.)
  (indirect object pronoun)
via (f.) *street, way, path*
viaggiare *to travel*
  viaggiare all'estero *to travel abroad*
viaggio (m.) *travel, trip*
  Buon viaggio. *Have a good trip.*
  fare un viaggio *to take a trip*
  viaggio organizzato *guided tour*
viale (m.) *avenue, path*
vicino *near*
  lì vicino *near there*
  qui vicino *nearby*
  vicino a … *near …*
video (m.) *monitor, screen*
villetta (f.) *small house*
vincere *to win*
vino (m.) *wine*
  lista (f.) dei vini *wine list*
  vino bianco *white wine*
  vino rosso *red wine*
viola (inv.) *purple*
visitare *to visit, to go sightseeing*
vista (f.) *view*

vita (f.) *life, waist*
  da una vita *for a very long time, since always*
  vita quotidiana *everyday life*
vitello (m.) *veal*
vivere *to live*
  vivere a … *to live in …*
voglia (f.) *wish, desire*
  avere voglia di … *to feel like …*
voi *you* (pl.) (subject pronoun); *you* (pl.) (direct object, disjunctive pronoun)
  a voi *to you* (pl.) (indirect object, disjunctive pronoun)
volentieri *gladly*
volere *to want*
  Ti voglio bene. *I care about you./I love you.*
  volerci *to take (time)*
  Vorrei … *I would like …*
volta (f.) *time*
  a volte *sometimes*
  due volte alla settimana *twice a week*
  ogni volta *every time*
  qualche volta *sometimes*
voltare *to turn*
vostro *your* (pl.)
votazione (f.) *grade*
voto (m.) *grade*
vuoto *empty*

W

water (m.) *toilet*
web log (blog) (m.) *web log (blog)*
web page (f.) *webpage*
weekend (m. sg./pl.) *weekend*

Z

zaino (m.) *backpack*
zero *zero*
zia (f.) *aunt*
zio (m.)/zii (m., pl.) *uncle*
zoo (m.)/zoo (m., pl.) *zoo*
zucchero (m.) *sugar*
zucchino (m.) *zucchini*

English-Italian

A

a *un/uno* (in front of s + consonant, z, ps, gn)/*una*
  a lot *parecchio/a* (m./f.), *molto/a* (m./f.) (noun)
  a lot of *tanto, parecchio, molto, un sacco di*
  a lot of stuff *un sacco di roba*
a.m. *di mattina, di notte*
  It's 11:15 a.m. *Sono le undici e un quarto di mattina.*
  It's 1:00 a.m. *È l'una di notte.*
ability *capacità* (f., pl. *capacità*)
able (to be) *riuscire, potere*
  able to … (to be) *riuscire a …*
about *circa, su*
  about it *ci, ne*
  about them *ne*
  I'll think about it. *Ci penserò.*
about to … (to be) *stare per …*
above all *soprattutto*
abroad *all'estero*
  travel abroad *viaggiare all'estero*
absolutely *assolutamente*
absorb (to) *assorbire*
abundant *abbondante*
accept (to) *accettare*
accessory *accessorio* (m.)
accommodating *accomodante*
accommodation *alloggio* (m.)
accompany (to) *accompagnare*
according to … *secondo …*
action *azione* (f.)
  action movies *film* (m. pl.) *d'azione*
activity *attività* (f., pl. *attività*)
actor *attore* (m.)
actress *attrice* (f.)
actually *veramente*
add (to) *aggiungere*
address *indirizzo* (m.)
adjective *aggettivo* (m.)
adorable *adorabile*
adult *adulto/a* (m./f.)
advance *anticipo* (m.)
  in advance *prima*
advice *consiglio* (m.)
  ask for advice (to) *chiedere (un) consiglio*
aerobic *aerobico*

afford (to) *permettersi*
afraid (to be) *avere paura*
  afraid of (to be) *avere paura di/essere impauriti da*
after *dopo*
afternoon *pomeriggio* (m.)
  Good afternoon. (from 1 p.m. to 6 p.m.) *Buon pomeriggio.*
  in the afternoon *di pomeriggio*
again *ancora, di nuovo*
  never again *mai più*
age *età* (f., pl. *età*)
agency *agenzia* (f.)
ago *fa*
  a month ago *un mese fa*
  two days ago *due giorni fa*
agree (to) *essere d'accordo*
agreed *d'accordo*
agreement *accordo* (m.)
ahead *avanti*
  Go ahead. *Va' avanti.*
aid *soccorso* (m.)
air *aria* (f.)
  air conditioning *aria condizionata*
airplane *aereo* (m.)
  by plane *in aereo*
airport *aeroporto* (m.)
all *tutto*
  above all *soprattutto*
  All right. *Va bene.*
  at all costs *a tutti i costi*
  first of all *prima di tutto*
  not … at all *non … affatto*
  of all *di tutti*
  open all day *orario* (m.) *continuato*
allow (to) *permettere, permettersi*
almost *quasi, ormai*
alone *solo*
along *lungo*
alpine *alpino*
  alpine skiing *sci* (m.) *alpino*
already *già*
also *anche*
alternate (to) *alternare*
although *benché*
always *sempre*
American *americano*
  American football *futbol americano* (m.)

among *fra, tra*
amusing *divertente*
ancient *antico*
and *e* (ed before a vowel)
  … and you? (fml.) *… e Lei?*
  … and you? (infml.) *… e tu?*
animal *animale* (m.)
ankle *caviglia* (f.)
anniversary *anniversario* (m.)
  Happy anniversary. *Buon anniversario.*
another *un altro/un'altra*
answer (to) *rispondere (a)*
  answer the phone (to) *rispondere al telefono*
anti-stress *antistress* (m., pl. *antistress*)
any *qualsiasi, qualunque, di + definite article*
anyone *chiunque, qualcuno*
anything *qualcosa*
  anything interesting/cool to do *qualcosa di bello da fare*
apartment *appartamento* (m.), *alloggio* (m.)
  apartment building *condominio* (m., pl.: *condomini*)
  apartment building (4-5 story building) *palazzo* (m.), *palazzina* (f.)
aperitif *aperitivo* (m.)
appetite *appetito* (m.)
appetizer *antipasto* (m.)
apple *mela* (f.)
appointment *appuntamento* (m.)
appropriate *adatto*
apricot *albicocca* (f.)
  apricot tree *albicocco* (m.)
April *aprile* (m.)
Arab *arabo*
archeological *archeologico* (m. pl *archeologici*)
architect *architetto* (m.)
arm *braccio* (m.)
arms *braccia* (f. pl.)
aroma *aroma* (m.)
around *attorno, intorno*
  around … *attorno a …*
  around midnight *intorno a mezzanotte*
  around the home/house *in giro per la casa*
  around the world *intorno al mondo*
  around town *in giro per la città*
arrive (to) *arrivare*
art *arte* (f.)
  modern art *arte moderna*

article *articolo* (m.)
artist *artista* (m./f.)
as *come*
 as a side dish *di/per contorno*
 as first course *per primo*
 as main course *di secondo*
 as many/much … as *tanto … quanto*
 as/so … as *così … come, sia … che*
 (One) might as well … *Tanto vale …*
ask (to), ask for (to) *chiedere*
 ask a question (to) *fare una domanda*
 ask for advice (to) *chiedere (un) consiglio*
assistant *assistente* (m./f.)
astronaut *astronauta* (m./f.)
at *a, da, in, presso*
 at all costs *a tutti i costi*
 at home *a casa*
 at least *almeno*
 at night, from midnight to 3 a.m *di notte*
 at seven thirty (7:30) *alle sette e mezza*
 at the beach *al mare*
 at the lake *al lago*
 at the same time *allo stesso tempo*
 not … at all *non … affatto*
athlete *atleta* (m./f.)
athletic *sportivo*
 athletic person *persona* (f.) *sportiva*
attach (to) *attaccare*
 attach (a file) (to) *allegare un file/documento*
attachment *allegato* (m.)
attend (to) *frequentare*
attention *attenzione* (f.)
 pay attention (to) *fare attenzione*
 Pay attention! *Sta' attento!*
attentive *attento*
August *agosto* (m.)
aunt *zia* (f.)
author *autore/trice* (m./f.)
availability *disponibilità* (f.)
available *disponibile*
avenue *viale* (m.)
average *media* (f.)
avocado *avocado* (m., pl. avocado)

B

baby *bambino/a* (m./f.)
back *schiena* (f.)
 go back (to) *ritornare, tornare*

back yard *cortile* (m.)
backpack *zaino* (m.)
bacon *pancetta* (f.)
bad *cattivo*
 It's bad. (weather) *Fa brutto.*
 Not bad. *Così, così.*
 Too bad! *Peccato!*
bad word *parolaccia* (f.)
badly *male*
bag *sacco* (m.), *borsa* (f.)
baked pork *maiale* (m.) *al forno*
bakery *pasticceria* (f.)
ball *palla* (f.), *pallone* (m.)
banana *banana* (f.)
band (music) *gruppo* (m.)
 British bands *gruppi* (pl.) *inglesi*
bandage *benda* (f.), *cerotto* (m.)
bank *banca* (f.)
banker *banchiere/a* (m./f.)
barbeque *alla brace*
baroque *barocco* (m.)
baseball *baseball* (m.)
basement *seminterrato* (m.), *sottopiano* (m.)
basil *basilico* (m.)
basketball *basket* (m.), *pallacanestro* (f.)
bath gel *bagnoschiuma* (m.), *docciaschiuma* (m.)
bath tub *vasca* (f.) *(da bagno)*
 take a bath (to) *fare il bagno*
bathing trunks/suit *costume* (m.) *da bagno*
bathroom *bagno* (m.), *servizio* (m.)
be (to) *essere, fare, stare*
beach *spiaggia* (f.)
beard *barba* (f.)
beat (to) *sbattere*
beautiful *bello*
 How beautiful! *Che bello!*
 It's beautiful. (weather) *Fa bello.*
 very beautiful *bellissimo*
 What a beautiful dish! *Che bel piatto!*
because *perché*
become (to) *diventare, farsi*
bed *letto* (m.)
 bed sheet *lenzuolo* (m.)
 bed sheets *lenzuola* (f. pl.)
 double bed *letto matrimoniale*
bedroom *camera* (f.), *camera da letto, stanza* (f.)
 da letto
beef *manzo* (m.)

beefsteak *bistecca* (f.)
beer *birra* (f.)
before *avanti*
   before ... *prima che ... , prima di ...*
begin (to) *cominciare*
   begin to ... (to) *cominciare a ...*
behind (n.) *sedere* (m.)
   behind (adv.) *dietro*
beige *beige* (inv.)
believe (to) *credere*
belly *pancia* (f.)
belong (It belongs to ...) *È di ...*
belt *cintura* (f.)
besides *inoltre*
best (the) *migliore, meglio*
better *meglio* (inv.)*, migliore, meglio*
   It's better. *Va meglio.*
between *fra, tra*
   between ... and ... *fra ... e ... /tra ... e ...*
bicycle *bicicletta* (f.)
   ride a bike (to) *andare in bicicletta*
big *grande*
   have a nice big meal (to) *farsi una bella mangiata*
bike *bici* (f., pl. *bici*)
biking *ciclismo* (m.)
bikini *bichini* (m.)
bill *conto* (m.)
billiards *biliardo* (m.)
billion *miliardo* (pl. *miliardi*)
biology *biologia* (f.)
birth *nascita* (f.)
birthday *compleanno* (m.)
   Happy birthday. *Buon compleanno.*
bitter *amaro*
bitterly *amaramente*
black *nero*
bleach *candeggina* (f.)
blender *frullatore* (m.)
blog *blog* (m.)
blood *sangue* (m.)
blouse *camicetta* (f.)
blue *blu* (inv.)
board *asse* (f.)
   ironing board *asse da stiro*
boat *barca* (f.)
boil (to) *bollire*
bone *osso* (m.)

bones *ossa* (f. pl.)
book *libro* (m.)
bookcase (in a house or office) *libreria* (f.)
bookstore *libreria* (f.)
bored (to get bored) *annoiarsi*
boring *noioso*
born (to be) *nascere*
   first-born *primogenito/a* (m./f.)
   second-born *secondogenito/a* (m./f.)
   third-born *terzogenito/a*
boss *capo/a* (m./f.)
both (of them) *entrambi/e*
   both ... and *sia ... che*
bottle *bottiglia* (f.)
bottom *fondo*
   the bottom of ... *in fondo a ...*
boutique *boutique* (f.)
bowl *ciotola* (f.)*, terrina* (f.)
   bowl (small, for one person) *scodella* (f.)
box *scatola* (f.)
boxers *mutande* (f. pl.)
boy (from 11 to 13 years old) *ragazzino* (m.)
   boy (from 14 to 35 years old) *ragazzo* (m.)
boyfriend *ragazzo* (m.)
   my boyfriend *il mio ragazzo*
bra *reggiseno* (m.)
bracelet *braccialetto* (m.)
brain *cervello* (m.)
bread *pane* (m.)
break *pausa* (f.)
   take a break (to) *fare una pausa*
break (to) *rompere*
   Break a leg! (lit. In the mouth of the wolf!) *In bocca al lupo!*
   Thank you. (lit. May the wolf die.) *Crepi il lupo.* (in response to *In bocca al lupo!*)
breakfast *colazione* (f.)
   have breakfast (to) *fare colazione*
breast *seno* (m.)
breathe (to) *respirare*
broccoli *broccolo* (m.)
brochure *opuscolo* (m.)
broom *scopa* (f.)
brother *fratello* (m.)
brown *marrone*
brown (to) *rosolare*
bruschetta *bruschetta* (f.)
building *edificio* (m.)

bus *autobus* (m.)
  tour bus *pullman* (m.)
business *affari* (m. pl.), *business* (m., pl.),
  commercio (m.)
  on business *per lavoro*
businessman *imprenditore* (m.), *uomo* (m.)
  d'affari
businesswoman *imprenditrice* (f.), *donna* (f.)
  d'affari
busy *impegnato, occupato*
  busy day *giornata* (f.) *piena*
but *ma, però*
butcher shop *macelleria* (f.)
butter *burro* (m.)
buy (to) *comprare*
by *per, in, a*
  by any chance *per caso*
  by car *in macchina*
  by now *ormai*
  by plane *in aereo*
  by seven (o'clock) *per le sette*
  by the way *a proposito*
  by train *in treno*
Bye-bye! *Ciao ciao!*

C

cabinet *camera* (f.)
  medicine cabinet *armadietto* (m.)
cable *cavo* (m.)
  cable (dsl) *cavo adsi*
café *bar* (m.)
cake *torta* (f.)
call (to) *chiamare, telefonare*
  call each other (on the phone) (to) *telefonarsi*
calm down (to) *tranquillizzare*
camera *macchina fotografica*
camping *campeggio* (m.)
  go camping (to) *fare il campeggio*
can *potere*
  Can I ... ? *Posso ... ?*
  How can this be! *Ma come!*
can (noun) *lattina* (f.)
cappuccino *cappuccino* (m.)
car *automobile* (f.), *macchina* (f.)
  by car *in macchina*
card *carta* (f.)
  credit card *carta di credito*
  play cards (to) *giocare a carte*

careful *attento*
  Be careful! *Sta' attento!*
carpenter *falegname* (m.)
carpet *tappeto* (m.)
  carpet (wall-to-wall) *moquette* (f.)
carrot *carota* (f.)
carry (to) *portare*
carton *scatola* (f.)
case *caso* (m.)
  in any case *comunque*
cashmere *cachemire* (m.)
  made out of cashmere *di cachemire*
cask *botte* (f.)
casual *sportivo*
CD-ROM *cd rom* (m.)
CD-ROM drive *lettore cd, lettore cd-rom*
ceiling *soffitto* (m.)
celebrate (to) *celebrare*
cell phone *cellulare* (m.), *telefonino* (m.)
center *centro* (m.)
  information center *centro informazioni*
centimeter *centimetro* (m.)
ceremony *cerimonia* (f.)
certain (ones) *certo/a* (m./f.)
certainly *certamente*
chair *sedia* (f.)
champion *campione/essa* (m./f.)
chance *caso* (m.)
  by any chance *per caso*
change (to) *cambiare*
channel *canale* (m.)
  flip channels (to) *cambiare canale*
chatroom *chatroom* (f.)
check *conto* (m.)
check (to) *controllare*
check in (to) *registrarsi (all'hotel)*
check out (to) *pagare il conto (dell'hotel)*
cheek *guancia* (f.)
cheese *formaggio* (m.)
chemical *chimico* (m. pl chimici)
chemistry *chimica* (f.)
chest *petto* (m.)
chicken *pollo* (m.)
child (from 0 to 10 years old) *bambino/a* (m./f.)
chin *mento* (m.)
China *Cina* (f.)
Chinese (language) *cinese* (m.)
  speak Chinese (to) *parlare cinese*

choice *scelta* (f.)
  variety of choices *varietà* (f.) *di scelta*
choose (to) *scegliere*
chop *braciola* (f.)
  pork chop *braciola di maiale*
Christmas *Natale* (m.)
  Merry Christmas. *Buon Natale.*
church *chiesa* (f.)
circle *giro* (m.)
circus *circo* (m.)
citizenship *cittadinanza* (f.)
city *città (f., pl. città)*
  in/to the city *in centro*
city hall *municipio* (m.)
civil *civile*
claim (to) *affermare*
classical *classico (m. pl. classici)*
  classical music *musica* (f.) *classica*
classroom, class *classe* (f.)
clean *pulito*
clean (to) *pulire*
  clean oneself (to) *pulirsi*
clear *chiaro*
clearly *chiaro, chiaramente*
clerk *impiegato/a* (m./f.)
climate *clima* (m.)
close *prossimo*
close (to) *chiudere*
  close a file (to) *chiudere un documento/file*
closet *armadio* (m.)
clothing *abbigliamento* (m.)
  clothing store *negozio* (m.) *di abbigliamento*
cloud *nuvola* (f.)
cloudy *nuvoloso*
  It's cloudy. *È nuvoloso.*
club *club (m., pl. club), discoteca* (f.)
coach *allenatore/trice* (m./f.)
coast *costa* (f.)
coat (above the knees) *giaccone* (m.)
  coat (to the knees or longer) *cappotto* (m.)
coffee *caffè (m., pl. caffè)*
coffee maker (stovetop) *caffettiera* (f.)
coffee shop *caffetteria* (f.), *caffè (m., pl. caffè)*
cold (noun) *freddo* (m.)
cold (to be) *avere freddo*
  It's cold. *Fa freddo.*
colleague *collega* (m./f.)
cologne *colonia* (f.)

come (to) *venire*
  come in (to) *entrare*
  come visit (to) *venire a trovare*
comedy *commedia* (f.)
comfortable *comodo*
command (to) *comandare*
commerce *commercio* (m.)
common *comune* (m.)
community *comunità (f., pl. comunità)*
company *compagnia* (f.)
competence *competenza* (f.)
complete (to) *compiere*
completely *affatto*
compliment *complimento* (m.)
computer *computer (m., pl computer);*
  informatico (adjective)
  computer science *informatica* (f.)
concert *concerto* (m.)
condition *patto* (m.), *condizione* (f.)
conditioning *condizionato*
confess (to) *confessare*
Congratulations! *Complimenti!*
construction worker *muratore/trice* (m./f.)
contemporary *contemporaneo*
  contemporary novels *romanzi* (m. pl.)
    contemporanei
continue (to) *continuare*
conversation *colloquio* (m.)
convince (to) *convincere*
  convince to … (to) *convincere a …*
convinced *convinto*
cook (to) *cucinare, cuocere*
cooking *cottura* (f.)
coordinate (to) *coordinare*
corduroy *velluto a coste*
  made out of corduroy *di velluto a coste*
correct *giusto*
correctly *giusto*
cost *costo* (m.)
  at all costs *a tutti i costi*
cost (to) *costare*
  How much does it cost? *Quanto costa?*
costume *costume* (m.)
cotton *cotone* (m.)
couch *divano* (m.), *sofà* (m.)
count (to) *contare*
country *campagna* (f.)
  to the country *in campagna*

countryside *campagna* (f.)
couple *coppia* (f.)
course *corso* (m.)
  as first course *per primo*
  as main course *di secondo*
  first course *primo (piatto)* (m.)
  main course *secondo (piatto)* (m.)
courtyard *cortile* (m.)
cousin *cugino/a* (m./f.)
cream *crema* (f.)
  shaving cream *crema da barba*
credit *credito* (m.)
  credit card *carta* (f.) *di credito*
cross-country skiing *sci* (m.) *di fondo*
crowded *affollato*
cucumber *cetriolo* (m.)
culture *cultura* (f.)
cup *tazza* (f.)
cupboard *credenza* (f.)
cure (to) *curare*
current *attuale*
currently *in questo periodo*
curtain *tenda* (f.)
customer *cliente* (m./f.)
cut (to) *tagliare*
cute *carino*

D

dad *papà* (m.)
  stay-at-home dad *casalingo* (m.)
daily *quotidiano*
dance *ballo* (m.)
dance (to) *ballare*
dangerous *pericoloso*
data *dati* (m. pl.)
date *data* (f.)
daughter *figlia* (f.)
day *giorno* (m.), *giornata* (f.), *data* (f.)
  a few day *pochi giorni* (m. pl.)
  a full day, a busy day *giornata* (f.) *piena*
  day trip *gita* (f.)
every day *tutti i giorni*
  Have a good day. *Buona giornata.*
  in a few days *fra qualche giorno*
  open all day *orario* (m.) *continuato*
  two days ago *due giorni fa*
December *dicembre* (m.)
decide (to) *decidere*

decide to … (to) *decidere di …*
deep *profondamente*
degree *grado* (m.), *laurea* (f.)
  high school degree *maturità* (f.)
  university degree *laurea* (f.)
delay *ritardo* (m.)
delete (to) *cancellare, eliminare*
delicious *delizioso, squisito*
dentist *dentista* (m./f.)
deodorant *deodorante* (m.)
department store *grande magazzino* (m.)
depressed *depresso*
describe (to) *descrivere*
desert *deserto* (m.)
desire *voglia* (f.)
desire (to) *desiderare*
desk *scrivania* (f.)
dessert *dolce* (m.)
destroy (to) *distruggere*
detergent *detersivo* (m.)
  dishwashing detergent *detersivo per i piatti*
  laundry detergent *detersivo per il bucato*
determine (to) *determinare*
die (to) *morire*
difference *differenza* (f.)
different *diverso*
difficult *difficile*
dining room *sala* (f.) *da pranzo*
dinner *cena* (f.)
  Enjoy your dinner./Have a good
    dinner. *Buona cena.*
diploma *diploma* (m.)
director *direttore* (m.)
  movie director *regista* (m./f.)
dirty *sporco*
disco *discoteca* (f.)
disease *malattia* (f.)
dish *piatto* (m.)
do the dishes (to) *lavare i piatti*
  What a beautiful dish! *Che bel piatto!*
dishwasher *lavapiatti* (f.), *lavastoviglie* (f.)
dishwashing detergent *detersivo* (m.) *per i
piatti*
displease (to) *dispiacere*
distant *lontano*
divorce … (someone) (to) *divorziarsi da …*
  get a divorce (to) *divorziarsi*
do (to) *fare*

do aerobics (to) *fare ginnastica aerobica*
do gardening (to) *fare giardinaggio*
do grocery shopping (to) *fare la spesa/le spese*
do the dishes (to) *lavare i piatti*
do the laundry (to) *fare il bucato*
How are you doing (fml.)? *Come sta?*
How are you doing (infml.)? *Come stai?*
things to do *cose* (f. pl.) *da fare*
What do you do? *Che lavoro fai?*
doctor *dottore/essa* (m./f.)
document *documento* (m.)
   save a document (to) *salvare un documento*
documentary *documentario* (m.)
dollar *dollaro* (m.)
   a million dollars *un milione di dollari*
door *porta* (f.)
double *doppio*
   double bed *letto* (m.) *matrimoniale*
   double room (one queen-size bed) *camera* (f.) *matrimoniale*
   double room (two twin-size beds) *camera* (f.) *doppia*
doubt (to) *dubitare*
downtown *in centro*
drain (to) *scolare*
drama *dramma* (m.)
draw (to) *tirare, fare pari*
drawer *cassetto* (m.)
dress *vestito* (m.), *abito* (m.)
dressed (to get dressed) *vestirsi*
drink *bevanda* (f.)
drink (to) *bere*
   something to drink *qualcosa da bere*
drive (to) *guidare*
drugstore *farmacia* (f.)
drunk *ubriaco*
dry *secco*
due *dovuto*
   due to ... *dovuto a ...*
DVD player *dvd* (m.)

E

each *ciascuno, ogni*
   each one *ciascuno/a* (m./f.)
ear *orecchio* (m.)
   ears *orecchi/orecchie* (m. pl./f. pl.)
early *presto*

early (to be) *essere in anticipo*
earn (to) *guadagnare*
earrings *orecchini* (m. pl.)
easy *facile*
eat (to) *mangiare*
   eat-in kitchen *cucina* (f.) *abitabile*
   nothing good to eat *niente di buono da mangiare*
economics *economia* (f.)
education *istruzione* (f.)
egg *uovo* (m.)
   eggs *uova* (f. pl.)
eggplant *melanzana* (f.)
eight *otto*
eighteen *diciotto*
eighth *ottavo*
eighty *ottanta*
elbow *gomito* (m.)
elder *maggiore*
electric *elettrico*
electrician *elettricista* (m.)
electrocardiogram *elettrocardiogramma* (m.)
electronics *elettronica* (f.)
   electronics store *negozio* (m.) *di elettronica*
elegant *elegante*
elegantly *elegantemente*
elementary *elementare*
   the first grade at elementary school *la prima elementare*
eleven *undici*
   It's 11:15 a.m. *Sono le undici e un quarto di mattina.*
eleventh *undicesimo*
e-mail *email, mail* (f., pl. *email, mail*), *posta* (f.) *elettronica*
   send an e-mail (to) *mandare un'email/una mail*
emergency room *pronto soccorso* (m.)
employee *impiegato/a* (m./f.)
empty *vuoto*
end (to) *per finire*
engaged *fidanzato*
engagement *impegno* (m.)
engineer *ingegnere* (m.)
English *inglese*
   British bands (music) *gruppi* (m. pl.) *inglesi*
English (language) *inglese* (m.)
enjoy oneself (to) *divertirsi*

Enjoy your dinner. *Buona cena.*
Enjoy your meal. *Buon appetito.*
Enjoy your walk. *Buona passeggiata.*
enormous *enorme*
enough *abbastanza*
  enough (to be) *bastare*
  That's enough! *Basta così!*
enroll (to) *iscrivere*
enthusiastically *entusiasticamente*
entire *intero*
equal *pari* (inv.)
espresso machine *macchina* (f.) *del caffè*
euro *euro* (m., pl. euro)
Europe *Europa* (f.)
European *europeo*
evening *sera* (f.), *serata* (f.)
  evening gown *vestito* (m.) *da sera*
  Good evening (from 6 to 11 p.m.). *Buona sera.*
  Have a good evening. *Buona serata.*
  in the evening *di sera*
  this evening *questa sera*
event *gara* (f.)
  in any event *in ogni caso*
ever *mai*
every *ogni*
  every day *tutti i giorni*
  every morning *tutte le mattine*
  every time *ogni volta*
  every year *tutti gli anni*
everyday life *vita* (f.) *quotidiana*
everyone *ognuno/a* (m./f.)
  everyone else *tutti gli altri*
exactly *giusto, proprio*
exaggerate (to) *esagerare*
exaggerated *esagerato*
exam *esame* (m.)
  fail (an exam) (to) *essere bocciato*
excellent *eccellente, ottimo*
exceptional *eccezionale*
exciting *stimolante*
excursion *escursione* (f.)
excuse (to) *scusare*
  Excuse me. (fml.) *(Mi) scusi.*
  Excuse me. (infml.) *Scusa.*
exercise (to) *fare ginnastica*
exhibition *mostra* (f.)
exist (to) *esistere*

expensive *caro, costoso, salato*
experience *esperienza* (f.)
expert *esperto/a* (m./f.)
exquisite *squisito*
extra *extra* (inv.)
eye *occhio* (m.)
eyebrow *sopracciglio* (m.)
  eyebrows *sopracciglia* (f. pl.)
eyeglasses *occhiali* (m. pl.)
eyelash *ciglio* (m.)
  eyelashes *ciglia* (f. pl.)

F

face *faccia* (f.)
facing … *di fronte a …*
fact *fatto* (m.)
  in fact *infatti*
factor *fattore* (m.)
factory *fabbrica* (f.)
fail (an exam) (to) *essere bocciato*
fairly *abbastanza*
fairy tale *favola* (f.), *fiaba* (f.)
fall *autunno* (m.)
  in the fall *in/d'autunno*
fall (to) *cadere*
  fall asleep (to) *addormentarsi*
false *falso*
family *famiglia* (f.)
  family style restaurant *trattoria* (f.)
  large family *famiglia numerosa*
famous *famoso*
fan *ventilatore* (m.)
fantastic *fantastico* (m. pl. fantastici)
far *lontano* (adverb)
  go too far (to) *esagerare*
farmer *contadino/a* (m./f.)
fashion *moda* (f.)
  fashion show *sfilata* (f.) *di moda*
fast *svelto, veloce, affrettato, pronto* (adjective); *veloce* (adverb)
fat *grasso* (m.) (noun); *grasso* (adjective)
father *padre* (m.)
father-in-law *suocero* (m.)
fault *torto* (m.)
favor *favore* (m.)
fax machine *fax* (m., pl. fax)
fear *paura* (f.)
February *febbraio* (m.)

feel (to) *sentirsi*
  feel like … (to) *sentirsi di … /avere voglia di …*
  feeling (to be) *stare*
female *femmina* (f.)
fettuccine *fettuccine* (f. pl.)
fever *febbre* (f.)
  have a fever (to) *avere la febbre*
few *poco/a* (m./f.) (noun); *poco* (adjective)
  a few *alcuni/e* (noun); *qualche, certo* (adjective)
  a few days *pochi giorni* (m. pl.)
  in a few days *fra qualche giorno*
fiancé(e) *fidanzato/a* (m./f.)
field *campo* (m.)
fifteen *quindici*
  It's 11:15 a.m. *Sono le undici e un quarto di mattina.*
  It's 3:15. *Sono le tre e quindici.*
fifth *quinto*
fifty *cinquanta*
figure *figura* (f.)
file *documento* (m.), *file* (m.), *cartella* (f.)
  attach a file (to) *allegare un documento/file*
  close a file (to) *chiudere un documento/file*
  open a file (to) *aprire un documento/file*
  send a file (to) *inviare un documento/file*
file cabinet *schedario* (m.)
fill (to) *riempire*
  fill up with … (to) *riempirsi di …*
film *film* (m., pl. *film*)
final *ultimo*
finalist *finalista* (m./f.)
finally *finalmente*
find (to) *trovare*
Fine, thanks. *(Sto) bene, grazie.*
finger *dito* (m.)
fingers *dita* (f. pl.)
finish (to) *finire*
  finish … ing (to) *finire di …*
  to finish *per finire*
first *primo*
  as first course *per primo*
  first course *primo (piatto)* (m.)
  first floor (second floor in the U.S.) *primo piano* (m.)
  first of all *prima di tutto*
  first-born *primogenito/a* (m./f.)
  the first grade at elementary school *la*

  prima elementare
fish *pesce* (m.)
  grilled fish *pesce alla griglia*
five *cinque*
  in five minutes *tra cinque minuti*
fixed *fisso*
flash (to) *lampeggiare*
flavor *sapore* (m.)
flip a coin (to) *fare testa o croce*
flip channels (to) *cambiare canale*
floor *piano* (m.)
  floor (inside a house or apartment) *pavimento* (m.)
  first floor (second floor in the U.S.) *primo piano*
  ground floor *pianterreno* (m.), *piano terra*
Florence *Firenze* (f.)
flower *fiore* (m.)
fog *nebbia* (f.)
  It's foggy. *C'è nebbia.*
follow (to) *seguire*
folly *follia* (f.)
food *cibo* (m.)
foot *piede* (m.)
  on foot *a piedi*
football *futbol* (m.)
  American football *futbol americano*
for *per, da*
  ask for (to) *chiedere*
  be looking for … (to) *essere in cerca di …*
  for a very long time *da una vita*
  go for a ride (to) *fare un giro*
  go for a walk (to) *fare un giro/fare un giro a piedi*
  look for (to) *cercare*
  passion for … *passione per …*
  wait for (to) *aspettare*
forehead *fronte* (f.)
foreign *straniero, estero*
foreign language *lingua* (f.) *straniera*
  foreign tourists *turisti* (m./f. pl.) *stranieri*
forest *foresta* (f.)
forget (to) *dimenticare*
  forget to … (do something) (to) *dimenticare di …*
form *forma* (f.)
forty *quaranta*
  from 10:45 a.m. to 3:00 p.m. *dalle undici meno*

un quarto alle tre
in forty-five minutes *fra tre quarti d'ora*
It's 3:45. *Sono le tre e quarantacinque./Sono le tre e tre quarti./Sono le quattro meno un quarto./Manca un quarto alle quattro.*
forward *avanti*
forward (to) *inoltrare*
four *quattro*
It's four (o'clock). *Sono le quattro.*
fourteen *quattordici*
fourth *quarto*
frankly *francamente*
free *libero*
free time *tempo* (m.) *libero*
French *francese*
fresh *fresco*
fresh fruit *frutta* (f.) *fresca*
Friday *venerdì* (m., pl.)
from Monday to Friday *dal lunedì al venerdì*
friend *amico* (m.)/*amici* (m., pl.)
friendly *simpatico*
friendship *amicizia* (f.)
From *da, di*
from ... to ... (time periods) *dalle ... alle ...*
from Monday to Friday *dal lunedì al venerdì*
from 10:45 a.m. to 3:00 p.m. *dalle undici meno un quarto alle tre*
I'm from ... *Sono di ...*
starting from ... *a partire da ...*
Where are you from? (fml.)/Where is he/she from? *Di dov'è?*
Where are you from? (infml.) *Di dove sei?*
fruit *frutta* (f.)
fresh fruit *frutta fresca*
fuchsia *fucsia* (inv.)
full *pieno*
a full day *giornata* (f.) *piena*
full-time *a tempo pieno*
fun (to have fun) *divertirsi*
funny *divertente*
furniture *mobili* (m. pl.)

G

gain weight (to) *ingrassare*
gallery *galleria* (f.)
game *partita* (f.)
garage *garage* (m., pl.)
garden *giardino* (m.)

gardening *giardinaggio* (m.)
do gardening (to) *fare giardinaggio*
gas *gas* (m., pl. *gas*)
general *generale*
genetic *genetico* (m. pl. *genetici*)
gentleman *signore* (m.)
Germany *Germania* (f.)
get (to) *farsi*
get a divorce (to) *divorziarsi*
get bored (to) *annoiarsi*
get dressed (to) *vestirsi*
get married (to) *sposarsi*
get nervous (to) *agitarsi*
get ready (to) *prepararsi*
get up (to) *alzarsi*
gift *regalo* (m.)
girl (from 11 to 13 years old) *ragazzina* (f.)
girl (from 14 to 35 years old) *ragazza* (f.)
girlfriend *ragazza* (f.)
my girlfriend *la mia ragazza*
give (to) *dare*
given that ... *visto che ...*
gladly *volentieri*
glass *bicchiere* (m.)
gloves *guanti* (m. pl.)
gnome *gnomo* (m.)
go (to) *andare*
go ... ing (to) *andare a ...*
Go ahead. *Va' avanti.*
go back (to) *ritornare, tornare*
go camping (to) *fare il campeggio*
go for a ride (to) *fare un giro*
go for a walk (to) *fare un giro/fare un giro a piedi*
go hiking (to) *fare un'escursione/camminare in montagna*
go on a vacation (to) *fare una vacanza*
go out (to) *uscire*
go shopping (to) *fare la spesa/le spese*
go sightseeing (to) *visitare*
Go there. *Vacci.*
go too far (to) *esagerare*
go visit (to) *andare a trovare*
How's it going? *Come va?*
Let's go there. *Andiamoci.*
good *buono* (buon before masculine nouns except when they begin with s followed by another consonant, or with z)

Good afternoon. (from 1 p.m. to 6 p.m.) *Buon pomeriggio.*
Good evening. *Buona sera.*
Good luck. *Buona fortuna.*
Good morning. *Buon giorno.*
Good night. *Buona notte.*
Good-bye (infml.) *Arrivederci./Ciao.*
Good-bye (fml.) *ArrivederLa.*
Have a good day. *Buona giornata.*
Have a good dinner. *Buona cena.*
Have a good evening. *Buona serata.*
Have a good rest. *Buon riposo.*
Have a good trip. *Buon viaggio.*
Have a good walk. *Buona passeggiata.*
make a good impression (to) *fare bella figura*
nothing good to eat *niente di buono da mangiare*
grade *votazione* (f.), *voto* (m.)
the first grade at elementary school *la prima elementare*
graduate (to) *laurearsi*
granddaughter *nipote* (m./f.)
grandfather *nonno* (m.)
grandmother *nonna* (f.)
grandson *nipote* (m./f.)
grapes *uva* (f.)
a bunch of grapes *un grappolo* (m.) *d'uva*
grass *erba* (f.)
grate (to) *grattugiare*
Greece *Grecia* (f.)
Greek *greco*
green *verde*
greet each other (to) *salutarsi*
greeting *saluto* (m.)
gray *grigio*
grill *griglia* (f.)
grilled/barbequed *alla brace*
grilled fish *pesce* (m.) *alla griglia*
grilled/barbequed meat *carne alla brace*
groceries *alimentari* (m. pl.)
do grocery shopping (to) *fare la spesa/le spese*
grocery store *negozio* (m.) *di alimentari*
ground (adjective) *terra* (inv.)
ground floor *piano* (m.) *terra, pianterreno*
group *gruppo* (m.)
grow (to) *coltivare, crescere*
grow old (to) *invecchiare*

guest *ospite* (m./f.)
guide *guida* (f.)
guided tour *viaggio* (m.) *organizzato*
guitar *chitarra* (f.)
gym(nasium) *palestra* (f.)
gymnastics *ginnastica* (f.)

H

habitable *abitabile*
hail (to) *grandinare*
It's hailing. *Grandina.*
hair *capelli* (m. pl.)
half, half hour *mezzo, mezz'ora*
half seasons (spring and fall) *mezze stagioni* (f. pl.)
in half an hour *fra mezz'ora*
two and a half hours *due ore e mezzo*
hall *ingresso* (m.)
hand *mano* (f., pl. mani)
happen (to) *succedere*
happy *contento, felice*
Happy anniversary. *Buon anniversario.*
Happy birthday. *Buon compleanno.*
Happy holidays. *Buone feste.*
happy to … *contento di …*
harbor *porto* (m.)
harmful *nocivo*
hat *cappello* (m.)
have (to) *avere*
have (food and drink) (to) *prendere*
Have a good day. *Buona giornata.*
Have a good dinner. *Buona cena.*
Have a good evening. *Buona serata.*
Have a good rest. *Buon riposo.*
Have a good trip. *Buon viaggio.*
Have a good walk. *Buona passeggiata.*
have a nice big meal (to) *farsi una bella mangiata*
have a tendency (to) *tendere*
have breakfast (to) *fare colazione*
have fun (to) *divertirsi*
have to (to) *dovere*
he (subject pronoun) *lui*
he/she who (relative pronoun) *chi*
head *testa* (f.)
health *salute* (f.)
health club *palestra* (f.)
healthy *sano*

hear (to) *sentire*
heart *cuore* (m.)
heart attack *infarto* (m.)
heat *caldo* (m.)
Hello. *Salve./Ciao.*
help *aiuto* (m.)
help (to) *aiutare*
 help … ing (to) *aiutare a …*
 help each other (to) *aiutarsi*
 How can I help you? (fml.) *Posso esserLe utile?*
her (direct object pronoun) *la*
 her (direct object, disjunctive pronoun) *lei*
 to her (indirect object pronoun) *le*
 to her (indirect object, disjunctive pronoun) *A lei*
 her (possessive) *suo/sua/suoi/sue, di lei*
 His/Her name is … *Si chiama …*
herbalist's shop *erboristeria* (f.)
here *ecco, qui, ci*
 here again *riecco*
 Here is … *Ecco …*
 Here we are again! *Rieccoci!*
herself *sé*
Hi. *Ciao.*
high school *liceo* (m.), *scuola* (f.) *superiore*
high school degree *maturità* (f.)
higher *superiore*
hike *escursione* (f.)
 go hiking (to) *fare un'escursione/camminare in montagna*
hill *collina* (f.)
him (direct object pronoun) *lo*
 him (direct object, disjunctive pronoun) *lui*
 to him (indirect object pronoun) *gli*
 to him (indirect object, disjunctive pronoun) *a lui*
himself *sé*
hip *fianco* (m.)
his *suo/sua/suoi/sue, di lui*
 His/Her name is … *Si chiama …*
history *storia* (f.)
hobby *hobby* (m., pl)
hockey *hockey* (m.)
 ice hockey *hockey su ghiaccio*
holiday *festa* (f.), *vacanza* (f.)
 Happy holidays. *Buone feste.*
home *casa* (f.)
 around the home *in giro per la casa*
 at home *a casa*

stay-at-home dad *casalingo* (m.)
stay-at-home mom *casalinga* (f.)
homeopathic *omeopatico* (m. pl. *omeopatici*)
homeopathy *omeopatia* (f.)
hometown *città* (f.) *natale*
honey *miele* (m.)
hope (to) *sperare*
 hope to … (to) *sperare di …*
hospital *ospedale* (m.)
hot (to be) *avere caldo*
 It's hot. *Fa caldo.*
hotel *albergo* (m.), *hotel* (m., pl. *hotel*)
hour *ora* (f.)
 half hour *mezzo*
 in half an hour *fra mezz'ora*
 shorter working hours *orario* (m.) *ridotto*
 two and a half hours *due ore e mezzo*
house *casa* (f.)
 around the house *in giro per la casa*
 small house *villetta* (f.)
how *come*
 how (exclamation) *che*
 How are you doing? (fml.) *Come sta?*
 How are you doing? (infml.) *Come stai?*
 How can I help you? (fml.) *Posso esserLe utile?*
 How do I look? *Come mi sta?*
 How is … ?/How are … ? *Com'è?/Come sono?*
 How long has it been since … ? *Da quanto tempo … ?*
 how many/much *quanto*
 How much does it cost? *Quanto costa?*
 How nice!/How beautiful! *Che bello!*
 How old are you? (infml.) *Quanti anni hai?*
 How's it going? *Come va?*
 How's it possible!/How can this be! *Ma come!*
 know how (to) *sapere*
however *però*
hug (to) *abbracciarsi*
hundred *cento*
hunger *fame* (f.)
hungry (to be) *avere fame*
hurricane *uragano* (m.)
hurry *fretta* (f.)
 in a hurry *in fretta*
 in a hurry (to be) *avere fretta*

husband *marito* (m.)
hygienic *igienico*

I *io*
ice *ghiaccio* (m.)
ice cream *gelato* (m.)
ice hockey *hockey* (m.) *su ghiaccio*
idea *idea* (f.)
 no idea *nessuna idea*
if *se*
ill *ammalato*
illustration *figura* (f.)
imagine (to) *immaginare*
immediately *subito*
imperfect *imperfetto* (m.)
important *importante*
impression (to make a good impression) *fare bella figura*
in *fra, tra, in, a*
 check in (to) *registrarsi (all'hotel)*
 come in (to) *entrare*
 in a few days *fra qualche giorno*
 in a hurry *in fretta*
 in advance *prima*
 in any case *comunque*
 in any event *in ogni caso*
 in fact *infatti*
 in five minutes *tra cinque minuti*
 in forty-five minutes *fra tre quarti d'ora*
 in front *davanti*
 in front of … *davanti a … /di fronte a …*
 in great shape *in ottima forma*
 in half an hour *fra mezz'ora*
 in love *innamorato/a*
 in order that *affinché*
 in person *di persona*
 in the afternoon, from 1 to 5 p.m. *di pomeriggio*
 in the city *in centro*
 in the evening, from 6 to 11 p.m. *di sera*
 in the fall *in/d'autunno*
 in the meantime *nel frattempo*
 in the morning, from 4 to 11 a.m. *di mattina*
 in the office *in ufficio*
 in the spring *in primavera*
 in the style of *a + definite article*
 in the summer *d'estate*
 in the world *del mondo*
 in this period *in questo periodo*
 in winter *d'inverno*
 live in … (to) *vivere a …*
 the way in which … *il modo in cui …*
indicate (to) *indicare*
influence *influenza* (f.)
ingredient *ingrediente* (m.)
inherit (to) *ereditare*
insist (to) *insistere*
instead *invece*
institute *istituto* (m.)
intellectual *intellettivo*
intelligence quotient (IQ) *quoziente* (m.) *intellettivo*
intelligent *intelligente*
intention *proposito* (m.)
interest *interesse* (m.)
interest (to) *interessare*
interesting *interessante*
 anything interesting/cool to do *qualcosa di bello da fare*
 very interesting *interessantissimo*
intermission *intervallo* (m.)
internet *internet* (m.)
internship *stage* (m., pl *stage*)
interrupt (to) *interrompere*
intersection *incrocio* (m.)
interview *colloquio* (m.), *intervista* (f.)
 job interview *colloquio di lavoro*
intestine *intestino* (m.)
introduce (to) *presentare*
introduction *presentazione* (f.)
invite (to) *invitare*
iron *ferro* (m.) (metal), *ferro da stiro* (appliance)
ironing board *asse* (f.) *da stiro*
island *isola* (f.)
it (direct object pronoun) *lo* (m.), *la* (f.)
 it (direct object, disjunctive pronoun) *lui* (m.), *lei* (f.)
 to it (indirect object pronoun) *gli* (m.), *le* (f.)
 to it (indirect object, disjunctive pronoun) *a lui* (m.), *a lei* (f.)
 about it *ci, ne*
 How long has it been since … ? *Da quanto tempo … ?*
 It hurts. *Fa male.*
 It's bad. (weather) *Fa brutto.*

It's beautiful. (weather) *Fa bello.*
It's better. *Va meglio.*
It's cloudy. *È nuvoloso.*
It's cold. *Fa freddo.*
It's 11:15 a.m. *Sono le undici e un quarto di mattina.*
It's foggy. *C'è nebbia.*
It's four (o'clock). *Sono le quattro.*
It's hailing. *Grandina.*
It's hot. *Fa caldo.*
It's midnight. *È mezzanotte.*
It's noon. *È mezzogiorno.*
It's 1:00 a.m. *È l'una di notte.*
It's raining. *Piove.*
It's snowing. *Nevica.*
It's stormy. *C'è un temporale.*
It's sunny. *C'è il sole.*
It's three (o'clock). *Sono le tre.*
It's 3:15. *Sono le tre e quindici.*
It's 3:45. *Sono le tre e quarantacinque./Sono le tre e tre quarti./Sono le quattro meno un quarto./Manca un quarto alle quattro.*
It's 3:30. *Sono le tre e trenta.*
It's time to … *È ora di …*
It's two (o'clock). *Sono le due.*
It's windy. *C'è vento./Tira vento.*
of it, on it *ci, ne*
What time is it? *Che ora è?/Che ore sono?*
Italian *italiano*
Italy *Italia* (f.)
its *suo/sua/suoi/sue*
itself *sé*

J

jacket *giacca* (f.)
January *gennaio* (m.)
jeans *blue jeans* (m. pl.)
job *lavoro* (m.)
　job interview *colloquio* (m.) *di lavoro*
　part-time job *lavoro part-time*
　steady job *lavoro fisso*
　summer job *lavoro temporaneo*
jog (to) *fare il footing*
jogging *footing* (m.)
joke *barzelletta* (f.)
journal *rivista* (f.)
journalist *giornalista* (m./f.)
juice *succo* (m.)

July *luglio* (m.)
jump (to) *saltare*
　jump rope (to) *saltare la corda*
June *giugno* (m.)
just *appena, proprio, solo*

K

keyboard *tastiera* (f.)
kidney *rene* (m.)
kilo *chilo* (m.)
kilometer *chilometro*
kind (adjective) *gentile*
kind (noun) *tipo* (m.)
kiss (to) *baciarsi*
kitchen *cucina* (f.)
　eat-in kitchen *cucina abitabile*
knee *ginocchio* (m.)
　knees *ginocchia/ginocchi* (f./m. pl.)
knife *coltello* (m.)
know (to) *sapere (a fact, how), conoscere (a person)*
　I know. *Lo so.*
　I don't know. *Non lo so.*
　know each other (to) *conoscersi*

L

lady *signora*
lake *lago* (m.)
　at the lake *al lago*
lamp *lampada* (f.)
lamp post *lampione* (m.)
land *terra* (f.)
language *lingua* (f.)
　foreign language *lingua straniera*
large *grosso; numeroso (family)*
　large dinner *cena* (f.) *abbondante*
　large family *famiglia* (f.) *numerosa*
lasagna *lasagne* (f. pl.)
last *scorso, ultimo*
　last night *ieri sera*
　last week *settimana* (f.) *scorsa*
　last year *anno* (m.) *scorso*
last (to) *durare*
late *tardi*
　late (to be) *essere in ritardo*
　until late *fino a tardi*
Latin American *latinoamericano*
laundry *bucato* (m.), *lavanderia* (f.)

do the laundry (to) *fare il bucato*
laundry detergent *detersivo* (m.) *per il bucato*
lawyer *avvocato* (m.)
learn (to) *apprendere, imparare*
leather *pelle* (f.)
  made out of leather *di pelle*
leave (to) *partire, lasciare*
left *sinistra* (f.)
  left (hand) *manca* (f.)
  on/to the left *(a) sinistra*
left-handed *mancino*
leg *gamba* (f.)
  Break a leg! (lit. In the mouth of the wolf!) *In bocca al lupo!*
  Thank you. (lit. May the wolf die.) *Crepi il lupo.* (in response to *In bocca al lupo!*)
less *meno*
  less ... than *meno ... di/che*
lesson *lezione* (f.)
let (to) *lasciare*
  Let me see. *Fammi vedere.*
  Let's go there. *Andiamoci.*
letter *lettera* (f.)
lettuce *lattuga* (f.)
level *livello* (m.)
library *biblioteca* (f.)
lie *bugia* (f.)
life *vita* (f.)
  everyday life *vita quotidiana*
light *leggero*
  light sweater *maglioncino* (m.)
lightning *lampo* (m.), *fulmine* (m.)
like (to) *piacere, amare*
  I like ... *Mi piace/piacciono ...* (sg./pl.)
  I would like ... *Vorrei ...*
likely *probabile*
linen *lino* (m.)
  made out of linen *di lino*
list *lista* (f.)
  wine list *lista dei vini*
listen to (to) *ascoltare*
liter *litro* (m.)
literature *letteratura* (f.)
little *poco/a* (m./f.) (noun); *poco* (adjective)
  a little *un poco/un po'*
live (to) *vivere, abitare*
  live in ... (to) *vivere a ...*
liver *fegato* (m.)

living room *salone* (m.), *soggiorno* (m.)
lobster *aragosta* (f.)
lonely *solo*
long *lungo*
  for a very long time *da una vita*
  How long has it been since ... ? *Da quanto tempo ... ?*
  long distance *di fondo*
  long time *molto tempo*
  take a nice long nap (to) *farsi una bella dormita*
look at (to) *guardare*
  How do I look? *Come mi sta?*
look for (to) *cercare*
  looking for ... (to be) *essere in cerca di ...*
lose (to) *perdere*
  lose weight (to) *dimagrire*
lottery *lotteria* (f.)
loudly *forte* (adverb)
Love *amore* (m.)
  in love *innamorato/a*
  love stories *storie* (f. pl.) *d'amore*
love (to) *amare*
  I love you. *Ti voglio bene. Ti amo.*
low *basso*
luck *fortuna* (f.)
  Good luck. *Buona fortuna.*
lucky *beato, fortunato*
  Lucky you. *Beati voi.* (pl.)
  Lucky you! *Beato te!*
lunch *pranzo* (m.)
lung *polmone* (m.)

M

machine *macchina* (f.)
magazine *rivista* (f.)
mail *posta* (f.) (noun); *postale* (adjective)
  e-mail *posta elettronica*
  send an e-mail (to) *mandare un'email/una mail*
main course *secondo (piatto)* (m.)
  as main course *di secondo*
make (to) *fare*
  made from plastic *di plastica*
  made out of cashmere *di cachemire*
  made out of corduroy *di velluto a coste*
  made out of leather *di pelle*
  made out of linen *di lino*

made out of silk *di seta*
make a good impression (to) *fare bella figura*
make friends (to) *fare amicizia*
make noise (to) *fare rumore*
male *maschio* (m.)
man *uomo* (m.)/*uomini* (pl.)
   men's suit *abito da uomo*
manage (to) *riuscire*
   manage to … (to) *riuscire a …*
manner *modo* (m.)
many *molto* (adjective); *molto/a* (m./f.) (noun)
   as many … as *tanto … quanto*
   how many *quanto*
   so many *tanto* (adjective); *tanto/a* (m./f.) (noun)
   too many *troppo* (adjective); *troppo/a* (m./f.)
      (noun)
map *cartina* (f.), *mappa* (f.), *piantina* (f.)
marathon *maratona* (f.)
March *marzo* (m.)
march *sfilata* (f.)
marital status *stato civile*
market *mercato* (m.)
married *sposato/a*
marry … (someone) (to) *sposarsi con …*
   get married (to) *sposarsi*
   He/She is getting married. *Si sposa.*
marvelous *meraviglioso*
math *matematica* (f.)
matrimonial *matrimoniale*
May *maggio* (m.)
May I … ? *Posso … ?*
maybe *forse*
mayor *sindaco* (m.)
me (direct object pronoun) *mi*
   me (direct object, disjunctive pronoun) *me*
   to me (indirect object pronoun) *mi*
   to me (indirect object, disjunctive pronoun) *a me*
meadow *prato* (m.)
means *mezzo* (m.)
   means of transportation *mezzo di trasporto*
meantime *frattempo*
   in the meantime *nel frattempo*
measure (to) *misurare*
Meat *carne* (f.)
   grilled/barbecued meat *carne alla brace*
   meat sauce *ragù* (m., pl.)
   sliced cold meat *affettato* (m.)
mechanic *meccanico* (m.)/*meccanici* (pl.)

medical doctor *medico* (m.)
medicine *medicina* (f.)
   medicine cabinet *armadietto* (m.)
meet (to) *vedere* (a person), *incontrare* (a person casually), *conoscere* (a person for the first time)
   meet each other (to) *incontrarsi*
   Pleased to meet you. *Piacere.*
   Pleased to meet you, too. *Piacere mio.*
   Very pleased to meet you! *Molto piacere!*
meeting *riunione* (f.)
   meeting room *sala* (f.) *delle riunioni*
melon *melone* (m.)
memory *memoria* (f.)
menu *menù* (m.)
Merry Christmas. *Buon Natale.*
message *messaggio* (m.)
   instant message *messaggio immediato*
meter *metro* (m.)
metro, subway *metrò* (m. in Milan/f. in Rome)
microwave *microonda* (f.)
   microwave oven *forno* (m.) *a microonde*
midnight *mezzanotte* (f.)
   around midnight *intorno a mezzanotte*
   It's midnight. *È mezzanotte.*
Might as well … *Tanto vale …*
Milan *Milano* (f.)
milk *latte* (m.)
million *milione* (m.)/*milioni* (pl.)
   a million dollars *milione di dollari*
mineral *minerale*
   mineral water *acqua* (f.) *minerale*
   still mineral water *acqua minerale naturale*
   sparkling mineral water *acqua minerale frizzante*
minute *minuto* (m.)
   in five minutes *tra cinque minuti*
   in forty-five minutes *fra tre quarti d'ora*
mirror *specchio* (m.)
mix (to) *mescolare*
mixed *misto*
   mixed cold cuts *affettati* (m. pl.) *misti*
   mixed salad *insalata* (f.) *mista*
model (fashion) *modello/a* (m./f.)
modem *modem* (m.)
modern *moderno*
   modern art *arte* (f.) *moderna*
mom *mamma* (f.)
   stay-at-home mom *casalinga* (f.)

moment *momento* (m.)

Monday *lunedì* (m., pl.)
  from Monday to Friday *dal lunedì al venerdì*
  on Mondays *il lunedì*

money *denaro* (m.), *soldi* (m. pl.)

monitor *monitor* (m.), *schermo* (m.), *video* (m.)

month *mese* (m.)
  a month ago *un mese fa*
  next month *mese prossimo*

monument *monumento* (m.)

moon *luna* (f.)

more *più*
  more/-er ... than *più ... di/che*
  no more *non ... più*

moreover *inoltre*

morning *mattina* (f.)
  every morning *tutte le mattine*
  Good morning. *Buon giorno.*
  in the morning, from 4 to 11 a.m. *di mattina*

mosque *moschea* (f.)

mother *madre* (f.)

mother-in-law *suocera* (f.)

motorbike *motocicletta* (f.), *moto* (f., pl.)

mountain *montagna* (f.)
  to the mountains *in montagna*

mouse *mouse* (m.) (computer)

mouse pad *tappetino* (m.)

mouth *bocca* (f.)

move (to) *muovere, trasferirsi*
  move (to a new house) (to) *traslocare, fare il traslocò*

movie *film* (m., pl.)
  action movies *film d'azione*
  movie director *regista* (m./f.)
  movie theater *cinema* (m., pl.: *cinema*)

Mr. *signore* (m.)

Mrs. *signora* (f.)

much *molto* (adjective); *molto/a* (m./f.) (noun)
  as much ... as *tanto ... quanto*
  how much *quanto*
  How much does it cost? *Quanto costa?*
  so much *tanto* (adjective); *tanto/a* (m./f.) (noun), *tanto* (adverb)
  too much *troppo* (adjective); *troppo/a* (m./f.) (noun)

municipal building *municipio* (m.)

muscle *muscolo* (m.)

museum *museo* (m.)

mushroom *fungo* (m.)

music *musica* (f.)
  classical music *musica classica*
  pop music *musica pop*

musician *musicista* (m./f.)

must *dovere*

my *mio/mia/miei/mie*
  My name is ... *Mi chiamo ...*

N

name *nome* (m.)
  His/Her name is ... *Si chiama ...*
  My name is ... *Mi chiamo ...*

named (to be) *chiamarsi*

nap *pisolino* (m.)
  take a nap (to) *fare un pisolino*
  take a nice long nap (to) *farsi una bella dormita*

Naples *Napoli* (f.)

native *natale*

natural *naturale*

nature *natura* (f.)

naughty *cattivo*

near *vicino*
  near ... *vicino a ...*
  near there *lì vicino*

nearby *qui vicino*

necessary *necessario*

neck *collo* (m.)

necklace *collana* (f.)

need *bisogno* (m.)
  need (to) *essere nel bisogno*
  need ... (to) *avere bisogno di ...*

neighborhood *quartiere* (m.)

nephew *nipote* (m./f.)

nervous *nervoso*
  get nervous (to) *agitarsi*

never *mai* (in negative sentences)
  Never! *Mai !*
  never again *mai più*

new *nuovo*

news *notizie* (f. pl.), *giornale radio* (m.) (on the radio), *telegiornale* (m.) (on TV), *TG* (m.) (on TV)

newspaper *giornale* (m.)

next *prossimo*
  next month *mese* (m.) *prossimo*
  next week *prossima settimana* (f.)

nice *simpatico, bravo*

have a nice big meal (to) *farsi una bella mangiata*
How nice! *Che bello!*
take a nice long nap (to) *farsi una bella dormita*
niece *nipote* (m./f.)
night *notte* (f.)
 at night, from midnight to 3 a.m. *di notte*
 Good night. *Buona notte.*
 last night *ieri sera*
nine *nove*
nineteen *diciannove*
ninth *nono*
ninety *novanta*
no *no* (adverb); *nessuno* (adjective)
 no idea *nessuna idea*
 no longer *non ... più*
 no more *non ... più*
nobody *nessuno/a* (m./f.)
noise *rumore* (m.)
 make noise (to) *fare rumore*
noisy *rumoroso*
none *nessuno/a* (m./f.)
noon *mezzogiorno* (m.)
 It's noon. *È mezzogiorno.*
normal *normale*
normally *normalmente*
Norwegian *norvegese* (m./f.)
nose *naso* (m.)
not *non*
 not ... at all *non ... affatto*
 Not bad. *Così, così.*
 not even *neanche, nemmeno*
notebook *quaderno* (m.)
nothing *niente, nulla*
 nothing good to eat *niente di buono da mangiare*
notice (to) *notare*
novel *romanzo* (m.)
 contemporary novels *romanzi* (pl.) *contemporanei*
November *novembre* (m.)
now *adesso*
 by now *ormai*
 right now *in questo momento*
number *numero* (m.)
numerous *numeroso*
nurse *infermiere/a* (m./f.)

O

O.K. *d'accordo*
obligation *impegno* (m.)
obvious *ovvio*
ocean *oceano* (m.)
October *ottobre* (m.)
of *di*
 first of all *prima di tutto*
 means of transportation *mezzo* (m.) *di trasporto*
 of all *di tutti*
 of it *ci, ne*
 of them *ne*
 out of town *fuori città*
 pair of shoes *paio* (m.) *di scarpe*
 speaking of ... *a proposito di ...*
 There are seven of us. *Siamo in sette.*
 There are three of them. *Ce ne sono tre.*
 variety of choices *varietà* (f.) *di scelta*
 works of art *opere* (f. pl.) *d'arte*
offer (to) *offrire*
office *ufficio* (m.), *studio* (m.)
 in the office *in ufficio*
often *spesso*
oil *olio* (m.)
old *vecchio*
 grow old (to) *invecchiare*
 How old are you? *Quanti anni hai?*
 I am ... years old. *Ho ... anni.*
older *maggiore*
olive *oliva* (f.)
on *in, su*
 on business *per lavoro*
 on foot *a piedi*
 on it *ci*
 on Mondays *il lunedì*
 on the contrary *anzi*
 on the left *a sinistra*
 on the right *a destra*
 on time (to be) *essere in orario, essere puntuale*
 on vacation *in ferie, in vacanza*
one *un/uno* (in front of s + consonant, z, ps, gn)/*una*
 one (impersonal pronoun) *si*
 one (number) *uno*
 It's 1:00 a.m. *È l'una di notte.*
 the one who, whoever (relative pronoun) *chi*

oneself *sé*
onion *cipolla* (f.)
only *soltanto, solo*
open *aperto*
  open all day *orario* (m.) *continuato*
open (to) *aprire*
  open a file (to) *aprire un documento/file*
opera *opera* (f.)
opposite *di fronte*
or *o*
orange *arancione* (inv.) *(color); arancia* (f.) *(fruit)*
orchard *orto* (m.)
order *ordine* (m.)
  in order that *affinché*
order (to) *ordinare*
organize (to) *organizzare*
osso buco *ossobuco* (m.)
other *altro*
our *nostro/nostra/nostri/nostre*
out of town *fuori città*
outdoors *all'aperto*
outside *fuori*
oven *forno* (m.)
  microwave oven *forno a microonde*
over *su*
overweight *sovrappeso* (m., pl.)
overweight (to be) *essere in sovrappeso*

P

p.m. *di pomeriggio, di sera*
pack (a suitcase) (to) *fare le valige/valigie*
page *pagina* (f.)
pain *dolore* (m.)
  have a pain in … (to) *avere un dolore a … /*
    avere male a …
painting *quadro* (m.)
pair *paio* (m.)
  pair of shoes *paio di scarpe*
pajamas *pigiama* (m.)
pan *pentola* (f.)
panorama *panorama* (m.)
pants *pantaloni* (m. pl.)
  pant suit *tailleur* (m.) *pantalone*
paper *carta* (f.)
  toilet paper *carta igienica*
parade *sfilata* (f.)
parent *genitore/trice* (m./f.)
Paris *Parigi* (f.)

park *parco* (m.)
park (to) *parcheggiare*
Parmesan cheese *parmigiano* (m.)
part *parte* (f.)
participate (to) *partecipare*
part-time *part-time*
  part-time job *lavoro* (m.) *part-time*
party *festa* (f.)
  have a party (to) *dare una festa*
pass (an exam) (to) *passare, essere promosso*
passion *passione* (f.)
  passion for … *passione per …*
passport *passaporto* (m.)
past (tense)
  past perfect *passato* (m.)
trapassato (m.) **prossimo**
pasta *pasta* (f.)
path *viale* (m.), *via* (f.)
patience *pazienza* (f.)
patient *paziente* (m./f.)
pay (to) *pagare*
  pay attention (to) *fare attenzione*
  Pay attention! *Sta' attento!*
peach *pesca* (f.)
pear *pera* (f.)
pediatrician *pediatra* (m./f.)
peel (to) *sbucciare*
penne (pasta) *penne* (f. pl.)
penthouse *attico* (m., pl. *attici*)
people *gente* (f.), *persone* (pl.)
people (impersonal pronoun) *si*
pepper (spice) *pepe* (m.) *(spice); peperone* (m.)
  (vegetable)
perfect *perfetto*
performance *spettacolo* (m.)
perfume *profumo* (m.)
perhaps *magari, forse*
period *periodo* (m.)
  in this period *in questo periodo*
permanent *fisso*
person *persona* (f.)
  athletic person *persona sportiva*
  in person *di persona*
personal information *dati* (m. pl.) *anagrafici*
pharmacy *farmacia* (f.)
photograph *foto* (f., pl.), *fotografia* (f.)
  take a picture (to) *fare una foto/fotografia*
photography *fotografia* (f.)

pianist *pianista* (m./f.)
piano *pianoforte* (m.)
  play the piano (to) *suonare il pianoforte*
pick up (to) *raccogliere*
picture *quadro* (m.) *(painting); foto* (f., pl.),
  fotografia (f.) *(photograph)*
  take a picture (to) *fare una foto/fotografia*
piece *pezzo* (m.)
pillow *cuscino* (m.)
pineapple *ananas (m., plural ananas)*
pink *rosa* (inv.)
place *luogo* (m.), *posto* (m.)
plan (to) *progettare*
planet *pianeta* (m.)
plant *pianta* (f.)
plant (to) *piantare*
plastic *plastica* (f.)
  made from plastic *di plastica*
plate *piatto* (m.)
play (theater) *spettacolo* (m.)
play (to) *giocare (sport, game); praticare (sport);*
  suonare (instrument)
  play a sport (to) *praticare uno sport*
  play cards (to) *giocare a carte*
  play tennis (to) *giocare a tennis*
  play the piano (to) *suonare il pianoforte*
player *giocatore/trice* (m./f.) *(person); lettore*
  (m.) *(machine)*
  CD player *lettore di cd (ci-di)*
  DVD player *dvd* (m.)
playground *parco giochi*
pleasant *piacevole*
Please. *Per favore.*
pleasing (to someone) (to be) *piacere*
  Pleased to meet you. *Piacere.*
  Pleased to meet you, too. *Piacere mio.*
  Very pleased to meet you! *Molto piacere!*
plentiful *abbondante*
plumber *idraulico/a* (m./f.)
plural *plurale* (m.)
poem *poema* (m.)
poker *poker* (m., pl.)
policeman *poliziotto* (m.)
  policewoman *donna* (f.) *poliziotto*
pond *stagno* (m.)
pool *biliardo* (m.)
pop *pop* (inv.)
  pop music *musica* (f.) *pop*

pork *maiale* (m.)
  baked pork *maiale al forno*
  pork chop *braciola* (f.) *di maiale*
possessive *possessivo*
possible *possibile*
  How's it possible! *Ma come!*
post office *ufficio* (m.) *postale*
pot *pentola* (f.)
potato *patata* (f.)
pour (to) *versare*
powder (talcum) *borotalco* (m.)
practice sports (to) *fare sport*
prefer (to) *preferire*
prepare (to) *preparare*
preposition *preposizione* (f.)
present (adjective) *presente*
  present perfect *passato* (m.) *prossimo*
  present subjunctive *congiuntivo* (m.) *presente*
present (to) *presentare*
pressure *pressione* (f.)
pretty *carino*
price *prezzo* (m.)
printer *stampante* (f.)
private *privato*
probably *probabilmente*
problem *problema* (m.)
product *prodotto* (m.)
production (theater) *messinscena* (f.)
professional
professional school *professionale*
istituto* (m.) tecnico*
professor *professore/essa* (m./f.)
program *trasmissione* (f.), *programma* (m.)
  television program *trasmissione televisiva*
prohibit (to) *proibire*
promise (to) *promettere*
  promise to ... (do something)
    (to) *promettere di ...*
promote (to) *promuovere*
pronoun *pronome* (m.)
provided that ... *a patto che ... / a condizione*
che ... / purché
province *provincia* (f.)
psychiatrist *psichiatra* (m./f.)
psychologist *psicologo* (m./f.)
publish (to) *pubblicare*
punctual *puntuale*
purple *viola* (inv.)

Glossary

purse *borsa* (f.)
put (to) *mettere*
put things away (to) *mettere in ordine*
put on (to) *mettersi*
He/She puts on ... (to) *Si mette ...*

Q

quarter *quarto* (m.)
question *domanda* (f.)
  ask a question (to) *fare una domanda*
quick *veloce*
quickly *velocemente, in fretta*
quit (to) *smettere*
quit ... ing (to) *smettere di ...*
quotient *quoziente* (m.)
  intelligence quotient (IQ) *quoziente intellettivo*

R

rain *pioggia* (f.)
rain (to) *piovere*
  It's raining. *Piove.*
raise (to) *crescere*
rarely *raramente*
rather *piuttosto*
ravioli *ravioli* (m. pl.)
razor *rasoio* (m.)
reach (to) *raggiungere*
read (to) *leggere*
reader *lettore* (m.)
ready *pronto*
  get ready (to) *prepararsi*
  ready to ... *pronto per ...*
really *veramente, davvero, proprio*
reason *motivo* (m.), *ragione* (f.)
  the reason why ... *il motivo per cui ... / la ragione per cui ...*
receive (to) *ricevere*
reception desk *accettazione* (f.), *reception* (f., pl.)
recipe *ricetta* (f.)
red *rosso*
  red wine *vino* (m.) *rosso*
reduced *ridotto*
refrigerator *frigorifero* (m.) *(frigo)*
regret (to) *pentirsi*
regularly *regolarmente*
reject (to) *bocciare*
relative *parente* (m./f.)

relax (to) *rilassarsi*
remain *rimanere*
remember (to) *ricordare*
  remember to ... (do something) (to) *ricordarsi di ...*
removal *trasloco* (m.)
Renaissance *Rinascimento* (m.) (noun); *rinascimentale* (adjective)
rent (to) *affittare*
repent (to) *pentirsi*
reply (to) *rispondere*
report card *scheda* (f.)
rescue *soccorso* (m.)
research *indagine* (f.)
researcher *ricercatore/trice* (m./f.)
reservation *prenotazione* (f.)
reserve (to) *prenotare*
residence *residenza* (f.)
respectively *rispettivamente*
rest *riposo* (m.)
  Have a good rest. *Buon riposo.*
restaurant *ristorante* (m.)
  family style restaurant *trattoria* (f.)
retired *pensionato/a* (m./f.)
return (to) *ritornare, tornare*
rib *costa* (f.)
rice *riso* (m.)
rich *ricco*
ride a bike (to) *andare in bicicletta*
right *destra* (f.) (noun); *vero, giusto* (adjective)
  on/to the right *(a) destra*
  right (to be) *avere ragione*
  right now *in questo momento*
ring *anello* (m.)
ring (a bell) (to) *suonare*
river *fiume* (m.)
road *strada* (f.)
roast *arrosto*
roast pork *maiale* (m.) *al forno*
rock *roccia* (f.)
romantic *romantico* (m., pl. *romantici*)
Rome *Roma* (f.)
room *sala* (f.), *camera* (f.), *stanza* (f.)
  bedroom *camera* (f.), *camera da letto, stanza* (f.) *da letto*
  dining room *sala da pranzo*
  double room (one queen-size bed) *camera matrimoniale*

double room (two twin-size beds) *camera doppia*
emergency room *pronto soccorso* (m.)
living room *salone* (m.), *soggiorno* (m.)
meeting room *sala delle riunioni*
single room (one twin bed) *camera singola*
study (room) *studio* (m.)
rope *corda* (f.)
  jump rope (to) *saltare la corda*
rug *tappeto* (m.)
run (to) *correre*
rural *rurale*
rushed *affrettato*

S

sad *triste*
sail *vela* (f.)
sail (to) *andare in barca a vela*
sailing *vela* (f.)
salad *insalata* (f.)
  mixed salad *insalata mista*
salary *salario* (m.)
salesman *venditore* (m.)
saleswoman *venditrice* (f.)
salt *sale* (m.)
same *stesso, pari* (inv.)
  at the same time *allo stesso tempo*
sand *sabbia* (f.)
sandwich *panino* (m.)
Sardinia *Sardegna* (f.)
satisfied *soddisfatto*
Saturday *sabato* (m.)
sauté (to) *rosolare*
save (to) *salvare*
  save a document (to) *salvare un documento*
say (to) *dire*
scare (to) *impaurire*
scarf *sciarpa* (f.) (long), *foulard* (m.) (square)
scary (to be) *fare paura*
scholastic *scolastico* (m. pl. *scolastici*)
school *scuola* (f.)
  high school *liceo* (m.), *scuola* (f.) *superiore*
  professional school *istituto* (m.) *tecnico*
  the first grade at elementary school *la prima elementare*
scientist *ricercatore/trice* (m./f.)
screen *monitor* (m.), *schermo* (m.), *video* (m.)
sculpture *scultura* (f.)

sea *mare* (m.)
seaside *mare* (m.)
season *stagione* (f.)
  half seasons (spring and fall) *mezze stagioni*
second *secondo*
  second-born *secondogenito/a* (m./f.)
secretary *segretario/a* (m./f.)
see (to) *vedere*
  Let me see. *Fammi vedere.*
  see each other (to) *vedersi*
  See you later. *A dopo.*
  See you soon. *A presto.*
seem (to) *sembrare*
send (to) *inviare, mandare, spedire*
  send a file (to) *inviare un documento/file*
  send an e-mail (to) *mandare un'email/una mail*
September *settembre* (m.)
serious *grave*
serve (to) *servire*
set (a table) (to) *apparecchiare*
settings *ambientazione* (f.)
seven *sette*
  at seven thirty (7:30) *alle sette e mezza*
  by seven (o'clock) *per le sette*
  There are seven of us. *Siamo in sette.*
seventeen *diciassette*
seventh *settimo*
seventy *settanta*
several *parecchio* (adjective); *parecchio/a* (m./f.) (noun)
shampoo *shampo* (m.)
shape *forma* (f.)
  in great shape *in ottima forma*
share (to) *condividere, avere in comune*
shave (to) *farsi la barba, radersi*
shaving cream *crema* (f.) *da barba*
she (subject pronoun) *lei*
  he/she who (relative pronoun) *chi*
shelf *scaffale* (m.)
  book shelf *scaffale (dei libri)*
shine (to) *splendere*
shirt *camicia* (f.)
shoes *scarpe* (f. pl.)
  pair of shoes *paio* (m.) *di scarpe*
  shoe store *negozio* (m.) *di scarpe*
  tennis shoes *scarpe da tennis*
shop (to) *fare spese*

shopping *spesa* (f.)
  go shopping (to), do grocery shopping
    (to) *fare la spesa/le spese*
shopping mall *centro acquisti, centro commerciale*
short *corto, basso*
  short trip *gita* (f.)
  shorter working hours *orario* (m.) *ridotto*
shoulder *spalla* (f.)
show (to) *mostrare, indicare, fare vedere*
shower *doccia* (f.)
  take a shower (to) *fare la doccia*
shrimp *gambero* (m.), *gamberetto* (m.)
Sicily *Sicilia* (f.)
sick *malato, ammalato*
side dish *contorno* (m.)
  as a side dish *di/per contorno*
sidewalk *marciapiede* (m.)
sightseeing (to go sightseeing) *visitare*
silent *silenzioso*
silk *seta* (f.)
  made out of silk *di seta*
silverware *posate* (f. pl.)
similar *simile*
simple *piano*
sin *peccato* (m.)
since *da*
  How long has it been since … ? *Da quanto tempo … ?*
  since … *visto che …*
  since always *da una vita*
sing (to) *cantare*
single *singolo*
  single (man) *celibe* (m.)
  single (woman) *nubile* (f.)
  single room (one twin bed) *camera* (f.) *singola*
sink (kitchen) *lavandino* (m.) *(kitchen); lavabo* (m.) *(wash basin)*
sister *sorella* (f.)
site *sito* (m.)
situation *condizione* (f.)
six *sei*
sixteen *sedici*
sixth *sesto*
sixty *sessanta*
size *taglia* (f.) *(dresses, pants), misura* (f.) *(shirts), numero* (m.) *(shoes)*

ski (to) *sciare*
skiing *sci* (m., pl.)
  alpine skiing *sci alpino*
  cross-country skiing *sci di fondo*
skillful *bravo*
skin *pelle* (f.)
skirt *gonna* (f.)
sky *cielo* (m.)
sleep *sonno* (m.)
sleep (to) *dormire*
sleepy *insonnolito*
  sleepy (to be) *avere sonno*
slice (to) *affettare, tagliare*
  sliced cold meat *affettato* (m.)
slowly *lentamente, piano*
small *piccolo*
smog *smog* (m.)
smoked *affumicato*
smooth *piano*
snack *spuntino* (m.)
sneakers *scarpe* (f. pl.) *da ginnastica, scarpe da tennis, sneakers* (m. pl.)
snow *neve* (f.)
snow (to) *nevicare*
  It's snowing. *Nevica.*
so *così, tanto, allora, quindi*
  I don't think so. *Non credo.*
  so … as *così … come/sia … che*
  so many *tanto/a* (m./f.) (noun); *tanto* (adjective)
  so much *tanto/a* (m./f.) (noun); *tanto* (adjective); *tanto* (adverb)
  So so. *Così, così.*
  so that *affinché*
soap (bar) *saponetta* (f.)
soccer *calcio* (m.)
social *sociale*
socks *calze* (f. pl.)
soda *bibita* (f.)
sofa *sofà* (m.), *divano* (m.)
soft drink *bibita* (f.)
softly *piano*
some *alcuni/e, qualche, certo, di + definite article*
someone *qualcuno*
something *qualcosa*
  something to drink *qualcosa da bere*
sometimes *qualche volta, a volte*
son *figlio* (m.)
song *canzone* (f.)

soon *presto*
  See you soon. *A presto.*
sooner *prima*
Sorry (I'm sorry.) *Mi dispiace./Scusami.*
soup *minestra* (f.)
sour *amaro*
spacious *spazioso, ampio*
spaghetti *spaghetti* (m. pl.)
sparkling wine *spumante* (m.)
spa *terme* (f. pl.)
speak (to) *parlare*
  speak Chinese (to) *parlare cinese*
  speaking of … *a proposito di …*
speech *discorso* (m.)
spend (to) *spendere*
spoon *cucchiaio* (m.)
sport *sport* (m., pl.)
  play a sport (to) *praticare uno sport*
  practice sports (to) *fare sport*
  watch sports on TV (to) *guardare lo sport in/ alla televisione*
spring *primavera* (f.)
  in the spring *in primavera*
square *piazza* (f.)
stadium *stadio* (m.)
staff *staff* (m.)
staircase *scala* (f.)
stairs *scale* (f.)
star *stella* (f.)
starting from … *a partire da …*
state *stato* (m.)
station *stazione* (f.)
  train station *stazione (dei treni)*
stay (to) *restare, stare*
  stay-at-home dad *casalingo* (m.)
  stay-at-home mom *casalinga* (f.)
steady job *lavoro* (m.) *fisso*
stepdaughter *figlia* (f.) *di mia moglie (di mio marito)*
stepfather *marito* (m.) *di mia madre*
stepmother *moglie* (f.) *di mio padre*
stepson *figlio* (m.) *di mia moglie (di mio marito)*
stereo *stereo* (m., pl.)
stew *spezzatino* (m.)
still *ancora*
stomach *stomaco* (m.) *(above the waist); ventre* (m.), *pancia* (f.) *(below the waist)*
stone *pietra* (f.)

stop (to) *fermarsi, smettere*
stop … ing (to) *smettere di …*
store *negozio* (m.)
  clothing store *negozio di abbigliamento*
  department store *grande magazzino* (m.)
  electronics store *negozio di elettronica*
  grocery store *negozio di alimentari*
  shoe store *negozio di scarpe*
storm *temporale* (m.)
  It's stormy. *C'è un temporale.*
story *storia* (f.)
  love stories *storie* (pl.) *d'amore*
stove (electric, gas) *cucina* (f.) *elettrica, cucina* (f.) *a gas*
straight *diritto*
  straight ahead *sempre diritto*
strange *strano*
strawberry *fragola* (f.)
street *strada* (f.), *via* (f.)
street light *semaforo* (m.)
stressed *stressato*
stressful *stressante*
strong *forte*
student *studente/essa* (m./f.)
  university student *studente universitario*
study *indagine* (f.), *studio* (m.) *(room)*
study (to) *studiare*
stuff *roba* (f.)
  a bunch/lot of stuff *un sacco di roba*
subject *materia* (f.)
subjunctive mood (grammar) *congiuntivo* (m.)
  present subjunctive *congiuntivo presente*
substance *sostanza* (f.)
substitute *sostituto/a* (m./f.)
suburban *periferico*
suburbs *periferia* (f.)
subway *metrò* (m. in Milan/f. in Rome)
suddenly *improvvisamente*
sugar *zucchero* (m.)
suit *abito* (m.) *(men's), tailleur* (m., pl.) *(women's)*
  men's suit *abito da uomo*
  pant suit *tailleur pantalone*
suitcase *valigia* (f.)
summer *estate* (f.)
  in the summer *d'estate*
  summer job *lavoro* (m.) *temporaneo*
sun *sole* (m.)
  It's sunny. *C'è il sole.*

Sunday *domenica* (f.)
sunglasses *occhiali da sole*
superior *superiore*
supermarket *supermercato* (m.)
sure *sicuro*
surprise *sorpresa* (f.)
   What a surprise! *Che sorpresa!*
surprise (to) *sorprendere*
sweater *maglione* (m.)
sweet *dolce*
swim (to) *nuotare*
swimming *nuoto* (m.)
symphony *sinfonia* (f.)
symptom *sintomo* (m.)
system *sistema* (m.)

T

table *tavolo* (m.)
tagliatelle (pasta) *tagliatelle* (f. pl.)
tail (of coin) *croce* (f.)
take (to) *portare, prendere*
   take (time) (to) *metterci, volerci*
   take a bath (to) *fare il bagno*
   take a break (to) *fare una pausa*
   take a nap (to) *fare un pisolino*
   take a nice long nap (to) *farsi una bella
      dormita*
   take a picture (to) *fare una foto/fotografia*
   take a shower (to) *fare la doccia*
   take a trip (to) *fare una gita, fare un viaggio*
   take a walk (to) *fare una passeggiata*
take off (to) *decollare*
talented *bravo, con talento; in gamba* (colloquial)
talk *discorso* (m.), *colloquio* (m.)
   talk show *interviste* (f. pl.) *alla televisione*
tall *alto*
taste *sapore* (m.)
taxi *taxi* (m.)
taxi driver *tassista* (m./f.)
tea *tè* (m.)
tea kettle *bollitore* (m.)
teach (to) *insegnare*
teacher *insegnante* (m./f.); *maestro/a* (m./f.)
   (nursery school and elementary school)
team *squadra* (f.)
technical *tecnico*
teenager *adolescente* (m./f.), *teenager* (m./f., pl.
   teenager)

telegram *telegramma* (m.)
telephone *telefono* (m.)
   answer the phone (to) *rispondere al telefono*
   cell phone *cellulare* (m.), *telefonino* (m.)
telephone (to) *telefonare, chiamare*
television *televisione* (f.), *tele* (f.), *tivù* (f.),
   televisore (m.) (noun); *televisivo* (adjective)
   television program *trasmissione* (f.) *televisiva*
   watch television (to)) *guardare la
      televisione/tele/ tivù*
   watch sports on TV (to) *guardare lo sport in/
      alla televisione*
tell (to) *raccontare, dire*
temperature *temperatura* (f.)
temple *tempio* (m.)
temporary *temporaneo*
ten *dieci*
   from 10:45 a.m. to 3:00 p.m. *dalle undici meno
      un quarto alle tre*
tendon *tendine* (m.)
tennis *tennis* (m., pl. *tennis*)
   play tennis (to) *giocare a tennis*
   tennis shoes *scarpe* (f. pl.) *da tennis*
tenth *decimo*
terrible *terribile*
test *test* (m.)
textbook *libro (di testo)*
than *di, che*
   less ... than *meno ... di/che*
   more/-er ... than *più ... di/che*
   than usual *del solito*
Thank you. *Grazie.*
Fine, thanks. *(Sto) bene, grazie.*
Thanks a lot. *Grazie mille.*
Very well, thanks. *Molto bene, grazie.*
that (conjunction) *che*
that (demonstrative) *quello*
that (relative pronoun) *che*
the *il* (m. sg.) (in front of a consonant); *lo* (m. sg.)
   (in front of s + consonant, z, ps, gn); *l'* (m. sg./f. sg.)
   (in front of a vowel); *la* (f. sg.) (in front of a
   consonant); *i* (m. pl.) (in front of consonants); *gli* (m.
   pl.) (in front of s + consonant, z, ps, gn, in front of
   vowels); *le* (f. pl.) (in front of consonants or vowels)
theater *teatro* (m.)
   movie theater *cinema* (m., pl.)
their *loro* (inv.)
them (direct object pronoun) *li/le* (m./f.)

them (direct object, disjunctive pronoun) *loro*
to them (indirect object pronoun) *gli*
to them (indirect object, disjunctive pronoun) *a loro*
then *poi, allora*
And then? *E poi?*
there *lì, ci*
Go there. *Vacci.*
Let's go there. *Andiamoci.*
near there *lì vicino*
There is … *C'è …*
There are … *Ci sono …*
There are seven of us. *Siamo in sette.*
There are three of them. *Ce ne sono tre.*
therefore *dunque, quindi*
thesis *tesi (f., pl. tesi)*
they (subject pronoun) *loro*
they (impersonal pronoun) *si*
thick *grosso*
thin *magro, sottile*
thin slice *fettina* (f.)
thing *cosa* (f.)
things to do *cose da fare*
tons of things, a thousand things *mille cose*
think (to) *pensare*
I don't think so. *Non credo.*
I'll think about it. *Ci penserò.*
think about … (doing somehing)
  (to) *pensare di …*
think about … (something/somebody)
  (to) *pensare a …*
third *terzo*
third-born *terzogenito/a*
thirst *sete* (f.)
thirsty (to be) *avere sete*
thirteen *tredici*
thirty *trenta*
at seven thirty (7:30) *alle sette e mezza*
It's 3:30. *Sono le tre e trenta.*
this *questo*
in this period *in questo periodo*
this evening *questa sera, stasera*
this week *questa settimana*
thousand *mille* (m.), *mila* (pl.)
two thousand *duemila*
three *tre*
from 10:45 a.m. to 3:00 p.m. *dalle undici meno un quarto alle tre*

It's three (o'clock). *Sono le tre.*
It's 3:15. *Sono le tre e quindici.*
It's 3:45. *Sono le tre e quarantacinque./Sono le tre e tre quarti./Sono le quattro meno un quarto./Manca un quarto alle quattro.*
It's 3:30. *Sono le tre e trenta.*
There are three of them. *Ce ne sono tre.*
through *per*
thumb *pollice* (m.)
thunder *tuono* (m.)
thunder (to) *tuonare*
Thursday *giovedì* (m., pl.)
ticket *biglietto* (m.)
tie *cravatta* (f.)
tie (to) *fare pari*
till *fino (a)*
time *tempo* (m.), *orario* (m.), *volta* (f.)
at the same time *allo stesso tempo*
every time *ogni volta*
for a very long time *da una vita*
free time *tempo libero*
full-time *a pieno tempo*
have time (to) *avere tempo*
It's time to … *È ora di …*
long time *molto tempo*
on time (to be) *essere in orario, essere puntuale*
part-time *part-time*
part-time job *lavoro part-time*
waste time (to) *perdere tempo*
What time is it? *Che ora è?/Che ore sono?*
tip *mancia* (f.)
tired *stanco*
title *titolo* (m.)
to *in, a, da*
from … to … (time periods) *dalle … alle …*
from Monday to Friday *dal lunedì al venerdì*
from 10:45 a.m. to 3:00 p.m. *dalle undici meno un quarto alle tre*
nothing good to eat *niente di buono da mangiare*
something to drink *qualcosa da bere*
things to do *cose* (f. pl.) *da fare*
to the city *in centro*
to the country *in campagna*
to the left *(a) sinistra*
to the mountains *in montagna*
to the right *(a) destra*

today *oggi*
toe (big) *alluce* (m.)
together *insieme*
  (together) with you *insieme a te*
toilet *water* (m.), *gabinetto* (m.)
toilet paper *carta* (f.) *igienica*
tomato *pomodoro* (m.)
tomorrow *domani*
tongue *lingua* (f.)
tonight *stasera*
tons of things *mille cose* (f. pl.)
too *anche*
  Pleased to meet you, too. *Piacere mio.*
too (much/many) *troppo/a* (m./f.) (noun); *troppo*
  (adjective)
  go too far (to) *esagerare*
  Too bad! *Peccato!*
tooth *dente* (m.)
tortellini *tortellini* (m. pl.)
tour *giro* (m.)
  guided tour *viaggio* (m.) *organizzato*
  tour bus *pullman* (m.)
tourist *turista* (m./f.)
  foreign tourists *turisti* (pl.) *stranieri*
towel *asciugamano* (m.)
tower *torre* (f.)
town *cittadina* (f.); *paese* (m.) *(small)*
  around town *in giro per la città*
  hometown *città* (f.) *natale*
  out of town *fuori città*
trade fair *fiera* (f.)
traditional *tradizionale*
traffic *traffico* (m.)
traffic light *semaforo* (m.)
train *treno* (m.)
  by train *in treno*
  train station *stazione* (f.) *(dei treni)*
training *formazione* (f.)
transfer (to) *trasferirsi*
transparent *trasparente*
transportation *trasporto* (m.)
  means of transportation *mezzo* (m.) *di
    trasporto*
travel *viaggio* (m.)
travel (to) *viaggiare*
  travel abroad (to) *viaggiare all'estero*
tread on (to) *calpestare*
treat (to) *curare*

tree *albero* (m.)
trip *viaggio* (m.)
  day trip *gita* (f.)
  Have a good trip. *Buon viaggio.*
  short trip *gita* (f.)
  take a trip (to) *fare un viaggio*
true *vero*
truth *verità* (f., pl.)
try (to) *provare*
  try on (to) *provare*
  try to … (to) *cercare di …*
t-shirt *maglietta* (f.)
tub *vasca* (f.)
  bath tub *vasca (da bagno)*
Tuesday *martedì* (m., pl. *martedì*)
turn (to) *girare, voltare*
twelve *dodici*
twenty *venti*
twenty-four *ventiquattro*
twenty-one *ventuno*
twenty-three *ventitré*
twenty-two *ventidue*
twice a week *due volte alla settimana*
two *due*
  It's two (o'clock). *Sono le due.*
  two and a half hours *due ore e mezzo*
  two days ago *due giorni fa*
  two thousand *duemila*
type *tipo* (m.)

U

ugly *brutto*
umbrella *ombrello* (m.)
uncle *zio* (m., pl. *zii*)
undecided *indeciso*
under *sotto*
  under stress *stressato*
underpants *slip* (m. pl.) *(men's)*; *mutandine* (f. pl.)
  (women's)
undershirt *canottiera* (f.)
understand (to) *capire*
unemployed *disoccupato/a* (m./f.)
unfortunately *purtroppo*
unfriendly *antipatico*
university *università* (f., pl. *università*) (noun);
  universitario (adjective)
  university degree *laurea* (f.)
  university student *studente* (m.) *universitario*

unless ... *a meno che ... non*
until *finché, fino (a)*
  until late *fino a tardi*
  until the end *fino in fondo*
up to *fino (a)*
upon *su*
upset (to) *dispiacere*
urban *urbano*
us (direct object pronoun) *ci*
  us (direct object, disjunctive pronoun) *noi*
  to us (indirect object pronoun) *ci*
  to us (indirect object, disjunctive pronoun) *a noi*
use (to) *usare*
useful *utile*
usual *solito*
  than usual *del solito*
usually *di solito*

V

vacation *ferie* (f. pl.), *vacanza* (f.)
  on vacation *in ferie, in vacanza*
vaguely *vagamente*
variety *varietà* (f.)
  variety of choices *varietà di scelta*
veal *vitello* (m.)
vegetable *verdura* (f.)
vegetable garden *orto* (m.)
velvet *velluto* (m.)
vendor *commerciante* (m./f.)
Venice *Venezia* (f.)
version *versione* (f.)
very *molto, tanto*
  for a very long time *da una vita*
  very beautiful *bellissimo*
  very interesting *interessantissimo*
  Very pleased to meet you! *Molto piacere!*
  Very well! *Benissimo!*
  Very well, thanks. *Molto bene, grazie.*
veterinarian *veterinario/a* (m./f.)
view *vista* (f.)
village *paese* (m.); *paesino* (m.) (small)
virgin *vergine* (f.)
visit (to) *visitare*
  come visit (to) *venire a trovare*
  go visit (to) *andare a trovare*
volleyball *palla* (f.) *a volo*

W

waist *vita* (f.)
wait for (to) *aspettare*
  Wait a second. *Un momento.*
waiter *cameriere* (m.)
waitress *cameriera* (f.)
wake up (to) *svegliarsi*
walk *passeggiata* (f.)
  Enjoy your walk./Have a good walk. *Buona passeggiata.*
  go for a walk (to) *fare un giro/fare un giro a piedi*
  take a walk (to) *fare una passeggiata*
walk (to) *camminare*
wall *parete* (f.), *muro* (m.)
want (to) *volere, desiderare*
wardrobe *armadio* (m.)
warehouse *magazzino* (m.)
wash (to) *lavare*
  wash oneself (to) *lavarsi*
washing machine *lavatrice* (f.), *lavabiancheria* (f.)
waste time (to) *perdere tempo*
watch *orologio* (m.)
watch (to) *guardare*
  Watch out! *Sta' attento!*
  watch sports on TV (to) *guardare lo sport in/alla televisione*
  watch television (to) *guardare la tivù/tele/televisione*
water *acqua* (f.)
  mineral water *acqua minerale*
  still mineral water *acqua minerale naturale*
  sparkling mineral water *acqua minerale frizzante*
way *via* (f.), *modo* (m.)
  by the way *a proposito*
  the way in which ... *il modo in cui ...*
we (subject pronoun) *noi*
weak *debole*
wear (to) *portare, indossare*
  He/She wears. *Si mette ...*
weather *tempo* (m.)
  What's the weather like? *Che tempo fa?*
web log *web log* (m.)
webpage *web page* (f.), *pagina* (f.) *web*
website *sito* (m.) *web*

wedding *matrimonio* (m.)
Wednesday *mercoledì* (m., pl.)
week *settimana* (f.)
　last week *settimana scorsa*
　next week *prossima settimana*
　this week *questa settimana*
　twice a week *due volte alla settimana*
weekend *fine settimana* (m., pl.), *weekend* (m., pl.)
welcome *benvenuto*
　You're welcome. *Prego.*
　Welcome back. *Bentornato.*
well *bene*
　I am well. *Mi sento bene.*
　(One) might as well … *Tanto vale …*
　Very well! *Benissimo!*
　Very well, thanks. *Molto bene, grazie.*
Well … *Beh …*
what *che*
　What? *Che cosa?*
　What a beautiful dish! *Che bel piatto!*
　What a surprise! *Che sorpresa!*
　What are you having? *Tu cosa prendi?*
　What do you do? *Che lavoro fai?*
　What time is it? *Che ora è?/Che ore sono?*
　What's the weather like? *Che tempo fa?*
when *quando*
where *dove*
　Where are you from? (fml.)/Where is he/she
　　from? *Di dov'è?*
　Where are you from? (infml.) *Di dove sei?*
　Where is … ?/Where are … ? *Dov'è … ?/*
　　Dove sono … ?
which *quale* (question); *cui, che* (relative pronoun)
　the way in which … *il modo in cui …*
while *mentre*
white *bianco*
　white wine *vino* (m.) *bianco*
who *chi* (question); *che* (relative pronoun)
whoever *chi*
whole *intero*
whom *che, cui*
Whose … is it ?/Whose … are they?
　Di chi è … ?/Di chi sono … ?
why *perché*
　the reason why … *il motivo per cui … / la*
　　ragione per cui …
wide *ampio*
wife *moglie* (f.)

wild *selvaggio*
win (to) *vincere*
wind *vento* (m.)
　It's windy. *C'è vento./Tira vento.*
window *finestra* (f.)
wine *vino* (m.)
　red wine *vino rosso*
　wine list *lista* (f.) *dei vini*
　white wine *vino bianco*
winter *inverno* (m.) (noun); *invernale* (adjective)
　in winter *d'inverno*
wish *voglia* (f.)
　I wish *magari*
with *con, presso*
　(together) with you *insieme a te*
without *senza*
　without … *senza che …*
wolf *lupo* (m.)
woman *donna* (f.)
　businesswoman *donna d'affari*
　policewoman *donna poliziotto*
　saleswoman *venditrice* (f.)
wonderful *meraviglioso*
　Wonderful! *Benissimo!*
wood *legno* (m.), *bosco* (m.)
wooden *di legno*
wool *lana* (f.)
work *lavoro* (m.), *opera* (f.)
　works of art *opere* (pl.) *d'arte*
work (to) *lavorare*
worker *operaio/a* (m./f.)
　construction worker *muratore/trice* (m./f.)
world *mondo* (m.)
　around the world *intorno al mondo*
　in the world *del mondo*
worry (to) *preoccupare*
　I'm worried. *Sono preoccupato.*
worth (to be) *valere*
wrist *polso* (m.)
write (to) *scrivere*
writer *scrittore/trice* (m./f.)
wrong (to be) *avere torto*

Y

year *anno* (m.)
　every year *tutti gli anni*
　I am … years old. *Ho … anni.*
　last year *anno scorso*

yellow *giallo*

yes *sì*

yesterday *ieri*

yet *ancora*

yolk *tuorlo* (m.)

you (subject pronoun) *Lei* (sg. fml.), *tu* (sg. infml.), *Loro* (pl. fml.), *voi* (pl.)

you (direct object pronoun) *La* (sg. fml.), *ti* (sg. infml.), *vi* (pl.)

you (direct object, disjunctive pronoun) *Lei* (sg. fml.), *te* (sg. infml.), *voi* (pl.)

to you (indirect object pronoun) *Le* (sg. fml.), *ti* (sg. infml.), *vi* (pl.)

to you (indirect object, disjunctive pronoun) *a Lei* (sg. fml.), *a te* (sg. infml.), *a voi* (pl.)

young *giovane*

younger *minore*

your *Suo/Sua/Suoi/Sue* (sg. fml.); *tuo/tua/tuoi/tue* (sg. infml.); *Loro/Loro* (pl. fml.); *vostro/vostra/vostri/vostre* (pl. infml.)

youth hostel *ostello* (m.)

Z

zero *zero*

zoo *zoo* (m., pl.)

zucchini *zucchino* (m.)